# Computer Art and Animation for the TRS-80

David L. Heiserman

PRENTICE-HALL, INC. Englewood Cliffs, New Jersey 07632

*Library of Congress Cataloging in Publication Data*

Heiserman, David L., (date)
Computer art and animation for the TRS-80.

(Prentice-Hall series in personal computing)
Includes index.
1. Computer graphics. 2. Computer art.
3. Computer animation. 4. TRS-80 (Computer)—
Programming. I. Title. II. Series.
T385.H44 1982 001.55′3 82-16592
ISBN 0-13-164749-0
ISBN 0-13-164731-8 (pbk.)

Editorial/Production Supervision
and Interior Design: *Lynn S. Frankel*
Cover Design: *Photo Plus Art*
Manufacturing Buyer: *Gordon Osbourne*



Printed in the United States of America

10 9 8 7 6 5 4 3 2 1

ISBN 0-13-164749-0 {CASE}
ISBN 0-13-164731-8 {PAPER}

Prentice-Hall International, Inc., *London*
Prentice-Hall of Australia Pty. Limited, *Sydney*
Editora Prentice-Hall do Brazil, Ltda., *Rio de Janeiro*
Prentice-Hall of Canada, Ltd., *Toronto*
Prentice-Hall of India Private Limited, *New Delhi*
Prentice-Hall of Japan, Inc., *Tokyo*
Prentice-Hall of Southeast Asia Pte. Ltd., *Singapore*
Whitehall Books Limited, *Wellington, New Zealand*

# CONTENTS

CHAPTER 3

## SELECTING CHARACTERS AND GETTING THEM ONTO THE SCREEN 17



CHAPTER 4

## COMPOSING SINGLE, STATIC FIGURES 25



CHAPTER 5

## SOME COMPOSITION TECHNIQUES 39

CHAPTER 6

## STRING-PACKING PROCEDURES 51



CHAPTER 7

## MORE ABOUT STRING PACKING 65



CHAPTER 8

## CUSTOMIZED CHARACTER SETS 85

CHAPTER 6



CHAPTER 7



CHAPTER 8

# Preface

Computer graphics plays a vital role in the successful application of home computer systems. Complex ideas are often better expressed in terms of animated graphics sequences, columns of dull data can be more meaningful when backed up with graphs or moving images, and, of course, computer games can be far more exciting when they are built around graphic razzle-dazzle.

The literature usually supplied with a home computer system, however, rarely reflects the full potential of its graphics system. The subject is often treated as a novelty to be exploited only by those who care to spend the time figuring things out for themselves.

This book treats TRS-80 computer graphics and animation as a topic worthy of considerable study and experimentation. The discussions and examples should help a programmer develop a sense of confidence in developing programs that employ some graphics features. The programs may be almost wholly graphic, serving as art for its own sake, or they may serve as a small part of a larger program that has a more practical purpose.

Whatever one's motivation might be, the study of computer graphics and animation can reap highly satisfying rewards. It's a matter of giving it the serious attention it requires. This book is a step in that direction.

**DAVID L. HEISERMAN**

# Setting the Stage

# 1

If your concept of computer art is limited to doodling complicated mathematical functions on a CRT, your understanding of the matter is about 20 years behind the times. Computer art, or graphics, is now a legitimate branch of computer science, and it certainly hasn't gained that stature by limiting itself to plotting purely abstract figures that a child can create with a simple drawing toy.

If you think it takes a great deal of expensive, special equipment to create computer animated sequences, you are in for a pleasant surprise. Cost and sophistication are relative terms, of course; assuming you already own a home computer system, the additional cost is just about nil, and there is no need for building or buying any additional equipment.

That is not to say that it is easy to produce satisfying computer art and animations. It is hard work, and it requires some learning and discipline. The purpose of this book is to point you toward the techniques that are most likely to produce the results you want. It is up to you to supply the creativity and hard work.

## THE REQUIRED EQUIPMENT

All of the discussions and examples cited in this book are oriented toward 16k, TRS–80 home computer systems; either the Model 1 with Level II BASIC, or the Model 3. It is assumed you will be using a cassette tape system for saving programs, although a disk-based TRS–80 system works equally well.

Aside from the standard drawing tools—pencils, a drawing compass, protractor, and a good supply of erasers— the only auxiliary materials of special importance are some clean cassette tapes and a couple of pads of Video Programming Worksheets (Radio Shack catalog number 28–2105).

## PROGRAMMING PREREQUISITES

All of the discussions are based on the BASIC programming language. A knowledge of BASIC is absolutely essential for getting any real benefit from the work presented here.

The graphics techniques featured throughout the book are slanted toward the application of string variables, dimensioned arrays, and DATA listings. If you happen to be weak in your understanding of any of those families of BASIC statements (as many home computer programmers are), you should take some time to polish your understanding as you work into the first few chapters.

## A WORD ABOUT LOW-RESOLUTION GRAPHICS

The TRS–80's graphics system is usually classified as a low-resolution system. It is virtually impossible, for instance, to draw a circle that doesn't have some geometric distortion and a rough, step-like appearance in most places. Therefore, unless the desired figure happens to be a rectangle that is situated so that its sides are parallel to the edges of the CRT screen, one has to settle for something less than a perfect rendition of a desired image. However, that ought to be taken as challenge rather than a point of discouragement.

The human brain is a marvelous perceptive organ, but it can be tricked. It is possible to fool the brain into thinking it is seeing something that isn't there; in the context of producing satisfying low-resolution pictures, that means it is possible to fool the brain into ignoring imperfections. With creative application of low-resolution graphics, a viewer can perceive the real essence of a figure or animation sequence without being bothered by geometric distortions that are inevitably present in it.

Viewed objectively, a TRS–80 image of a girl standing in the middle of the screen can look terrible. The figure is necessarily made up of sharp right angles, relatively large rectangles of black and white, with none of the smooth curves a traditional artist would like to use. However, if you take time and care in preparing the figure, if you take the trouble to introduce some novel and interesting elements, the brain will attempt to interpret the image as something rather nice and meaningful. It will attempt to view the image as the artist intended, reaching for the essence of the image rather than dwelling on its objective appearance. Furthermore, the effect is enhanced when the image is animated in real time.

Along the same lines, the TRS-80 systems featured here are limited to black and white drawings. There are no shades of gray. That, too, poses no problem when one consciously introduces strokes of black and white that merely represent shades of gray. So what if the shadow cast by a figure is white instead of black or gray? The visual impression—especially if animated—can still be quite effective. It is a matter of taking the trouble to try it.

## HOW TO USE THIS BOOK

Take the book one step at a time. A number of special graphics techniques are developed over a number of chapters; attempting to jump into the middle of the book without studying the preceding material is courting disaster. So start from the beginning and move along as rapidly as you wish, making sure you are grasping the essence of the material as you go along.

There are a good many specific programming examples suggested through these chapters. They are intended to be just that—examples. This is not a collection of finished programs that stand on their own merits. It is up to you to develop such programs yourself. Try the examples in order to convince yourself that the topic at hand really fulfills its purpose. Study the programs themselves to make sure you understand exactly how they work and what the function of every statement is. I hope you will find some of the specific program listings interesting and even a little amusing, but you will be selling yourself short if you make no attempt to generate programs of your own as you go through the book.

# 2 The TRS-80 Graphic Characters

The graphic characters available on the TRS–80 are the elementary components of any image that can be drawn on the CRT screen. No picture can be created without them, so a discussion of those characters is a logical starting point for any presentation of TRS–80 graphics and animation.

An imaginative, creative selection of graphic elements goes a long way toward creating satisfying images on the screen. Anything less than a thorough appreciation of all those characters—exactly how they look and how to get them onto the screen—is bound to diminish the quality of the final works.

Even if you have worked with the TRS–80 graphic characters before, you will do well to study this chapter because it goes into a finer level of detail than does most of the standard literature on the subject. It is this eye for detail that promises to open new horizons for graphic achievement.

This chapter is not concerned with putting the graphic characters into a desired place on the screen, nor with stringing characters to create larger and more complex figures. That begins in Chapter 3. For now, use the programs merely to view the characters they place onto the screen. It's not necessary yet to figure out how the programs work. You will have an abundance of program analysis later on.

## CHARACTER SPACES

For our immediate purposes, the TRS–80's graphics are divided into two categories: the alphanumeric characters, including punctuation marks and special symbols, and the unique TRS–80 graphic elements. There are 64 of each kind, and in this chapter you will get to know all 128 of them rather well.

The CRT screen has a rectangular *graphics field.* That is the working space for all the characters, leaving a black border around the edges where nothing can be printed. That character field is divided into 1024 separate character locations, on each horizontal line of text or graphics, and 16 lines running from top to bottom of the field. Any character, alphanumeric or special graphic, has to fit into one of those character locations in the field. There are no in-between places.

Each of those 1024 character locations is further divided into 6 smaller segments called *pixels.* As indicated in Fig. 2–1, the pixels are arranged in a 2 × 3 format.

The smallest graphic that can be plotted is one that fills out just one pixel. Some of the keyboard punctuation marks (comma, period, and apostrophe, for instance) fill only a portion of one pixel, but they cannot be drawn without excluding any other graphics from the rest of that character space. Since the pixels are the elementary building blocks for screen graphics, they are worthy of closer study.

Obviously the pixels are not square. Using simple eyeball reckoning, and perhaps a natural desire to make things as simple as possible, one might assume that each pixel is about twice as tall as it is wide. But that is not the case. The relative dimensions of each pixel is actually $1 \times \frac{7}{3}$: it is $2\frac{1}{3}$ times taller than wide.

An important implication of the rectangular pixel shape is that lines drawn vertically can be much narrower than those drawn horizontally. Horizontal resolution, in other words, is far better than vertical resolution. If you have played with some SET and RESET graphics, you have doubtless noticed that fact. It is something that TRS–80 graphics artists must contend with constantly.

So each pixel in a graphic character space has relative dimensions of $1 \times \frac{7}{3}$. Since the pixels are arranged in a $2 \times 3$ pattern within each character space, it follows that the relative dimensions of each character space are $2 \times 7$. A character space is thus $3\frac{1}{2}$ times taller than it is wide. When it comes to printing graphics from the alphanumeric character

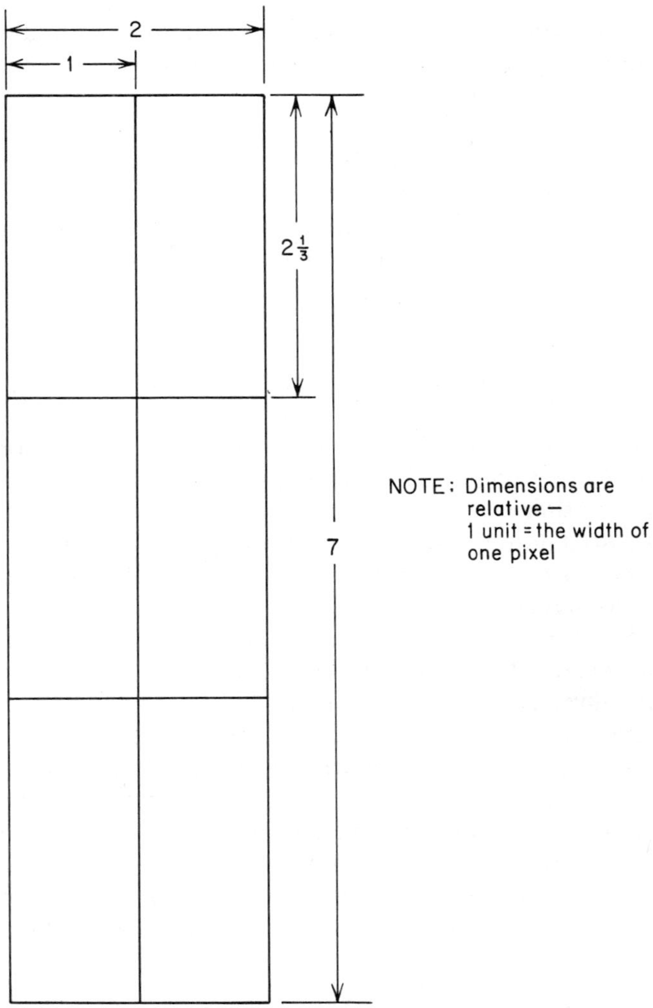


**FIGURE 2-1** A TRS-80 character space showing the relative dimensions of that space and its pixels

generator, each character will dominate a 2 × 7 space in the field. The space in that case will always be black and the character itself will be white. No other graphic can be slipped into that same space as long as the character is there.

Finally, since there are 64 character spaces in each field line and 16 lines in the field, the relative dimensions of the field is 8 × 7. The field is slightly wider than it is tall.

No doubt matters would be much simpler if everything were square—pixels, character spaces, and the field. Things aren't that simple, however, and if we are to set the stage for a complete acquaintance with this system of graphics, even details such as the relative dimensions of the basic elements can be important.

Incidentally, your CRT might suffer from some *astigmatic distortion.* The symptom of this malady is a change in character-space dimensions from one place on the screen to another. Astigmatic distortion is generally too slight to be of any concern, but if it ever grows to distressing proportions, your local Radio Shack computer dealer ought to be able to fix it for you.

## THE TRS-80 GRAPHICS SET

The TRS-80 system has an unique, built-in graphics generator. It allows you to specify any one of 64 possible graphic characters in terms of a special number that is assigned to each of them. In fact, the only way to get them printed onto the screen is by calling them out by their assigned numbers; there are no keys on the keyboard assembly for directly typing them onto the screen.

Figure 2–2 shows the pixel arrangement in a single character space. It is the same arrangement illustrated in Fig. 2–1, but this time I have included some numbers in each pixel space.

When you call up one of the special TRS-80 graphics, it either will fill each pixel with a spot of light or will clear it to black. Since there are 6 pixels and each can be either black or white, it figures that there are 64 possible combinations. For example, all pixels can be black. That's one possibility. Then pixel number 0 could be white, and the rest can be black. That is possibility number 2. Or, for possibility number 3, pixel number 1 can be white and the rest black. Or pixels 0 and 1 can be white and the rest

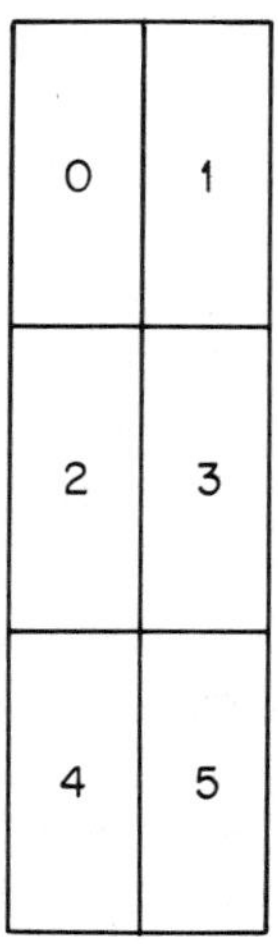


**FIGURE 2-2** The six pixels in a character space; the numerals indicate the place values for determining the graphic character code number

black. On and on it goes, up to 64 possible combinations of black and white pixels in that one character space.

All of the possible graphics combinations are shown in Fig. 2-3. Count them, if you wish. There are 64 of them.

The number shown below each graphic is the number one has to call in order to print it onto the screen. An all-black graphic is called by number 128, and an all-white graphic is called by 191. The other combinations use the integer values between those two.

If you aren't already aware of the fact, you should know that pictures are assembled by calling out appropriate combinations of these graphics numbers. The information in Fig. 2-3 can be quite valuable, and you will probably refer to it any number of times.

In order to make it easier for you to find this information at a later time, the figures are duplicated in the Appendices.

If you would like to take a look at the graphics on your own computer, consider Projects 2-1 and 2-2.

## PROJECT 2-1

Listing 2-1 is a short program that lets you ENTER a decimal graphic code number, then see the graphic printed in the upper left-hand corner of the screen. If you ENTER a number outside the range of 128 to 191, the program will give you an error message and an opportunity to try again.

```
10 REM **  PROJECT  2-1 **
15 CLS
20 DEFINT C:CLS
30 INPUT "WHAT GRAPHIC CODE NUMBER (128-191)";C
40 IF C>=128 AND C<=191 THEN 60
50 PRINT:PRINT "ENTRY ERROR ... TRY AGAIN":GOTO 20
60 CLS:PRINT CHR$(C);C
70 PRINT:PRINT:GOTO  30
```

**LISTING 2-1** Programming for Project 2-1

The program runs endlessly, and the best way to get out of it is by striking the BREAK key.

## PROJECT 2-2

Listing 2-2 lets you view the special TRS-80 graphics and their corresponding code numbers in a fashion akin to that in Fig. 2-3. The graphics and their code numbers are printed down the left side of the screen, six at a time. Striking the ENTER key lets you view the next six characters and code numbers.

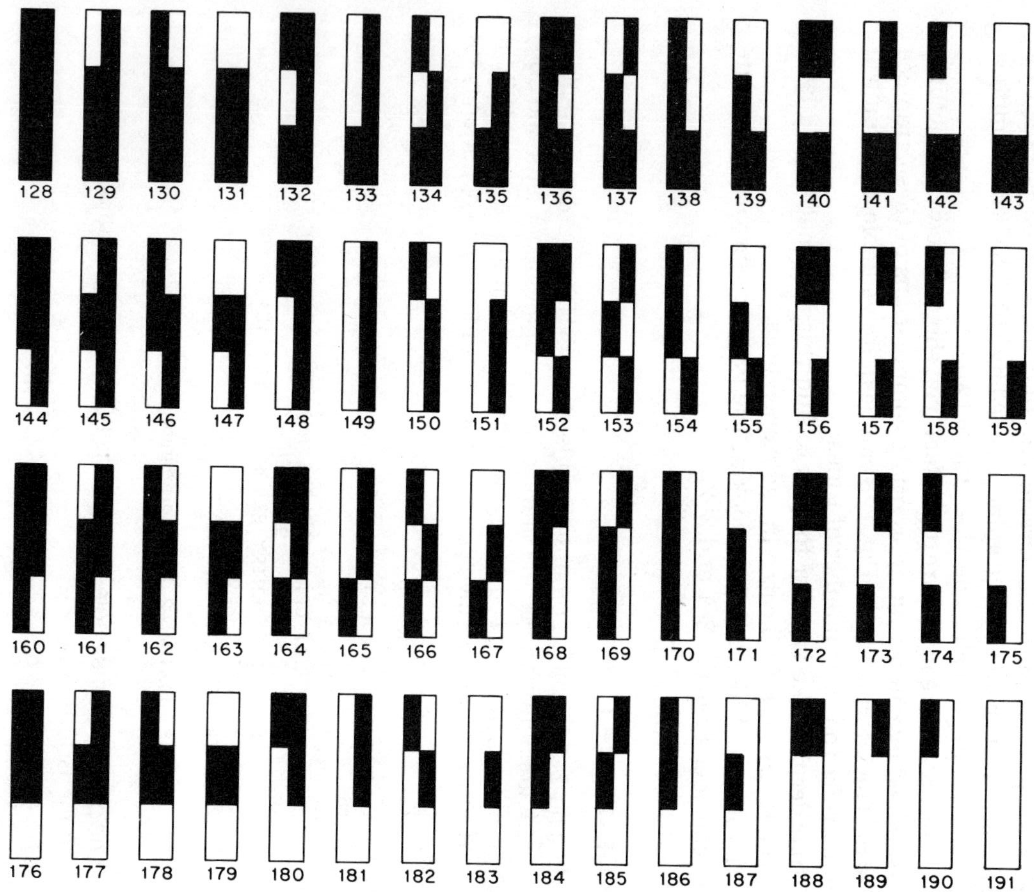


**FIGURE 2-3** The 64 special TRS-80 graphic characters; also see the version in Appendix A

```
10 REM ** PROJECT 2-2 **
20 CLS:C=128
30 FOR N=0 TO 6
40 PRINT CHR$(C);C
50 C=C+1:IF C>191 THEN PRINT:INPUT S$:GOTO 20
60 PRINT
70 NEXT N
80 INPUT S$:CLS:GOTO 30
```

**LISTING 2-2** Programming for Project 2-2

This program also runs endlessly. Terminate it at any time by striking the BREAK key.

## the meaning of the graphics and their code numbers

You have seen that the 64 TRS-80 special graphics characters represent all possible combinations of black and white pixels within a character space. The code numbers assigned to each of those graphics are not arbitrarily chosen, nor, for that matter, are the patterns of blacks and whites.

The graphics characters are generated according to a standard, 6-bit binary counting sequence. Each of the six pixels represents a binary place value that is assigned as shown in Fig. 2-2. The pixel in the upper left-hand corner of the character space has a place value of zero. The one in the upper right-hand corner has a place value of 1. The place-value numbering continues in that left-to-right and top-to-bottom fashion until the pixel in the lower right-hand corner, which has a place value of 5.

Keeping that in mind, also consider that a white pixel is assigned a numeric value of 1 when it is white, and a numeric value of 0 when it is black.

Now, each pixel has a certain place value assigned to it. That value never changes. Each pixel also has assigned to it a numeric value, 0 or 1, depending on whether that pixel is to be white or black.

To determine the character code for each graphic, work through the following procedure:

- Step 1: For each of the six pixels:
  - A. Find $2^p$, where p is the place value. (The powers-of-2 shown in Table 2-1 can be helpful here.)
  - B. Multiply the result by the numeric value of that pixel (by 0 if it is black, by 1 if it is white).
- Step 2: Sum the results for all six pixels as determined by the operations in Step 1.

- Step 3: Add 128 to the result of Step 2. That number will be that particular graphic's code number.

Try out the procedure on a specific graphic; say number 156.

- Step 1: For pixel 0—$0.2^0 = 0$
  For pixel 1—$0.2^1 = 0$
  For pixel 2—$0.2^2 = 4$
  For pixel 3—$1.2^3 = 8$
  For pixel 4—$1.2^4 = 16$
  For pixel 5—$0.2^5 = 0$
- Step 2: $0 + 0 + 4 + 8 + 16 = 28$
- Step 3: $128 + 28 = 156$

Sure enough, the procedure works. There is a definite mathematical relationship between the configuration of each graphic and its assigned code number. Try it on any other graphic.

If you are already familiar with the process of converting 6-bit binary numbers (combinations of 1s and 0s) into a decimal format, the procedure should look rather familiar—familiar, because that's what it is. The only significant variation on the old binary-to-decimal conversion theme is the need to add 128 at the end of the procedure.

That is a purely mathematical procedure, and since you have a computer sitting there, and since computers are supposed to be good at doing mathematical operations, you might as well let it do the figuring for you.

The program for Project 2-3 is really something more than a simple demonstration program. Later on you will find it to be an invaluable aid for determining the graphic code numbers for your drawings on the screen. Using this program certainly is better than having to look up the graphic code number for the dozens, and perhaps hundreds, of graphic elements you will be using in a display. In short, the program makes the

**TABLE 2-1**

POWER-OF-2 VALUES FOR DETERMINING GRAPHIC CODE NUMBERS

| |
|---|
| $2^0 = 1$ |
| $2^1 = 2$ |
| $2^2 = 4$ |
| $2^3 = 8$ |
| $2^4 = 16$ |
| $2^5 = 32$ |

**summary of graphic figures in Fig. 2–3 obsolete. Now your computer does all that searching for you.**

## PROJECT 2–3

The program in Listing 2–3 lets you specify or determine a graphic code number by simply typing in the 1 or 0 value for the six pixels in any desired graphic figure. When you have done that, the computer displays your original combination of 1s and 0s, the graphic code those combinations represent, and the graphic itself.

```
10 REM ** PROJECT 2-3 **
20 CLS:C=0
30 PRINT "TYPE THE NUMERIC VALUE FOR EACH PIXEL"
35 PRINT TAB(5);"(0 FOR BLACK, 1 FOR WHITE)":PRINT "?"
40 FOR  P=0 TO 5
50 S$=INKEY$:IF S$="" THEN 50
60 S=ASC(S$)-48:IF NOT(S=0 OR S=1) THEN  50
70 S(P)=S:PRINT S;
80 NEXT P
90 CLS:FOR P=0 TO 5
100 PRINT S(P);
110 C=C+S(P)*2[P
120 NEXT P
130 PRINT:PRINT C+128,CHR$(C+128)
140 INPUT S$:GOTO 20
150 '
160 '
170 'NOTE:  [=UP ARROW
```

**LISTING 2–3** Programming for Project 2–3

When you RUN this program, you first see a prompting message:

TYPE THE NUMERIC VALUE FOR EACH PIXEL
(0 FOR BLACK, 1 FOR WHITE)

Respond by typing the 1s and 0s in the desired graphic figure, using the left-to-right, top-to-bottom sequence described a bit earlier in this discussion. The keyboard is "live" through this process, so you do not have to strike the ENTER key after typing each digit. In fact, you shouldn't strike the ENTER key at all. If you happen to strike the wrong key, you have to restart the sequence, either by RUNning from the beginning or by typing in any combination of 1s and 0s until the program recycles to start another entry process.

After you've typed in the final digit, the program automatically summarizes your entry and shows the correct code number and a picture of the little graphic. Then, after having a chance to view the results, you should strike the ENTER key to start with another series of pixel values.

### complementing the codes, or reversing blacks and whites

As the following chapter will describe, you can build pictures from the elementary graphic characters by stringing the characters together to compose a larger and more complex figure. It seems more natural to think in terms of plotting white figures onto a black background than white onto black and I imagine that is the perspective that was taken by those who devised the TRS–80 graphics set. However, the visual impression of many kinds of graphics can be greatly enhanced if that thinking is reversed—thinking in terms of black figures being plotted onto a white background. And of equal importance is the notion that it might be necessary at times to reverse the black-and-white patterns already composed at some previous time.

Since the pixel patterns in the TRS–80 graphic characters have an underlying binary configuration, it should be possible to complement the binary values—exchange all the 1s for 0s and the 0s for 1s—and come up with a graphic that has the same general configuration but a reversal of the black and white pixels. Indeed, that can be done.

To see this idea at work, select any TRS–80 graphic from Fig. 2–3 and subtract its code number from 319. Use the numeric result as a new code number, and look up its graphic. Lo! the two graphic characters are negatives of one another.

*To reverse the blacks and whites for any TRS–80 graphic, subtract the original code number from 319. The result will be the code number for the reversed black-and-white graphic.*

Perhaps this matter of coming up with a black-and-white reversal of a graphic character is of purely academic significance at this point. However, by writing the conversion—subtracting code number from 319—into a drawing program, you can see the picture with reversed colors, though the image will retain the same form.

It is unfortunate that this cannot be done with the printable keyboard characters that are to be described next.

## THE ALPHANUMERIC CHARACTER SET

Virtually all home computers generate the same set of alphanumeric characters: letters of the alphabet, numerals 0 through 9, standard punctuation marks, and a few special symbols. All of these characters have standard ASCII code numbers (decimal 32 through 95) assigned to them, and most are directly printable from the keyboard. The lower-case alphabetical characters that are normally assigned ASCII decimal codes 96 through 127 are not used in this book. Readers who happen to have the lower-case hardware installed in their systems can use those characters, however.

The typical listing of keyboard characters and their corresponding decimal ASCII codes is shown in Fig. 2-4.

The alphanumeric characters occupy the upper four pixels in their character spaces. The lower set of pixels is always set to black, thereby forming a space that separates lines of printed text on the CRT.

Many of the alphanumeric characters, especially some of the special symbols, can be made into interesting parts of wholly graphic figures. The arrows, for instance, can be shot across the screen from a cupid's bow,

| *CODE* | *CHARACTER* | *CODE* | *CHARACTER* |
|---|---|---|---|
| 32 | space | 64 | @ |
| 33 | ! | 65 | A |
| 34 | " | 66 | B |
| 35 | # | 67 | C |
| 36 | $ | 68 | D |
| 37 | % | 69 | E |
| 38 | & | 70 | F |
| 39 | ' | 71 | G |
| 40 | ( | 72 | H |
| 41 | ) | 73 | I |
| 42 | * | 74 | J |
| 43 | + | 75 | K |
| 44 | , | 76 | L |
| 45 | - | 77 | M |
| 46 | . | 78 | N |
| 47 | / | 79 | O |
| 48 | 0 | 80 | P |
| 49 | 1 | 81 | Q |
| 50 | 2 | 82 | R |
| 51 | 3 | 83 | S |
| 52 | 4 | 84 | T |
| 53 | 5 | 85 | U |
| 54 | 6 | 86 | V |
| 55 | 7 | 87 | W |
| 56 | 8 | 88 | X |
| 57 | 9 | 89 | Y |
| 58 | : | 90 | Z |
| 59 | ; | 91 | ↑ |
| 60 | < | 92 | ↓ |
| 61 | = | 93 | ← |
| 62 | > | 94 | → |
| 63 | ? | 95 | — |

**FIGURE 2-4** TRS-80 alphanumeric characters having ASCII decimal codes 32 through 95

periods and asterisks can be printed as stars in a nighttime sky, and commas can be tears from the eyes of a crying face. The applications are limited only by one's own imagination and creative skill.

These alphanumeric characters are always printed as white on a black background. There is no way that can be changed without installing special hardware. What's more, each character totally dominates one complete character space on the screen. Even when a tiny character such as a period occupies just one pixel, the remaining five pixels in the character location are automatically set to black—nothing else can be printed in those "unused" pixels. You can see that using the special TRS-80 graphics gives one greater control over the screen than using the alphanumerics does.

# 3 Selecting Characters and Getting Them Onto the Screen

The main purpose of this chapter is to make sure you understand the basic principles for selecting a character and printing it at the desired place on the CRT screen. The examples are necessarily simple ones. Procedures for generating more elaborate images will be introduced in the chapter that follows.

## THE TRS-80 VIDEO DISPLAY WORKSHEET

Throughout your experiences with TRS-80 graphics, the selection of special graphic characters, the placement of any character onto the screen, and, indeed, the organization of virtually all images rest heavily on the use of Radio Shack's Video Display Worksheet (Radio Shack catalog number 26-2105). See Fig. 3-1.

The worksheet shows the pixel configuration for every character

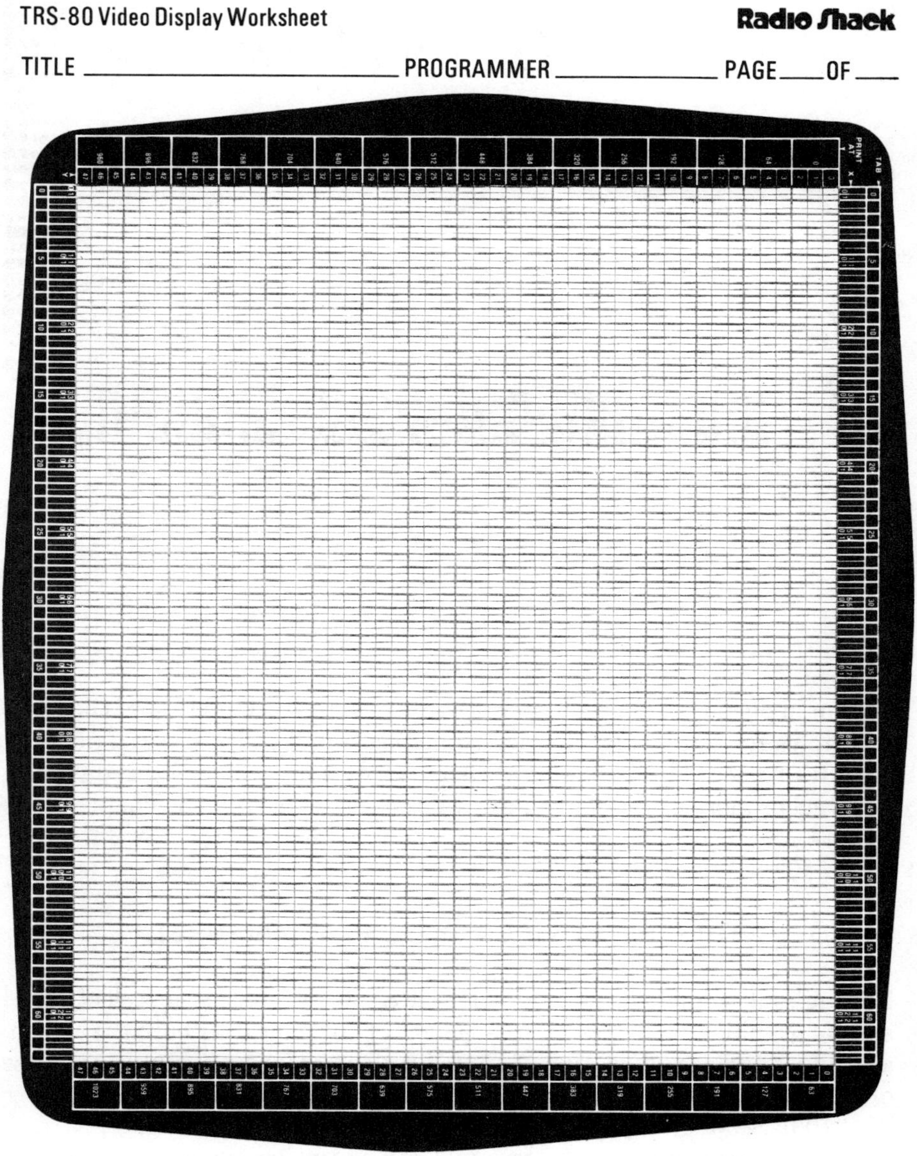


**FIGURE 3-1** The TRS-80 Video Display Worksheet

space on the screen and, what is even more important, the numbers used for designating the character positions.

Generally speaking, a picture is first sketched onto one of the video worksheets. Since the worksheets are scored with the exact dimensions of the pixels, character spaces, and field, this preliminary drawing step gives you a chance to determine the actual sizes, positions, and spacings of all elements of the picture.

After making the preliminary sketch, you modify the drawing, making as few compromises as possible while conforming to the pixel and character-space configurations.

Then you determine which graphic is to be used in the character spaces and assign a position number to each of them. Finally, you devise a computer program that causes your picture to be drawn onto the screen.

There is a lot to be said about the video worksheet and the suggested drawing procedure, but it is sufficient at this point to indicate the importance of the worksheet.

## POSITIONING CHARACTERS WITH THE PRINT @ STATEMENT

As described in the previous chapter, the CRT drawing field is divided into 1024 character spaces. Those character spaces are clearly outlined on the video worksheet.

Running down the left side of the worksheet is a series of PRINT AT numbers—0 through 960 in increments of 64. When you are using PRINT @ statements to position characters on the screen, those numbers indicate the first character position on each line. So if you want to print the letter *A* at the beginning of the second line from the top of the screen, you would use a statement such as:

```
PRINT @ 64,"A"
```

If you want to position a letter *B* near the middle, left-hand edge of the screen, you could do this:

```
PRINT @ 448,"B"
```

There are also some PRINT AT numbers along the right-hand edge of the video worksheet. They start at 63 and run through 1023 at intervals of 64. Those are the PRINT @ positions for characters to be printed along the right-hand edge of the field. If, for example, you want to place a *C* in the upper right-hand corner of the screen, an appropriate PRINT @ statement would be:

```
PRINT @ 63,"C"
```

Thus the first PRINT @ line begins at 0 and ends at 63. The second line begins at 64 and ends at 127. All 16 PRINT @ lines are labeled in that fashion.

But what if you want to print a character somewhere besides the extreme left or right side of the field? Well, there are 64 character spaces in each line, and they can be numbered consecutively, beginning with the PRINT AT number on the left side of the worksheet. The TAB numbers along the top of the worksheet help determine where the character is to be positioned on each line.

The position numbers for plotting a character with a PRINT @ statement can be viewed as the result of using an X–Y coordinate system. The Y, or vertical position, is determined by the PRINT AT number along the left side of the worksheet. The X, or horizontal position, is determined by the TAB number along the top of the worksheet. You can print a letter *X* near the middle of the screen by this statement:

```
PRINT @ 448 + 31,"X"
```

The position number for the PRINT @ statement is reckoned by summing the PRINT AT line number with the TAB space number. Of course you could do the summing operation yourself, using this statement to do exactly the same thing:

```
PRINT @ 479,"X"
```

Use the procedure that suits your own style and manner of thinking.

### printing the special graphics

Any of the printable keyboard characters can be plotted on the screen via PRINT @ statement if the character is enclosed in quotes. The special TRS–80 graphics characters, however, cannot be printed in that fashion, simply because those characters are not directly represented anywhere on the keyboard.

The special graphics must be printed with reference to their code numbers, 128 through 191. In order to fit one of those code numbers into a PRINT @ statement, it must be altered by means of a CHR$ function. Thus, printing graphic 153 at PRINT AT position 448 calls for a BASIC statement of this form:

```
PRINT @ 448,CHR$(153)
```

To put graphic 191 near the middle of the screen, try this:

```
PRINT @ 448 + 32,CHR$(191)
```

Thus, the PRINT @ statement can be used for positioning and plotting any of the 64 special TRS-80 graphics as long as the graphic code number is treated with a CHR$ function.

Incidentally, the ASCII keyboard characters can be printed that way, too. You can, if you wish, print the letter *A* at character position 580 by doing this:

```
PRINT @ 580,CHR$(65)
```

Simply apply the CHR$ function to the ASCII code number for the character you want to print. Whether you use this CHR$ approach, or actually show the character enclosed in a set of quotes, depends largely on the situation at hand. No such option exists for the special graphic characters, however; they must be printed with the CHR$ function.

### avoiding the scrolling effect

Whenever a TRS-80 BASIC program comes to a conclusion, the system automatically prints READY at the beginning of the next line, and a greater-than prompt symbol on the line after that. In other words, BASIC programs conclude by committing two additional lines of text to the READY and prompt symbol.

Further consider that the TRS-80 is set up to scroll lines of text upward, one line at a time, whenever additional lines of text would otherwise cause the printing to take place below the bottom of the screen. When the screen is full of text, the next line to be printed goes to the bottom line, all previous lines are moved up, and the top line is lost. That's not a bad feature when you are writing BASIC programs, but it can cause havoc when you are trying to fix a picture on the screen.

Try this:

```
PRINT @ 896,CHR$(191)
```

That statement supposedly prints a graphic 191—a full character space of white—at the beginning of the second line from the bottom of the screen. The computer will do precisely that; but when the statement has been executed and the system automatically returns to the BASIC monitor, the READY message and prompt symbol will appear at the beginning of the next two lines. That will scroll the display up one line, and your graphic-191 figure will appear at 832 instead of 896.

The scrolling problem isn't critical if the last PRINT @ statement puts a character somewhere else besides the last two lines, but it can be a problem if you want to print something down there.

There are two ways to get around the hazards of the scrolling effect.

One is to make sure the last-used PRINT @ statement does not put a character anywhere on the last two lines. The other, perhaps more suitable in most instances, is to prevent the program from coming to a conclusion until you are finished viewing the picture on the screen.

The following program sequence lets you print a graphic 191 at position 960—at the beginning of the last line—without kicking it out of place when the program ends:

```
10 PRINT @ 960,CHR$(191)
20 PRINT @ 0,""
```

Line 20 puts the cursor at position 0 and prints the null character (nothing). The sequence thus ends with the READY and prompt symbol in the upper left-hand corner of the screen. The graphic-191 character is printed in the lower left-hand corner, and its position is not disturbed at the conclusion of the program.

The alternate approach looks like this:

```
10 PRINT @ 960,CHR$(191)
20 GOTO 20
```

That is a case of preventing the program from concluding. Graphic 191 will appear at the beginning of the bottom line, and it will remain there indefinitely. Actually, the program "buzzes" on line 20, and the most suitable way to get out of the program is by striking the BREAK key. The READY message and prompt symbols will appear after doing the BREAK; but until then, you can view the graphic to your heart's content.

## POSITIONING CHARACTERS WITH POKE STATEMENTS

POKE statements can be used for plotting keyboard characters and graphics in much the same way PRINT @ statements are used. The screen is still viewed as 1024 character spaces that are organized into 16 lines having 64 characters in each line. Only the scaling is different.

The PRINT @ screen format uses position numbers 0 through 1023. POKE graphics does the same thing using position numbers 15360 through 16383. In fact, it is perfectly legitimate to convert a PRINT @ character position to a POKE position by simply adding 15360. Conversely, a POKE position number can be converted to a PRINT @ number by subtracting 15360. It can be important to remember those conversions, especially considering that the TRS-80 video worksheet does not show POKE-oriented screen-position numbers.

## plotting the special graphics with POKE statements

A typical POKE statement has this general form:

```
POKE 15360,153
```

That will plot graphic 153 at POKE position 15360—at the extreme upper left-hand corner of the screen. By way of a slight variation of the idea, suppose you want to plot a graphic 191 near the middle of the screen. Here is one convenient way to go about it:

```
POKE(15360 + 448 + 31),191
```

The 191 in that statement is, of course, the desired graphic code number. The computer, however, is left to calculate the POKE position: the 448 and 31 come from the PRINT AT and TAB figures on the video worksheet (together, they represent the PRINT @ position), and the 15360 is added to convert the number into a POKE position. If you care to do the position calculation yourself, this statement does the same job:

```
POKE 15839,191
```

Any of the 64 special graphic characters can be POKEd that way—with a POKE position followed by a comma and the graphic code number.

## plotting keyboard characters with POKE statements

The graphic to be POKEd into a designated position on the screen must be presented as a numeric value. That requirement suits the special TRS-80 graphic symbols quite nicely, but one has to be careful when selecting one of the printable keyboard characters.

The data to be POKEd must be represented as an ASCII character code. Printing letter *A* at the upper left-hand corner of the screen is thus a matter of executing this statement:

```
POKE 15360,65
```

Alternately:

```
POKE 15360,ASC("A")
```

In the latter instance, the keyboard string character *A*, is transformed into its ASCII counterpart by means of the ASC function. To be sure, it is an awkward procedure, and perhaps its only redeeming feature is that it saves you the trouble of looking up the ASCII code number for the character you want to POKE onto the screen.

### avoiding the scrolling effect and printover

POKEing graphics into the two lower lines on the screen does not, in itself, cause any scrolling. Scrolling, as described earlier, is the result of some kinds of PRINT operations in those two lower lines. Even when using only POKE graphics, however, scrolling can occur *when the program comes to an end* and the system returns to the BASIC monitor—when it prints the READY message and prompt symbol. Scrolling will occur if the program comes to an end and the PRINT cursor (whether used or not during the program) happens to be resting on one of the two lower lines on the screen.

The most effective way to get around that situation is by starting a POKE-drawing routine with a CLS statement. Doing a CLS clears the screen and sends the PRINT cursor (although invisible) to the upper left-hand corner of the screen. And as long as no PRINT statements are used in the drawing program, the invisible cursor will remain in that corner. Thus there will be no chance of scrolling when the POKE routine comes to an end and the system returns to the BASIC monitor.

Then there is another kind of problem. Suppose you write a drawing program that uses only POKE graphics. Maybe the picture occupies the entire graphic field. When the drawing routine is done, the program comes to a conclusion, and then that pesky READY and prompt symbol messes up the picture. What is the cure for this printover effect? It's simple: don't let the program come to a conclusion until you are ready for it to do so. And that is best accomplished by putting the program into an endless loop. Here is a simple example:

```
10 CLS:POKE 15424,191
20 GOTO 20
```

The little routine prints a graphic 191, but then latches up at line 20, executing that line again and again. The program never comes to an end, so the graphic is not messed up by the unwanted appearance of the READY message and BASIC prompt symbol. You terminate the program when you're ready by simply striking the BREAK key.

# 4 Composing Single, Static Figures

This chapter illustrates the techniques most often used for composing *static,* or nonanimated, figures on the screen. The relative complexity of the picture is irrelevant here; the figures may be made up of a mere handful of graphic characters or a thousand. The procedures are tailored to one-of-a kind images that can be interesting or esthetically pleasing in their own right.

This marks a good starting point for a discussion of TRS–80 graphics techniques because the programming principles are about as straightforward as any can be. A good understanding of standard BASIC and elementary programming procedures suffices in this case. The only trade-off is the relatively slow drawing speed, but that is not a real problem with nonanimated, one-of-a-kind drawings.

That is not to say, however, that the techniques offered here are used only for static drawings. Some of the elements can be used in animated pictures to some extent.

## STARTING WITH THE VIDEO WORKSHEET

Fig. 4-1 shows a simple graphic design that will be used as a model for demonstrating the various ways to go about stringing together its character elements and positioning them on the screen. The characters and their screen positions will be the same for each of the techniques described, so no matter which technique you decide is best for this particular image, you will need the same preliminary analysis of its elements.

The first step in composing a picture of this sort is to draw it onto the video worksheet, making it conform to the arrangement of character spaces and pixels. It is equally important at this time to designate the areas that are to be black and those that are to be white. In this case the figure is to be white on a black background.

The image is also shown in the exact position it is to have on the CRT screen. As demonstrated in the next chapter, it isn't always necessary to make a worksheet drawing that shows the exact position of the figure. Here, however, the image is to be centered on the screen, and it is shown that way by the PRINT @ numbers on the worksheet: the middle of the worksheet is between PRINT @ lines 448 and 512, and between TAB positions 31 and 32.

After you draw the picture onto the video worksheet, it is time to specify exactly which graphics are to be used. This is perhaps the most tedious and time-consuming step; it requires studying each character space and determining the graphic code for its particular combination of white and black pixels.

If you look at the first line of characters in this image and study them from left to right, you will find that the graphic-code sequence is this:

```
188, 191, 143, 143, 191, 188
```

The second line of characters is:

```
139, 191, 188, 188, 191, 135
```

With these graphic codes thus defined and arranged in a systematic, left-to-right, line-by-line fashion, the next step is to determine their respective positions on the screen.

In order to center this image, the first graphic in the first line should be located at PRINT @ position 477. Once you know that, the other positions fall into place. With the first line of graphics beginning at 477, the second one in that line must be at 478, the next at 479, then 480, 481, and 482.

The worksheet drawing shows that the second line of graphics begins at PRINT @ position 541, so its remaining characters spaces occupy locations 542, 543, 544, 545, and 546, respectively.

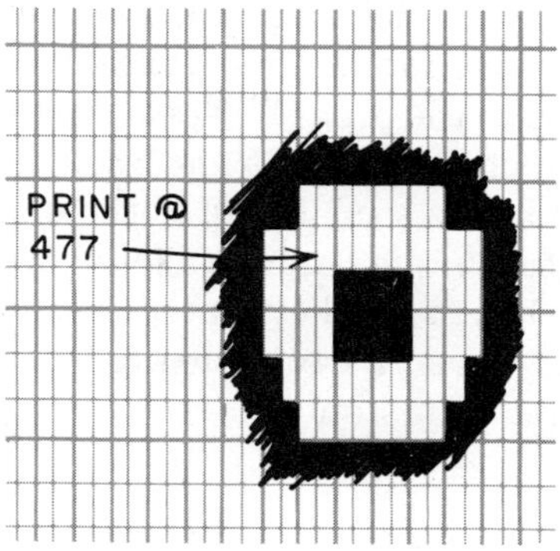


**FIGURE 4-1** A simple worksheet figure

The analysis defines the exact screen positions for all 12 graphics used in this particular image. You will soon find, however, that it is rarely necessary to determine all the character positions: it is usually sufficient to know just the starting position of each line that is used.

At any rate, the image is now completely specified in terms of the graphic characters to be used and their positions on the screen. It is finally time to begin writing BASIC programs for getting that information into the computer and transformed into the desired picture on the CRT screen.

The following sections describe four different approaches to generating the appropriate program. Conspicuous by their absence are POKE and machine-language graphic statement; those are generally reserved for drawing animated figures.

## USING A PRINT @ STATEMENT FOR EACH CHARACTER

## PROJECT 4–1

Write a BASIC program for drawing the image in Fig. 4–1, using a PRINT @/CHR$ combination for each character. See the suggested listing in Listing 4–1.

```
10 REM ** PROJECT 4-1
15 REM          SIMPLE FIGURE
20 CLS
25 PRINT @ 477,CHR$(188):PRINT @ 478,CHR$(191):PRINT @ 479,CHR$(143)
30 PRINT @ 480,CHR$(143):PRINT @ 481,CHR$(191):PRINT @ 482,CHR$(188)
35 PRINT @ 541,CHR$(139):PRINT @ 542,CHR$(191):PRINT @ 543,CHR$(188)
40 PRINT @ 544,CHR$(188):PRINT @ 545,CHR$(191):PRINT @ 546,CHR$(135)
```

**LISTING 4–1** Programming for Project 4–1

This is hardly the simplest way to go about writing a graphics program. Each element in the picture occupies a PRINT @ and CHR$ statement. Line 25 in the program, for instance, sets the screen positions and character types for the first three characters in the picture. In a similar way, line 30 in the program specifies the remaining characters in the first line of the picture. Lines 35 and 36 in the program do the same task for the characters in the second line of the image.

This technique requires a lot of typing at the keyboard, and the more typing one has to do, the greater the chances of making a programming error. It is, however, a workable procedure that can have some applications in a few limited instances.

## TAKING ADVANTAGE OF AUTOMATIC CURSOR MOVEMENT

It is possible to use the same general approach suggested by Project 4–1 and yet modify it so that it is easier to type into the computer. This modification also requires less program memory.

Unless directed otherwise, any sort of PRINT statement, including the PRINT @ statement, concludes by automatically moving the printing cursor down to the beginning of the next line on the screen. A subsequent PRINT statement (not a PRINT @) would begin printing from that place.

However, if the PRINT or PRINT @ statement is directed to suppress the automatic linefeed/carriage return feature, the statement concludes with the cursor resting at the next character position on the same line. The simplest way to suppress the automatic linefeed/carriage return is to include a semicolon at the end of that PRINT or PRINT @ statement.

What bearing does this have on the topic at hand? It means that it is possible to write image-drawing programs that use PRINT @ statements only to specify the starting point of each line in the image. The remaining characters on a given line can be specified without any direct reference to their position; the computer itself keeps track of the next character position. Consider the following project.

### PROJECT 4–2

Modify Listing 4–1 so that a PRINT @ statement appears only where a new line is to begin in the drawing. See the result in Listing 4–2.

```
10 REM ** PROJECT 4-2
15 REM          SIMPLE FIGURE
20 CLS
25 PRINT @ 477,CHR$(188);CHR$(191);CHR$(143);CHR$(143);CHR$(191);CHR$(188)
30 PRINT @ 541,CHR$(139);CHR$(191);CHR$(188);CHR$(188);CHR$(191);CHR$(135)
```

**LISTING 4–2** Programming for Project 4–2

Line 25 in the program completely specifies the positions and graphics for the first line of characters in the image. The first part of that line points to the position of the first character, but after that the semicolons inserted ahead of each CHR$ function allows the cursor to move to the next character position on that same line. Once the starting point of the line is specified with the initial PRINT @ statement, the combinations of semicolons and CHR$ functions take care of setting the graphics for the remainder of that line.

Line 30 uses the same technique for drawing the elements of the second line in the image.

This is clearly a simpler program than the one used in Project 4-1. It is also easier to debug and modify.

Using this technique, it is still necessary to figure out the graphic code for each character space involved in the picture. However, when it comes to specifying the positions, you need be concerned only with the position of the first characters in each line.

## COMPRESSING THE PROGRAM FURTHER WITH THE STRING$ FUNCTION

Looking over the specifications for the graphics to be used in Fig. 4-1, you can see that a particular graphic is used twice in succession on two different occasions. In the first line of the image, there are two 143s in succession, and in the second line there are two 188s used in succession.

Whenever there is more than one graphic of the same kind appearing in succession, a STRING$ function can save some programming time and memory space. A STRING$ function has this general form:

STRING$(N,T)
where N is the number of identical characters to be printed in succession;
T is the character code number.

So a statement such as PRINT @ 512,STRING$(16,191) will print a row of sixteen 191 graphics, beginning at the PRINT @ location 512. Using that statement is certainly easier than having to type sixteen CHR$(191) statements in succession.

A single STRING$ function can handle up to 255 successive characters. Doing PRINT STRING$(255,191), for example, will call for printing 255 graphic 191s in succession. That is almost four full lines of them (four lines less 1 character space). But if you type in that command on your TRS-80, you just might get an OS error—out of string space. Why is that? What can be done about it?

When the TRS–80 is first turned on, or whenever any sort of action brings up the MEMORY SIZE initialization routine, it automatically sets aside 50 bytes in memory for string characters. That means the largest workable STRING$ statement is one calling for 50 successive characters. And that is why the system turns up an OS error when you try to print strings longer than 50 characters.

To set aside more memory space for strings, simply type a CLEAR *n* command, where *n* is the number of bytes you want to reserve for strings. Doing CLEAR 256, for instance, makes it possible to execute the PRINT STRING$(255,191) statement. Always set aside a number of string bytes that equals or exceeds the number you will be using in the program.

Doing a CLEAR 1024 from the keyboard will clear quite a bit of memory for strings. Once that is done, it remains in force until the computer is initialized to MEMORY SIZE again, or until you change the value by doing another CLEAR command. It need not be written into every little program you write, just as long as you do the CLEAR command at the beginning of your work session. However, if you plan to save the program on tape or disk, it is a good idea to include an appropriate CLEAR *n* command at the very beginning of the program. That way, the program will run properly, even if you load it immediately after turning on the computer.

Thus if you see the OS error while you are experimenting with graphics programs, simply take a moment to do a CLEAR command that specifies a larger number of string bytes.

As illustrated in the next project, STRING$ functions can be imbedded in a series of CHR$ functions.

## PROJECT 4–3

Use STRING$ functions to compress the program from Project 4–2. See the result in Listing 4–3.

```
10 REM  ** PROJECT 4-3
15 REM         SIMPLE FIGURE
20 CLS
25 PRINT @ 477,CHR$(188);CHR$(191);STRING$(2,143);CHR$(191);CHR$(188)
30 PRINT @ 541,CHR$(139);CHR$(191);STRING$(2,188);CHR$(191);CHR$(135)
```

**LISTING 4–3** Programming for Project 4–3

In this case, the program doesn't appear to be significantly shorter than the version in Listing 4–2. There would be a much more noticeable difference if the original program called for using the same graphic a relatively large number of times in succession.

There is no need to execute the CLEAR command in this case

because none of the STRING$ statements calls for using more than 50 characters in succession.

This CHR$/STRING$ technique is one that can be used for generating any sort of static pictures on the screen. It is a fairly straightforward technique, and the programming is easy to follow. The overall procedure can be summarized as follows:

- Draw the desired image on the video worksheet.
- Determine the character codes for all the graphics to be used, preferably arranging them in a left-to-right, line-by-line pattern on a sheet of paper.
- Determine the PRINT @ position for the first graphic in each line of the image.
- Write a BASIC program that:
  - CLEARs sufficient string space if any STRING$ function calls for more than 50 characters.
  - Indicates the beginning of each line in the image with a PRINT @ statement.
  - Uses CHR$ functions where side-by-side characters are different.
  - Uses STRING$ functions to compress character codes in instances where the same character is used more than one time in succession.

## PROJECT 4–4

Use the procedure just outlined to write a BASIC program that draws the white-on-black image of a burning candle that is shown in Fig. 4–2. The worksheet analysis is represented in Table 4–1, and the suggested program is in Listing 4–4.

```
10 REM **  PROJECT 4-4
20 REM          FLAMING CANDLE
30 CLS
40 PRINT @ 209,CHR$(176)
50 PRINT @ 270,CHR$(184);CHR$(190);STRING$(2,191);CHR$(148)
60 PRINT @ 334,CHR$(175);STRING$(3,191);CHR$(133)
70 PRINT @ 399,CHR$(147)
80 PRINT @ 460,CHR$(191);CHR$(188);CHR$(176);CHR$(177);CHR$(176)
90 PRINT @ 524,STRING$(6,191);CHR$(149)
100 PRINT @ 588,STRING$(7,191);CHR$(149)
110 PRINT @ 652,STRING$(6,191);CHR$(159);CHR$(149)
120 PRINT @ 716,STRING$(6,191);CHR$(133)
130 PRINT @ 780,STRING$(6,191)
140 PRINT @ 844,STRING$(6,191)
150 PRINT @ 908,STRING$(6,191)
160 GOTO 160
```

**LISTING 4-4** Programming for the flaming candle in Project 4-4

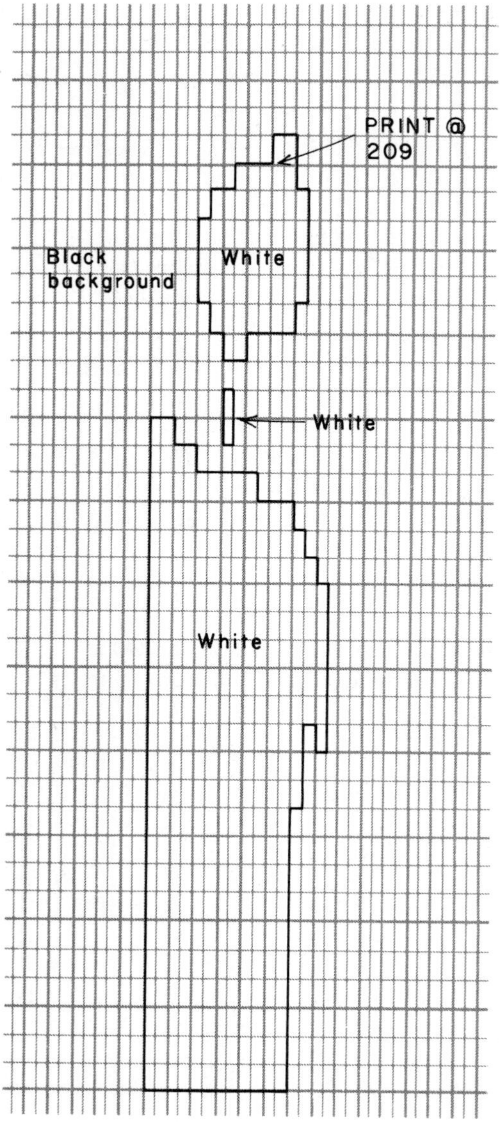


**FIGURE 4-2** Worksheet drawing for the flaming candle, Project 4-4

If you can understand the rationale behind the development of the worksheet analysis and every part of the program listing in that project, you are in a good position to begin composing static images of your own design.

**TABLE 4-1**

WORKSHEET ANALYSIS FOR THE FLAMING CANDLE IN PROJECT 4-4

| *Image Line* | *Start At* | *Character Codes* |
|---|---|---|
| 1 | 209 | 176 |
| 2 | 270 | 184,190,191,191,148 |
| 3 | 334 | 175,191,191,191,133 |
| 4 | 399 | 147 |
| 5 | 460 | 191,188,176,177,176 |
| 6 | 524 | 191,191,191,191,191,191,149 |
| 7 | 588 | 191,191,191,191,191,191,191,149 |
| 8 | 652 | 191,191,191,191,191,191,159,149 |
| 9 | 716 | 191,191,191,191,191,191,133 |
| 10 | 780 | 191,191,191,191,191,191 |
| 11 | 844 | 191,191,191,191,191,191 |
| 12 | 908 | 191,191,191,191,191,191 |

## CARRYING THE GRAPHIC CODES AS DATA ELEMENTS

It can become quite tedious to type long lists of CHR$ and STRING$ statements for every line in a large and complicated figure. The procedure suggested in the next project simplifies matters by using just one PRINT @ and one CHR$ statement for each line in the image to be drawn. All the character codes are carried in DATA lists and are called, one at a time, to the appropriate CHR$ function as they are needed.

The operation of this program isn't quite as straightforward as the preceding ones, so it may require some special explanation.

## PROJECT 4–5

Rewrite the program for drawing the image in Fig. 4–1 in such a way that it uses a single PRINT @ statement, one CHR$ function, and one DATA line for each line of characters in the picture. See Listing 4–5.

```
10 REM **  PROJECT 4-5
15 REM          SIMPLE FIGURE
20 CLS
25 READ A:PRINT @ 477,CHR$(A);:P=6:GOSUB 50
30 READ A:PRINT @ 541,CHR$(A);:P=6:GOSUB 50
35 END
50 FOR N=1 TO P-1:READ A:PRINT CHR$(A);:NEXT N:RETURN
125 DATA 188,191,143,143,191,188
130 DATA 139,191,188,188,191,135
```

**LISTING 4-5** Programming for Project 4-5

The program can be divided into three sections, and no matter how complex the picture might be, those three sections prevail. That is one of the hallmarks of the technique.

The section that hasn't been used thus far is the DATA section. There are two DATA lines in this particular case—one for each line of characters in the image. Furthermore, each DATA line is composed of the graphic code numbers, in a left-to-right order, for that line. That's helpful because the DATA lines look very much like the series of character codes you generate while making up the specifications from the original video worksheet; that means it is easier to locate incorrect codes or change some of them after the original programming has been done.

A second major section of the program appears in lines 25 and 30. In essence, these lines specify the starting position and the number of characters in each line of the picture. There are just two lines in the image, so there are just two program lines dedicated to this purpose. Line 25 in the program handles the first line in the image, and line 30 handles the second.

The first statement in those lines, READ A, reads the first item in the appropriate DATA list and assigns the value to variable A. Immediately after that, the PRINT @ statement and its CHR$ function plot that character into the first position of the line. After that, the number of characters in that line is assigned to variable P; there are six characters in each line of this image.

With the number of characters to be printed in the line thus assigned to variable P, the program does a GOSUB 50. Line 50 is a one-line subroutine that calls the remaining character codes from the appropriate DATA list and prints them onto the screen.

By the time the system completes its execution of lines 25 and 30, the drawing is done.

This approach has some nice features. As mentioned earlier, it is no small advantage to be able to show all the graphics to be printed as items in a DATA list. That makes the matter of debugging the character code numbers a rather simple one.

Another good feature of this approach is that there is just one three-statement program line that is used for setting the starting position, plotting the first character, and setting the number of characters to be printed in each line of the picture. If the picture happened to be composed of 12 lines of characters, instead of just 2 as shown here, there would be 12 of those three-statement program lines. In each case, variable A is read from the DATA list and represents a character code number, and P is the number of characters in that line. If a line happened to have 56 different characters in it, P would be set to 56.

Line 50, the drawing subroutine for all but the first character in each line, remains unchanged, no matter how complicated the picture might be.

In the light of some previous illustrations, the only disadvantage of this approach is that the STRING$, data-compression procedures cannot be applied. (Actually they can be applied, but that tends to destroy the simplicity of the whole approach). Therefore if an image calls for printing 16 graphic-150 symbols in succession, the corresponding DATA line would have to show 16 150s in a row.

Here is how you can apply this approach to your own needs. First, assume you have broken down the image this way:

1. The PRINT AT starting position for each line of characters
2. The graphic codes for each character in each line
3. The number of graphics in each line

Then type in a controlling line for each line in the picture, using this general format:

READ A:PRINT @ *s*, CHR$(A);:P = *n*: GOSUB *x*

where *s* is the PRINT AT starting position for the line
*n* is the number of characters in that line
*x* is the BASIC program line number for the FOR . . . NEXT subroutine.

After that, type in the printing subroutine just as it is shown in line 50 of Listing 4–5. Finally, type in the DATA lists, using one program line for each line in the picture.

Whenever it is necessary to add or delete a character at one of the DATA lines in the program, be sure to adjust the value of the P variable in the corresponding controlling line of the program.

This is the most complex figure yet described in this book, but it hardly represents the limit of complexity for the suggested drawing and programming procedures. The real test of your understanding of the matters is to attempt a drawing of your own.

## PROJECT 4–6

Use the DATA procedure just described to generate a BASIC program for drawing the aircraft figure in Fig. 4–3. The worksheet analysis appears in Table 4–2, and the suggested program is in Listing 4–6.

```
10 REM ** PROJECT 4-6
15 REM           AIRCRAFT
20 CLS
25 READ A:PRINT @ 192+30,CHR$(A);:P=4:GOSUB 500
30 READ A:PRINT @ 286,CHR$(A);:P=4:GOSUB 500
35 READ A:PRINT @ 351,CHR$(A);:P=2:GOSUB 500
40 READ A:PRINT @ 384+30,CHR$(A);:P=4:GOSUB 500
```

(*cont.*)

```
45 READ A:PRINT @ 448+26,CHR$(A);:P=12:GOSUB 500
50 READ A:PRINT @ 535,CHR$(A);:P=18:GOSUB 500
55 READ A:PRINT @ 599,CHR$(A);:P=18:GOSUB 500
60 READ A:PRINT @ 663,CHR$(A);:P=18:GOSUB 500
400 GOTO 400
500 FOR N=1 TO P-1:READ A:PRINT CHR$(A);:NEXT N:RETURN
525 DATA 160,190,189,144
530 DATA 191,177,178,191
535 DATA 191,191
540 DATA 168,191,191,148
545 DATA 160,180,160,184,151,191,191,171,180,144,184,144
550 DATA 160,180,128,186,175,175,191,149,191
552 DATA 191,170,191,191,175,181,128,184,144
555 DATA 186,191,191,191,188,184,191,181,191
557 DATA 191,186,191,189,184,191,191,191,181
560 DATA 128,130,130,130,130,128,128,128,191
562 DATA 191,128,128,128,129,129,129,129,128
```

**LISTING 4-6** Programming for the aircraft figure in Project 4-6

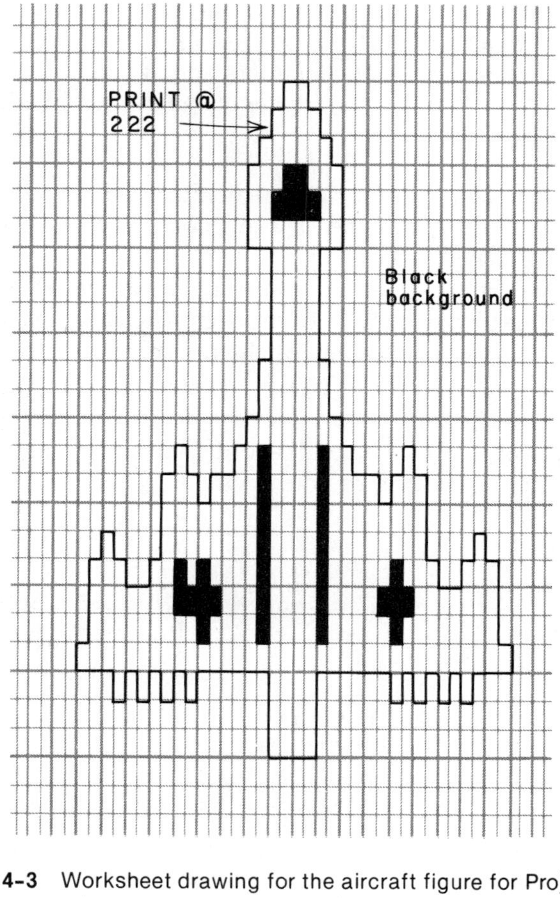


**FIGURE 4-3** Worksheet drawing for the aircraft figure for Project 4-6

**TABLE 4-2**
WORKSHEET ANALYSIS FOR THE AIRCRAFT FIGURE IN PROJECT 4-6

| Image Line | Start At | Character Codes |
|---|---|---|
| 1 | 192 + 30 | 160,190,189,144 |
| 2 | 286 | 191,177,178,191 |
| 3 | 351 | 191,191 |
| 4 | 384 + 30 | 168,191,191,148 |
| 5 | 448 + 26 | 160,180,160,184,151,191,191,171, 180,144,184,144 |
| 6 | 535 | 160,180,128,186,175,175,191,149,191 191,170,191,191,175,181,128,184,144 |
| 7 | 599 | 186,191,191,191,188,184,191,181,191 191,186,191,189,184,191,191,191,181 |
| 8 | 663 | 128,130,130,130,130,128,128,128,191 191,129,128,128,129,129,129,129,128 |

## BACK-SPACE CODE COMPRESSION

Drawing situations often call for plotting a number of full-black, or blank, character spaces in succession. The graphic code for a blank is 128, and the ASCII version is a 32. Thus, doing a PRINT CHR$(128) or PRINT CHR$(32) will plot a fully black character space on the screen.

It is possible, of course, to plot a series of blanks by means of a STRING$ function, doing something such as PRINT STRING$(12,128). That will plot 12 blank spaces in succession. There is really nothing wrong with the notion of plotting a series of blanks with the STRING$ function. The idea does not suit the DATA list technique however: that technique uses only CHR$ functions.

TRS-80 engineers have built in a handy procedure for plotting successive blanks; they use code numbers 192 to 255 to do the job. In the TRS-80 user's manual, they are called *space compression codes.* Here is how they work.

Doing a PRINT CHR$(192) does nothing at all (that, in itself, can be handy at times). Doing a PRINT CHR$(193) prints one blank space, and doing PRINT CHR$(194) plots two blank spaces in succession. A CHR$ function can be used for printing from 0 to 63 successive blank spaces. All you have to do is a statement such as PRINT CHR$(192 + $n$), where $n$ is the number of successive blanks you want to print. Just remember that $n$ cannot exceed 63 without bringing up an FC (function code) error.

Thus doing something such as PRINT CHR$(202) accomplishes the same task as doing a PRINT STRING$(10,128)—they both plot 10 blank spaces in succession. The advantage of the space-compression version is that its code numbers can be inserted into DATA lists and implemented with CHR$ functions.

# 5 Some Composition Techniques

It is possible to use the drawing techniques described thus far to compose full-screen pictures of great complexity. The general idea is to plot the entire picture onto the video worksheet, analyze it, line by line, into the appropriate series of graphic codes, and then develop a BASIC program that generates the image on the screen, line by line and character by character. The real composition is done on the video worksheet, and the matter of getting the information into the computer and onto the screen is a purely routine one.

That approach is entirely satisfactory when one is working with simple figures, but it can get in the way when one is attempting to compose pictures having a lot of individual elements, including background detail as well as some central figures. The techniques offered in this chapter make it possible to rearrange simpler individual figures once they are defined in the BASIC program. The individual elements of the picture can be clearly defined and analyzed on the video worksheet but arranged on the screen after their individual drawing elements have been entered into the computer. The procedure is analogous to cutting the individual elements of a picture from pieces of paper, then arranging them on a larger sheet of paper to come up with a complete composition. If nothing else, the procedure allows the graphic artist a degree of spontaneity in composing the overall picture. In computer jargon, the idea is one of in-line graphic composition.

The individual images described in this chapter are still rather simple ones, but you will find that the composition techniques are suitable for collecting those simple images into a much larger and more complex picture.

## RELOCATABLE STATIC FIGURES

The key to doing on-screen picture composition is to create picture elements that can be relocated on the screen with a minimal amount of program manipulation. This is done by keeping the PRINT @ position numbers in a very general form.

Fig. 5-1 shows a worksheet version of a simple figure that will be called SPACE CREATURE. The graphic codes used for generating the figure are still important, but the PRINT AT positions are not.

First, note the dashed line that is drawn vertically along the left-hand side of the image. That line is not to be drawn on the screen; rather, it marks the leftmost starting point for a line of characters. The leftmost starting line will not be shown in future images in this book, but you should assume that an imaginary version of it exists.

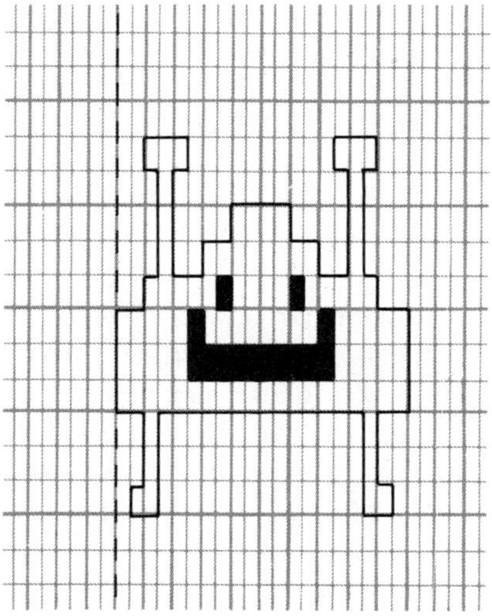

**FIGURE 5-1** Space Creature figure

But here is the important point. Notice that the first graphic character in the first of four lines in the image is indented one space to the right of the reference line; the same is true for the first graphic character in the second line. The first characters in the two lower lines, however, are situated in the space that is defined by the reference line. The PRINT @ statements for marking the beginning of each of the four lines in this picture can thus take this general form:

PRINT @ D + 1, . . . characters for first line
PRINT @ D + 1 + 64, . . . characters for second line
PRINT @ D + 128, . . . characters for third line
PRINT @ D + 192, . . . characters for fourth line

Variable D determines where the image will be printed on the screen. If, for example, D is set to zero, the first line of graphics will begin at PRINT @ position 1, the second line will begin at position 65, the third will begin at 128, and the fourth will begin at 192. With D equal to 0, the image will be drawn in the extreme upper left-hand corner of the graphics field, but if D is set to 350, the image will be drawn near the middle of the screen.

The value of D (the *displacement variable*) actually marks the PRINT @ position for the upper left-hand corner of the image. It might be a virtual position—no graphic actually plotted—but that's the general idea. The image can then be respositioned simply by one's changing the value of the displacement variable just prior to executing the PRINT @ statements that use it.

## PROJECT 5–1

Develop a relocatable version of the SPACE CREATURE image in Fig. 5–1. See the worksheet analysis in Table 5–1 and the suggested program in Listing 5–1.

```
10 REM ** PROJECT 5-1
15 REM          SPACE CREATURE
20 CLS
25 D=0
30 READ A:PRINT @ D+1,CHR$(A);:P=5:GOSUB 100
35 READ A:PRINT @ D+65,CHR$(A);:P=8:GOSUB 100
40 READ A:PRINT @ D+128,CHR$(A);:P=10:GOSUB 100
45 READ A:PRINT @ D+192,CHR$(A);:P=5:GOSUB 100
50 GOTO 50
100 FOR N=1 TO P-1:READ A:PRINT CHR$(A);:NEXT N:RETURN
125 DATA 172,132,196,136,156
130 DATA 186,176,156,191,191,172,176,181
135 DATA 191,191,181,179,179,179,179,186,191,191
140 DATA 160,149,198,170,144
```

**LISTING 5–1** Programming for Project 5–1

**TABLE 5-1**
WORKSHEET ANALYSIS FOR THE SPACE CREATURE

| *Image Line* | *PRINT @* | *Graphic DATA* |
|---|---|---|
| 1 | D+1 | 172,132,196,136,156 |
| 2 | D+65 | 186,176,156,191,191,172,176,181 |
| 3 | D+128 | 191,191,181,179,179,179,179,186 191,191 |
| 4 | D+192 | 160,149,198,170,144 |

The character codes from the worksheet analysis are built into the program's DATA lists, using space compression codes to replace successive blanks, or graphic 128s. The feature important to the present discussion, however, is the use of the displacement term, D. It is defined in line 25, then used thereafter to mark the starting point of the drawing for each new line in the image.

Change the value assigned to variable D in line 25, RUN the program, and note the new image position on the screen. If you happen to assign certain values to D, you will notice the creature figure being split between the right- and left-hand sides of the screen. Or, you might get an FC error that indicates you are trying to plot the image too close to the bottom of the screen. Those two undesirable effects can be avoided if you take a moment to think through the drawing procedure, noting for yourself whether the figure will be too close to the right side or bottom of the screen. Even if you do run the figure off the screen, there's no harm done; just assign a smaller value to variable D and try again.

Make up some simple images of your own, and test your understanding of making up BASIC programs for drawing relocatable images.

## MAKING MULTIPLE COPIES OF THE SAME IMAGE

You can draw relocatable figures a number of times on the screen by simply executing the drawing routine a number of times, using a different displacement value in each case.

## PROJECT 5–2

Revise Listing 5–1 so that it will print eight SPACE CREATURE images at eight different locations on the screen.

```
10 REM ** PROJECT 5-2
15 REM    MULTIPLE SPACE CREATURES
20 CLS
25 D=0:GOSUB 50:D=450:GOSUB 50
30 D=94:GOSUB 50:D=50:GOSUB 50
35 D=202:GOSUB 50:D=345:GOSUB 50
40 D=370:GOSUB 50:D=719:GOSUB 50
45 GOTO 45
50 READ A:PRINT @ D+1,CHR$(A);:P=5:GOSUB 100
55 READ A:PRINT @ D+65,CHR$(A);:P=8:GOSUB 100
60 READ A:PRINT @ D+128,CHR$(A);:P=10:GOSUB 100
65 READ A:PRINT @ D+192,CHR$(A);:P=5:GOSUB 100
70 RESTORE:RETURN
100 FOR N=1 TO P-1:READ A:PRINT CHR$(A);:NEXT N:RETURN
125 DATA 172,132,196,136,156
130 DATA 186,176,156,191,191,172,176,181
135 DATA 191,191,181,179,179,179,179,186,191,191
140 DATA 160,149,198,170,144
```

**LISTING 5-2** Programming for Project 5-2

Here, the drawing statements are rewritten as a subroutine that begins at line 50. Since it is a subroutine that is called by some control statements in lines 25 through 40, it must conclude with a RETURN statement. And since the DATA lists are read each time the drawing subroutine is called, it must also include a RESTORE statement.

The drawing control portion of the program simply sets a displacement value, D, then calls the drawing subroutine. Only the values of D are changed just prior to drawing another SPACE CREATURE image.

Any image can be specified just once in a program but then duplicated as long as sufficient room remains on the screen. This method is certainly better than writing the same series of PRINT @ drawing statements for each copy of the image.

## CREATING MULTIPLE-IMAGE COMPOSITIONS

Knowing how to relocate a single image on the screen opens the door for making multiple-image compositions—full-screen pictures that include two or more separate images. If you know how to generate one image, you can certainly make two or more of them; and if you know how to relocate one image on the screen, you can relocate more than one of them. The composition technique described here lets you work out the main elements of a full-screen picture one at a time, gradually working them into a single composition.

Of course it is possible to work out the entire composition on a video worksheet, analyze the whole thing into 16 lines of character codes, and then transform them into one big BASIC drawing program. But that tends to kill off an important sense of creative spontaneity. It is far more exciting to develop a complex, full-screen picture in a piecemeal fashion, modifying the images and experimenting with new ideas while the picture is taking shape on the screen.

The following series of projects demonstrate the technique for composing multiple-image, full-screen pictures. You will see that it is an evolutionary process that stimulates a sense of creativity rather than subduing it under a large-scale worksheet analysis and a tedious program listing.

The picture to be created in these projects is that of a little space creature landing in a flying saucer. Those are the two main elements of the picture. After you get those two images situated on the screen, you will touch up the picture with some background detail, some foreground elements and the inevitable message, "Take me to your leader."

The space creature will be the same one developed through the earlier projects in this chapter (a fact suggesting that images created at one time can be saved and used in later compositions). The flying saucer, however, has to be worked out from scratch in this case. Its worksheet drawing is shown in Fig. 5-2.

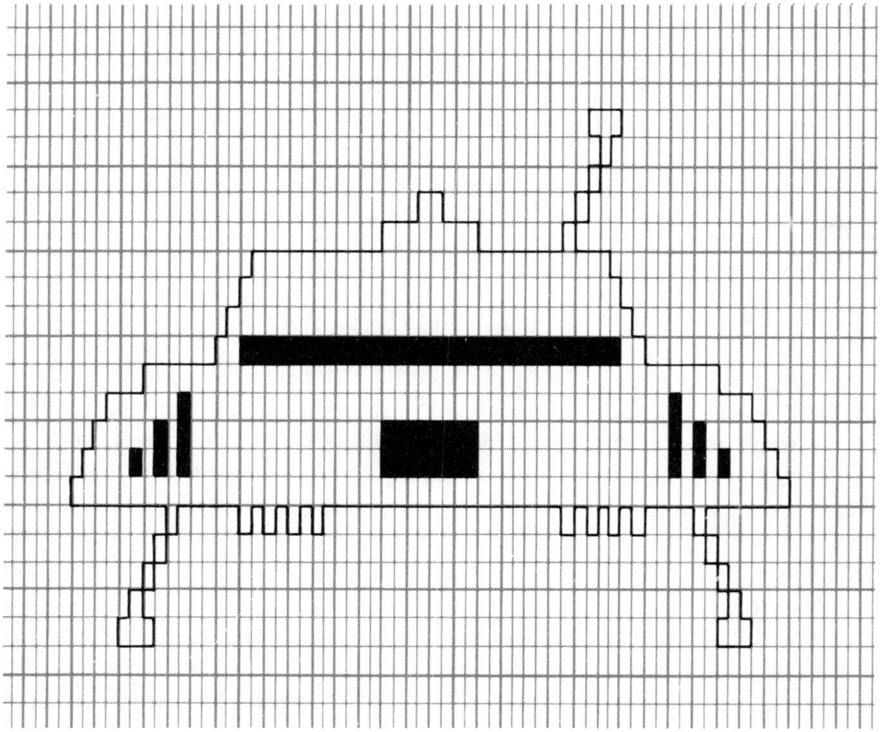

**FIGURE 5-2** Spacecraft figure

The flying saucer is basically a white image placed onto a black background. There is no need to darken the background on the worksheet as long as you can identify the pixels and character spaces that are to be white or black. The black detail within the flying saucer image is darkened, however, to get a better idea of how it will appear on the screen.

## PROJECT 5–3

Generate a BASIC program for drawing the flying saucer image shown in Fig. 5–2. See the suggested program in Listing 5–3.

```
10 REM **  PROJECT 5-3
15 REM          SPACECRAFT
20 CLS
25 D=0:GOSUB 1010
30 GOTO 30
1000 REM  ** DRAWING SUBROUTINES
1005 REM         SPACECRAFT
1010 READ A:PRINT @ D+20,CHR$(A);:P=2:GOSUB 1500
1015 READ A:PRINT @ D+76,CHR$(A);:P=7:GOSUB 1500
1020 READ A:PRINT @ D+134,CHR$(A);:P=18:GOSUB 1500
1025 READ A:PRINT @ D+193,CHR$(A);:P=28:GOSUB 1500
1030 READ A:PRINT @ D+256,CHR$(A);:P=30:GOSUB 1500
1035 READ A:PRINT @ D+323,CHR$(A);:P=15:GOSUB 1500
1040 READ A:PRINT @ D+386,CHR$(A);:P=5:GOSUB 1500
1045 RETURN
1500 FOR N=1 TO P-1:READ A:PRINT CHR$(A);:NEXT N:RETURN
2000 REM ** DATA LISTS
2005 REM         SPACECRAFT
2010 DATA 136,156
2015 DATA 176,184,180,176,195,160,134
2020 DATA 160,190,191,191,191,191,191,191,191
2022 DATA 191,191,191,191,191,191,191,189,144
2025 DATA 160,176,188,156,188,191,188,188,188,188,188,188,188,188
2027 DATA 188,188,188,188,188,188,188,188,191,188,172,188,176,176
2030 DATA 184,191,183,181,181,191,191,191,191,191,191,191,191,176,176
2032 DATA 176,176,191,191,191,191,191,191,191,191,186,186,187,191,180
2035 DATA 152,129,194,129,129,129,129,201,130,130,130,130,194,137,144
2040 DATA 142,132,215,142,132
```

**LISTING 5–3** Programming for Project 5–3

Load the program into your system and take a look at the SPACECRAFT figure. Debug the program, if necessary, and tinker around with the location of the figure by changing around the value assigned to the displacement variable in line 25.

The next step is to get the SPACE CREATURE into the same picture.

Listing 5–4 suggests a way to get both the SPACECRAFT and SPACE CREATURE figures onto the screen. The SPACECRAFT is drawn by means of the drawing subroutine in lines 1010 through 1045. The corresponding DATA lists occupy lines 2010 through 2040. As far as

## PROJECT 5–4

Expand the SPACECRAFT drawing program to include the space creature from Fig. 5–1.

```
10 REM **  PROJECT 5-4
15 REM          SPACECRAFT AND CREATURE
20 CLS
25 D=156:GOSUB 1010
30 D=592:GOSUB 1055
35 GOTO 35
1000 REM  ** DRAWING SUBROUTINES
1005 REM        SPACECRAFT
1010 READ A:PRINT @ D+20,CHR$(A);:P=2:GOSUB 1500
1015 READ A:PRINT @ D+76,CHR$(A);:P=7:GOSUB 1500
1020 READ A:PRINT @ D+134,CHR$(A);:P=18:GOSUB 1500
1025 READ A:PRINT @ D+193,CHR$(A);:P=28:GOSUB 1500
1030 READ A:PRINT @ D+256,CHR$(A);:P=30:GOSUB 1500
1035 READ A:PRINT @ D+323,CHR$(A);:P=15:GOSUB 1500
1040 READ A:PRINT @ D+386,CHR$(A);:P=5:GOSUB 1500
1045 RETURN
1050 REM        SPACE CREATURE
1055 READ A:PRINT @ D+1,CHR$(A);:P=5:GOSUB 1500
1060 READ A:PRINT @ D+65,CHR$(A);:P=8:GOSUB 1500
1065 READ A:PRINT @ D+128,CHR$(A);:P=10:GOSUB 1500
1070 READ A:PRINT @ D+192,CHR$(A);:P=5:GOSUB 1500
1075 RETURN
1500 FOR N=1 TO P-1:READ A:PRINT CHR$(A);:NEXT N:RETURN
2000 REM ** DATA LISTS
2005 REM        SPACECRAFT
2010 DATA 136,156
2015 DATA 176,184,180,176,195,160,134
2020 DATA 160,190,191,191,191,191,191,191,191
2022 DATA 191,191,191,191,191,191,191,189,144
2025 DATA 160,176,188,156,188,191,188,188,188,188,188,188,188,188
2027 DATA 188,188,188,188,188,188,188,188,191,188,172,188,176,176
2030 DATA 184,191,183,181,181,191,191,191,191,191,191,191,191,176,176
2032 DATA 176,176,191,191,191,191,191,191,191,191,186,186,187,191,180
2035 DATA 152,129,194,129,129,129,129,201,130,130,130,130,194,137,144
2040 DATA 142,132,215,142,132
2045 REM        SPACE CREATURE
2050 DATA 172,132,196,136,156
2055 DATA 186,176,156,191,191,172,176,181
2060 DATA 191,191,181,179,179,179,179,186,191,191
2065 DATA 160,149,198,170,144
3040 DATA 142,132,215,142,132
```

**LISTING 5-4** Programming for Project 5-4

the SPACE CREATURE is concerned, its drawing subroutine is at lines 1055 through 1075, and the corresponding DATA lines are from 2050 through 3040.

Thus any statement that calls a subroutine at 1010 will draw the SPACECRAFT figure, and a GOSUB 1055 will draw the SPACE CREATURE. Those routines are called from lines 25 and 30 in this example, and setting the value of the displacement variable, D, just prior to calling the subroutines effectively sets the figures' locations. Play around with both of those displacement values, RUNning the program after each change. Maybe you can come up with some arrangements for the two figures that please you more than these do.

Basically, this is a workable technique for positioning more than one image on the screen. The general idea is to develop the main elements of the picture separately, perhaps writing some smaller programs to test your ideas. Then the next step is to write a composite program, one that includes the drawing subroutine and DATA listing for each of them. Of course it is important to arrange the figures' drawing subroutine and DATA listings in the same order. Having the SPACECRAFT drawing subroutine refer to DATA for the SPACE CREATURE would certainly yield some confusing results.

Before carrying this composition any further, note that the program is divided into three main sections: a control section that positions the figures and calls the drawing subroutines, a drawing section that actually does the drawing tasks, and a DATA section for the drawing subroutines. Also take note of the fact that I began the drawing subroutines section at a fairly high line number. Doing that, I have a lot of BASIC programming space—through line number 999—for touching up the composition with background detail and anything else that happens to strike my fancy as the composition progresses.

## PROJECT 5–5

Complete the composition from Listing 5–4 to include some other details.

```
10 REM **  PROJECT 5-5
15 REM          SPACE INVASION PICTURE
20 CLS
25 REM  ** DRAW STARRY BACKGROUND
30 FOR N=0 TO 100:POKE 15360+RND(512),ASC(".")：NEXT N
35 REM ** DRAW ROCKY BACKGROUND
40 D=0
45 FOR N=1 TO 16:PRINT @ 384+D+RND(63),CHR$(RND(63)+128):NEXT N
50 FOR N=0 TO 63:PRINT @ 448+D+N,CHR$(RND(63)+128):NEXT N
55 REM ** DRAW PATH
60 D=554
65 FOR N=1 TO 6:PRINT @ D+60*N,STRING$(6," ");:NEXT N
70 REM  ** DRAW BIG STARS
75 FOR N=1 TO 8:POKE 15360+RND(512),ASC("*"):NEXT N
80 REM ** PRINT MESSAGE
85 D=936
90 PRINT @ D,"TAKE ME TO YOUR LEADER"
100 REM ** DRAW SPACECRAFT
105 D=156:GOSUB 1010
110 REM ** DRAW SPACE CREATURE
115 D=592:GOSUB 1055
120 GOTO 120
```

(cont.)

```
1000 REM  ** DRAWING SUBROUTINES
1005 REM        SPACECRAFT
1010 READ A:PRINT @ D+20,CHR$(A);:P=2:GOSUB 1500
1015 READ A:PRINT @ D+76,CHR$(A);:P=7:GOSUB 1500
1020 READ A:PRINT @ D+134,CHR$(A);:P=18:GOSUB 1500
1025 READ A:PRINT @ D+193,CHR$(A);:P=28:GOSUB 1500
1030 READ A:PRINT @ D+256,CHR$(A);:P=30:GOSUB 1500
1035 READ A:PRINT @ D+323,CHR$(A);:P=15:GOSUB 1500
1040 READ A:PRINT @ D+386,CHR$(A);:P=5:GOSUB 1500
1045 RETURN
1050 REM        SPACE CREATURE
1055 READ A:PRINT @ D+1,CHR$(A);:P=5:GOSUB 1500
1060 READ A:PRINT @ D+65,CHR$(A);:P=8:GOSUB 1500
1065 READ A:PRINT @ D+128,CHR$(A);:P=10:GOSUB 1500
1070 READ A:PRINT @ D+192,CHR$(A);:P=5:GOSUB 1500
1075 RETURN
1500 FOR N=1 TO P-1:READ A:PRINT CHR$(A);:NEXT N:RETURN
2000 REM ** DATA LISTS
2005 REM        SPACECRAFT
2010 DATA 136,156
2015 DATA 176,184,180,176,195,160,134
2020 DATA 160,190,191,191,191,191,191,191,191
2022 DATA 191,191,191,191,191,191,191,189,144
2025 DATA 160,176,188,156,188,191,188,188,188,188,188,188,188,188
2027 DATA 188,188,188,188,188,188,188,188,191,188,172,188,176,176
2030 DATA 184,191,183,181,181,191,191,191,191,191,191,191,191,176,176
2032 DATA 176,176,191,191,191,191,191,191,191,191,186,186,187,191,180
2035 DATA 152,129,194,129,129,129,129,201,130,130,130,130,194,137,144
2040 DATA 142,132,215,142,132
2045 REM        SPACE CREATURE
2050 DATA 172,132,196,136,156
2055 DATA 186,176,156,191,191,172,176,181
2060 DATA 191,191,181,179,179,179,179,186,191,191
2065 DATA 160,149,198,170,144
3040 DATA 142,132,215,142,132
```

**LISTING 5-5** Programming for Project 5-5

It seems appropriate that a picture such as this one would be enhanced by some stars put into a background sky. So I moved the SPACECRAFT and SPACE CREATURE positioning and subroutine-calling statements down to lines 100 through 115. Then I added a starry-sky drawing routine at line 30.

The picture needed some better definition for a horizon, so I added some quasi-random things in lines 40 through 50. Note the displacement value in line 40; I included that in the event I wanted to move the horizon up or down at some later time.

Lines 55 through 65 draw a little path between the SPACECRAFT and SPACE CREATURE figures. If you have relocated either of those main figures, you will have to relocate the PATH figure as well. How? by adjusting the value of D in line 60.

The background sky needed a few larger stars, so that is handled by line 75. And finally, I added the TAKE ME TO YOUR LEADER MESSAGE in lines 80 through 90.

I hope you can appreciate the flexibility of this approach to composing full-screen pictures. I certainly encourage you to tinker around with it, adding more detail of your own.

At the risk of insulting your intelligence, I should point out that it is important to structure the program so that the background elements are printed before the foreground images are. Sometimes that means moving some of the BASIC lines from one place to another, but if you locate the complex images (their drawing subroutines and DATA lists) at relatively high line numbers, all the line changing that is necessary ought to be an easy task.

# 6 String-Packing Procedures

The drawing procedures described in all the previous projects plot the images on the screen directly from raw character codes in the BASIC program. The character codes are assigned to a CHR$ or STRING$ function and PRINTed from there. The picture is built up on the screen either by reading and plotting one character at a time (as with the CHR$ function), or by reading and plotting relatively small groups of identical characters (as with the STRING$ function).

That might seem to be a very natural way to go about doing TRS-80 graphics; indeed, it is a straightforward approach that is fairly easy to understand and master. However, there is an attractive alternative that offers some distinct advantages.

Rather than reading the raw character codes and plotting them directly onto the screen, the program can read the codes and assign them, one full line at a time, to a string variable. The image can thus be defined as a relatively small number of string variables, each representing a full line of character information. After that process is completed, the picture can be drawn onto the screen by the printing string variables. Once those string variables are defined, the image can be drawn again any number of times without making any further reference to the raw character data.

The process of defining string variables from raw character codes is called *string packing.* The *string* variables are *packed* with character codes. The actual drawing is deferred until the strings are defined, and thereafter there is no further use for the raw character information: the entire image is carried as a set of more or less complex string variables.

As you might imagine, a computer can print a long string, one defined as a string variable, much faster than it can read raw character codes one at a time and plot them onto the screen. If nothing else, you are going to notice a distinct increase in image-drawing speed. You are also going to find that it is easier to manipulate string variables than large amounts of raw character data.

## CHARACTER CODES AND STRING VARIABLES

Anyone who has worked with BASIC programming ought to be familiar with this sort of routine:

```
M$ = "HELLO"
PRINT M$
```

The first statement defines string variable M$ as HELLO. The PRINT statement then prints the content of that variable; it causes HELLO to appear on the screen. Changing the string assigned to M$ in the first statement will cause a different expression to be printed by the second statement.

Alternately, the same message can be printed this way:

```
M$ = CHR$(72) + CHR$(69) + STRING$(2,76) + CHR$(79)
PRINT M$
```

In that case, the string variable is defined in terms of a set of *concatenated* ASCII codes. CHR$(72) defines the letter *H,* CHR$(69 defines the letter *E,* STRING$(2,76) defines two *L*s in succession, and CHR$(79) defines the letter *O.* Those characters are concatenated to create a single variable, M$. When the PRINT M$ statement is executed, the HELLO message appears on the screen.

String packing is not limited to the alphanumeric character codes. The TRS-80 graphic codes can be packed into a string variable, too.

## PROJECT 6–1

Write a program that packs all 64 TRS–80 graphics codes into a single string variable, then print the content of that variable onto the screen. See the suggested program in Listing 6–1.

```
10 REM ** PROJECT 6-1
15 REM    PACKED GRAPHCS SET
20 CLEAR 128
25 M$=""
30 FOR N=128 TO 191
35 M$=M$+CHR$(N)
40 NEXT N
45 CLS
50 PRINT @ 256,M$
```

**LISTING 6–1** Programming for Project 6–1

The CLEAR statement in line 20 clears 128 bytes of memory for the string operations. As mentioned in earlier discussions, the TRS–80 normally assigns only 50 bytes of memory for string variables; this particular project calls for at least 65 bytes—thus the need for a special effort to expand the available string space.

Line 25 makes sure the string variable to be packed is clear. If it should happen to contain any characters before the packing operation begins, they will appear in the PRINTed version of the string later on. Doing an M$ = "" statement ensures that the string to be packed is empty—it is set to the *null* string.

The actual string-packing operation occupies program lines 30 through 40. The FOR . . . NEXT statements define the TRS–80 graphics codes one at a time, and line 35 packs them (also one at a time) into string variable M$. As that FOR . . . NEXT loop is executed, the M$ variable grows longer and longer. It begins with nothing, then grows one CHR$ character at a time until it is 64 characters long.

By the time the program reaches line 45, the string is fully defined and it can then be PRINTed at any later time. Here, the string is printed by the statement in line 50.

When the RUN this program, you will notice a short delay before the screen is cleared (program line 45) and the string is printed (program line 50). One of the hallmarks of a string-packing procedure is an initial time delay required for packing the strings. Once the string-packing operation is done, however, the string variables can be PRINTed rather quickly. Note how quickly the image is printed, once that initial delay is over.

It can be instructive at this point to compare the printing of a string-packed variable with a drawing routine that is representative of those described in earlier chapters. Try adding this sequence to Listing 6–1:

```
55 FOR N=128 TO 191
60 PRINT CHR$(N);
65 NEXT N
```

In this case, the 64 TRS–80 graphics are printed onto the screen as they are defined by the FOR . . . NEXT routine. The printing is not deferred as it is when using a packed string.

Now, when you run this expanded version of the program, you will see two identical lines of graphic characters appearing on the screen. The first comes from the packed string, M$, and the second comes directly from the FOR . . . NEXT routine that has been added at lines 55 through 65.

Run the routine several times. You will see that the first line prints somewhat faster than the second. Clearly, string-packed variables draw faster than images generated directly from raw information.

In a manner of speaking, using string-packed variables stores lines of characters into the computer memory, and as long as nothing is done to clear the string variables, those strings remain intact in memory. To demonstrate this fact, run the program just described. When it is done, strike the CLEAR key to clear the screen, and then ENTER this statement: PRINT M$. There it is! the string is printed onto the screen, even though the program itself isn't being executed. That cannot be done with any of the previous drawing procedures.

## STRING PACKING A SINGLE STATIC IMAGE

Fig. 6–1 shows a worksheet drawing, FISH. The following project demonstrates how to generate a string-packed version of it.

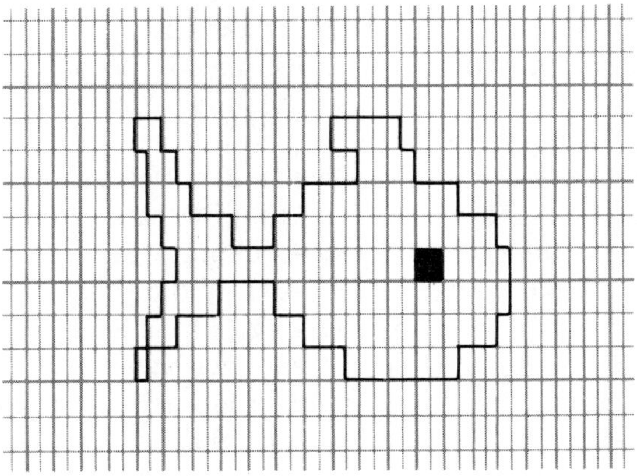

**FIGURE 6–1** Fish figure

## PROJECT 6-2

Write a BASIC program that uses string-packing procedures to draw the FISH in Fig. 6-1.

```
10 REM ** PROJECT 6-2
15 REM          FISH
20 CLEAR 256
25 GOSUB 1000
30 REM ** CONTROL ROUTINE
35 CLS
40 D=0:GOSUB 55
45 GOTO 45
50 REM ** DRAWING SUBROUTINE
55 PRINT @ D,F1$;
60 PRINT @ D+64,F2$;
65 PRINT @ D+128,F3$;
70 RETURN
1000 REM ** STRING-PACKING SUBROUTINE
1005 P=7:GOSUB 1500:F1$=L$
1010 P=14:GOSUB 1500:F2$=L$
1015 P=13:GOSUB 1500:F3$=L$
1020 RETURN
1500 L$="":FOR N=1 TO P:READ A:L$=L$+CHR$(A):NEXT N:RETURN
2000 REM ** DATA LINES
2030 DATA 172,144,197,140,188,180,196
2035 DATA 130,175,188,180,176,188,191,191,191,191,143,189,188,144
2040 DATA 152,135,131,194,131,143,175,191,191,191,159,143,129
```

**LISTING 6-2** Programming for Project 6-2

This program, and all other string-packing programs for that matter, is divided into five essential sections. One is a set of DATA lines that look like and serve the same function as those used in earlier projects. Here, the DATA lines for FISH occupy program lines 2030 through 2040. There is really nothing new at that point.

A second major section of a string-packing program is the packing routine itself. In this case, the string packing is done with a subroutine in lines 1005 through 1500. The FISH figure is composed of three lines of characters, and those lines are ultimately packed into three different string variables: F1$, F2$, and F3$.

First, note how variable F1$ is packed at program line 1005. Variable P, used as it was in earlier procedures, tells the system how many characters are to be packed into the line. P is set to 7, and if you look at the FISH figure, you will see that the first line is composed of seven graphic characters.

After setting the number of characters to be packed (concatenated) into the first line, the routine does a GOSUB 1500 statement. Line 1500 is a one-line subroutine that does the actual string-packing task. First, a general-purpose string variable, L$, is nulled; then the first seven items in the DATA list are packed into string L$—the FOR . . . NEXT sequence in line 1500 does that, as described a bit earlier in this chapter. Line 1500 concludes with a RETURN statement that returns operations to the end of line 1005.

When the routine returns from line 1500, L$ is the packed string variable. The final statement in line 1005 assigns that string to another variable that is peculiar to the first line in the FISH figure, variable F1$.

That sequence of operations is repeated in lines 1010 and 1015: variable P is assigned the number of characters to be packed in one line, subroutine 1500 packs the characters from the DATA list into string L$, and when the routine returns to its calling line, the value of L$ is assigned to the appropriate line variable.

By the time the routine reaches the RETURN statement in line 1020, the packing for the FISH image is done.

From the string-packing routine, the program returns to the beginning of another major section of the program, the control routine. Beginning at program line 35, the control routine clears the screen, sets a displacement value (the same expression used for relocatable images as described in the last chapter), and calls a subroutine at line 55.

The fourth major section is the drawing subroutine, which, in this particular project, begins at line 55 and runs through its RETURN statement in line 70. This section simply prints the packed strings in their proper sequence and at their designated positions on the screen. When the drawing routine has been executed, the image is on the screen, and control returns to line 45 of the control routine. Here, the program simply loops on that line to preserve the image until the user strikes the BREAK key to end it.

Finally, there is always a need for a short initialization routine. It is placed at the very beginning of the program (lines 20 and 25 in this example), and its purpose is to CLEAR an adequate amount of string space and call the string-packing routine. If the program happens to use dimensioned array variables—which this one does not—the arrays are defined in that initialization section.

The foregoing discussion deals with the five major sections of the program in the order they are executed. Before going to the next topic, you might find it helpful to study the major sections in the order I suggest they appear in the program for any string-packed drawing routine.

### the initialization routine

This short routine must appear first in a string-packed drawing program. The purpose is to set up the computer for running the program at hand. This includes:

- CLEARing the necessary amount of memory space for the strings. The amount to be cleared must be equal to or greater than the number of elements in the DATA listings plus the number of string variables cited in the program. Rather than counting out the number of DATA elements and strings, it is usually sufficient to CLEAR some arbitrarily large number of spaces. You know you haven't cleared enough string space when the execution of the string-packing routine turns up an OS error.

- DIMensioning any arrays used in the program. Arrays have not been used in any of the previous projects, but they will appear in future versions. String-packed variables are sometimes expressed as arrays—F$(6) for the sixth line in a figure defined by string variable F$, or F$(2,6) for the sixth line in version 2 of a set of figures defined by variable F$.
- Defining variable types with statements such as DEFSTR. Defining a set of variable names in this fashion saves you the trouble of attaching a dollar-sign symbol to indicate a string variable.
- Calling the string-packing subroutine by means of a GOSUB statement.

### the control routine

The control routine determines what is to be done with the string-packed images that are available to it. This is the real workhorse of the program.

In its most elementary form, the control routine first clears the screen, then sets the displacement value for a figure and calls the appropriate drawing subroutine. Finally, it concludes with a statement that ends the program.

As you will see later in this chapter, the control routine is all that is usually modified in order to change the ways the figures are presented. This part of the program, for example, is used for PRINTing any number of identical images, placing multiple images onto the screen, doing time delay operations, and even doing some simple animation sequences.

Once all the other major sections are written and entered into the computer, the control section is the one that is set aside for determining what is to be done with the figures that are available.

### the drawing subroutines

A portion of the program listing must be set aside for doing the actual drawing operations. Assuming that the images have been packed into well-defined string variables, the drawing subroutines simply do line-by-line PRINT operations that refer to those variables.

There will be one drawing subroutine for each unique figure to be drawn on the screen, and they are all called from the control routine.

It is a good idea to begin the drawing subroutines at rather high BASIC line numbers, thus leaving plenty of lower-numbered lines for tinkering with the control routines.

### the string-packing subroutine

The string-packing subroutine is called from the initialization routine, and it is responsible for packing the designated string variables. This subroutine defines the line-by-line string variables and packs them with character codes from the DATA list.

The string-packing routine is run only one time—at the beginning of the program. Once the strings are defined and packed, there is no need for repeating the process until the program is RUN from the beginning again.

There will be one three-part line in the subroutine for every line of characters in each unique image in the drawing. Those three parts include:

- Setting a variable equal to the number of characters to be packed into a given string.
- Calling a line-packing routine (such as line 1500 in Listing 6–2). That routine is the same for every string-packed drawing program, no matter how large or small it might be.
- Setting a specific line variable equal to the general-purpose string that is packed by the second step.

A RETURN statement concludes the string-packing subroutine, returning program control to the control routine.

### DATA listings

Throughout this book, the DATA listings appear in groups of the highest-numbered BASIC program lines. The DATA lines carry the sequences of character codes for every unique image to be PRINTed on the screen. They are READ by sections of the string-packing routines; once the strings are packed, the DATA items have served their purpose.

The DATA listings are organized in the same way as described in Chapter 5.

## DUPLICATING A STRING-PACKED FIGURE

As mentioned in the previous section, the actual function of the program is determined by the nature of its control routine. The drawing, string-packing, and DATA routines that define and draw the figures need not be changed in most instances. Altering a string-packed drawing routine to make it duplicate the same figure at different places on the screen is largely a matter of revising just the control routine.

## PROJECT 6–3

Revise Listing 6–2 so that it will print six Fish figures on the screen. See the program in Listing 6–3.

```
10 REM ** PROJECT 6-3
15 REM         LOTS OF FISH
20 CLEAR 256:DEFSTR F,L
25 GOSUB 1000
30 REM ** CONTROL ROUTINE
35 CLS
40 D=0:GOSUB 110:D=90:GOSUB 110
45 D=175:GOSUB 110:D=579:GOSUB 110
50 D=478:GOSUB 110:D=393:GOSUB 110
95 GOTO 95
100  REM ** DRAWING SUBROUTINE
105    DRAW  FISH
110 PRINT @ D,F1;
115 PRINT @ D+64,F2;
120 PRINT @ D+128,F3;
125 RETURN
1000 REM ** STRING-PACKING SUBROUTINE
1005 P=7:GOSUB 1500:F1=L
1010 P=14:GOSUB 1500:F2=L
1015 P=13:GOSUB 1500:F3=L
1020 RETURN
1500 L="":FOR N=1 TO P:READ A:L=L+CHR$(A):NEXT N:RETURN
2000 REM ** DATA LINES
2030 DATA 172,144,197,140,188,180,196
2035 DATA 130,175,188,180,176,188,191,191,191,191,143,189,188,144
2040 DATA 152,135,131,194,131,143,175,191,191,191,159,143,129
```

**LISTING 6–3** Programming for Project 6–3

The fact that six versions of FISH are drawn on the screen is determined by the changes in the control portion of the program. See how the job is done in lines 40 through 50. In each case, a displacement value is assigned to variable D, and the drawing subroutine (not at lines 110 through 125) is called.

Give it a try.

The five-part format described earlier for string-packed drawing programs now breaks down this way:

Initialization routine (lines 20 and 25)

- CLEAR 256 string locations in memory.
- DEFine variables F and L as string variables.
- Call the string-packing subroutine at line 1000.

Control routine (lines 35 through 95).

- Clear the screen.
- Set the displacement value and call the drawing subroutine for each of the six FISH figures.
- GOTO line 95 to put the program into an endless loop.

Drawing subroutine (lines 110 through 125)

- PRINT the three lines of characters for the FISH figure at the designated displacement locations.

String-packing subroutine (lines 1005 through 1500)

- Pack the general-purpose string variable, L, with the designated number of characters, P.

DATA listing (lines 2030 through 2040)

- Define the character codes for each character in the FISH figure.

## CREATING STRING-PACKED COMPOSITIONS

As was described earlier in this chapter, any worksheet image can be packed into a series of string variables, where each variable represents one line of graphic characters in the image. There is, however, nothing to prevent you from creating more than one string-packed image; what's even more fun is tinkering with the control section of a multi-image program to compose a full-screen picture.

The general idea is to work out some main images to be placed into a composition and then write some programming for the string-packing and drawing subroutines for each one. Of course, it is necessary to assign a different string variable to each line of each image to be used.

With that part of the job done, all that remains is to devise a control section—a section that places the individual images at desired places on the screen and calls the drawing subroutines for plotting them at those places.

## PROJECT 6–4

Use the FISH in Fig. 6–1 as a starting point for developing a multi-image composition. Invent a LITTLE FISH as well, and make some bubbles, a large WATER PLANT, and some BOTTOM STUFF. The suggested program, FISH COMPOSITION, is shown in Listing 6–4.

```
10 REM ** PROJECT 6-4
15 REM          FISH COMPOSITION
20 REM ** INITIALIZATION ROUTINE
25 CLEAR 512:DEFSTR F,L
30 GOSUB 1000
100 REM ** CONTROL ROUTINE
105 CLS
110 D=208:GOSUB 510:D=473:GOSUB 510
115 D=183:GOSUB 535:D=307:GOSUB 535
120 D=363:GOSUB 535:D=562:GOSUB 535
125 D=687:GOSUB 535
130 D=159:GOSUB 590:D=424:GOSUB 590
135 D=362:GOSUB 605:D=685:GOSUB 605
140 D=385:GOSUB 545
145 D=832:GOSUB 615
495 GOTO 495
500 REM ** DRAWING SUBROUTINES
505 CLS
510 PRINT @ D,F1(1);
515 PRINT @ D+64,F1(2);
520 PRINT @ D+128,F1(3);
525 RETURN
530 REM          LITTLE FISH
535 PRINT @ D,F2;:RETURN
540 REM          WATER PLANT
545 PRINT @ D+2,F3(1);
550 PRINT @ D+65,F3(2);
555 PRINT @ D+130,F3(3);
560 PRINT @ D+193,F3(4);
565 PRINT @ D+256,F3(5);
570 PRINT @ D+320,F3(6);
575 PRINT @ D+389,F3(7);
580 RETURN
585 REM          BIG BUBBLES
590 PRINT @ D-1,"O";:PRINT @ D+64,"O";
595 PRINT @ D+128,"O";:RETURN
600 REM          LITTLE BUBBLES
605 PRINT @ D,":";:RETURN
610 REM          BOTTOM STUFF
615 PRINT @ D,F6(1)+F6(2);:RETURN
1000 REM ** STRING-PACKING SUBROUTINES
1005 REM         BIG FISH
1010 P=7:GOSUB 1500:F1(1)=L
1015 P=14:GOSUB 1500:F1(2)=L
1020 P=13:GOSUB 1500:F1(3)=L
1025 REM         LITTLE FISH
1030 P=5:GOSUB 1500:F2=L
1035 REM         WATER PLANT
1040 P=6:GOSUB 1500:F3(1)=L
1045 P=8:GOSUB 1500:F3(2)=L
1050 P=8:GOSUB 1500:F3(3)=L
1055 P=8:GOSUB 1500:F3(4)=L
1060 P=9:GOSUB 1500:F3(5)=L
1065 P=10:GOSUB 1500:F3(6)=L
1070 P=2:GOSUB 1500:F3(7)=L
1075 REM         BOTTOM STUFF
1080 F6(1)="":FOR N=1 TO 64:F6(1)=F6(1)+CHR$(RND(2)+128):NEXT N
1085 F6(2)="":FOR N=1 TO 64:F6(2)=F6(2)+CHR$(RND(64)+128):NEXT N
1495 RETURN
1500 L="":FOR N=1 TO P:READ A:L=L+CHR$(A):NEXT N:RETURN
```

```
2000 REM ** DATA LISTINGS
2005 REM          BIG FISH
2010 DATA 172,144,197,140,188,180,196
2015 DATA 130,175,188,180,176,188,191,191,191,191,143,189,188,144
2020 DATA 152,135,131,194,131,143,175,191,191,191,159,143,129
2025 REM          LITTLE FISH
2030 DATA 174,187,191,140,183
2035 REM          WATER PLANT
2040 DATA 136,144,130,148,128,148
2045 DATA 160,128,173,170,128,154,128,160
2050 DATA 165,130,171,128,148,160,133,152
2055 DATA 144,138,180,186,176,181,150,131
2060 DATA 160,138,140,140,148,191,176,184,129
2065 DATA 130,139,173,176,178,191,160,156,140,133
2070 DATA 191,131
```

**LISTING 6-4** Programming for Project 6-4

Here is how the individual images are defined and drawn:

- **BIG FISH.** BIG FISH is packed by program lines 1010 through 1020, and those lines use the DATA from lines 2010 through 2020. When the packing is done, BIG FISH is defined as variables F1(1), F1(2), and F1(3). It is drawn by calling its drawing subroutine at line 510.
- **LITTLE FISH.** An image of a smaller fish is packed at program line 535, and it uses the DATA in line 2030. Anytime after that, LITTLE FISH can be drawn by calling its drawing subroutine at line 535. The string variable in this case is F2.
- **BIG BUBBLES.** BIG BUBBLES for the BIG FISH are not packed into a string variable; they are too simple to bother with that. Rather, the BIG BUBBLES are defined *and* drawn by calling a subroutine at line 590.
- **LITTLE BUBBLES.** As is indicated by the combined definition and drawing routine at program line 605, LITTLE BUBBLES are simply a colon figure.
- **WATER PLANT.** This is a relatively complicated image that is defined by the string-packing routine in lines 1040 through 1065. That routine uses the DATA elements in lines 2040 through 2070; when the packing is done, WATER PLANT is carried by string variables F3(1) through F3(7)—seven individual lines that are assigned to figure 3 in the composition. The WATER PLANT is drawn by calling its drawing subroutine at line 545.
- **BOTTOM STUFF.** BOTTOM STUFF is packed into string variables F6(1) and F6(2) at program lines 1080 and 1085. Although the exact configuration of BOTTOM STUFF is determined by a set of random functions, it remains unchanged after its

strings are packed. BOTTOM STUFF is drawn by calling its drawing subroutine at line 615.

The foregoing discussion actually describes the purpose of program lines 500 through the end of the listing. Clearly, the matter of packing the string variables and setting up the drawing subroutines accounts for a majority of the work involved in writing this particular composition program. The string-packing subroutines and associated DATA lists occupy program lines 1000 through 2070, and the drawing subroutines use program lines 500 through 580.

All that remains is a short initialization routine and a control routine. As far as the initialization routine is concerned (program lines 25 and 30), the idea is to clear some space for the string variables and define any variable name beginning with F or L as a string variable. The latter feature makes it possible to specify all the string variables without having to type a dollar sign after each of them. The last step in the initialization routine (line 30) is to call the string-packing subroutine.

The control routine occupies program lines 105 through 495. This part of the program determines where each image will appear and how many identical images are to be used.

The control routine makes sense only if you keep track of the drawing subroutine numbers:

510 for BIG FISH
535 for LITTLE FISH
590 for BIG BUBBLES
605 for LITTLE BUBBLES
545 for WATER PLANT
615 for BOTTOM STUFF

Using those drawing subroutine numbers as a guide, you can see how the control routine does its job:

Line 105: Clear the screen for doing the drawing.
Line 110: Draw two BIG FISH at PRINT @ positions 208 and 473.
Lines 115–125: Draw five LITTLE FISH.
Line 130: Draw two sets of BIG BUBBLES for the BIG FISH.
Line 135: Draw two sets of LITTLE BUBBLES for a couple of LITTLE FISH. Add more if you wish.
Line 140: Draw the WATER PLANT at position 385.

Line 145: Draw the BOTTOM STUFF.

Line 495: Lock the program into an endless loop so that a READY message doesn't destroy the composition.

When this program is run, you will notice an initial time delay of about seven seconds. That is the time required for packing the strings. Once the string packing is done, though, the image is drawn fairly rapidly on the screen. Some of the projects suggested in the next chapter clearly demonstrate the advantage of being able to plot packed variables in rapid succession.

# 7 More About String Packing

The discussions in Chapter 6 suggest that string-packing procedures can be a vital part of good TRS–80 graphics, especially when it comes to creating multi-image or complex compositions. The material in this chapter carries the idea even further, offering some new ideas and paving the way toward doing some higher-performance POKE and machine-language graphics.

## THE IMPORTANCE OF THE CONTROL SECTION

A program that runs string-packed images is made up of five basic sections. Three of them determine *what* figures are to be drawn; those are the sections defined earlier as the drawing subroutines, the string-packing subroutine, and the DATA listings. A fourth section, the initialization section, is largely responsible for setting up the computer to run the program,

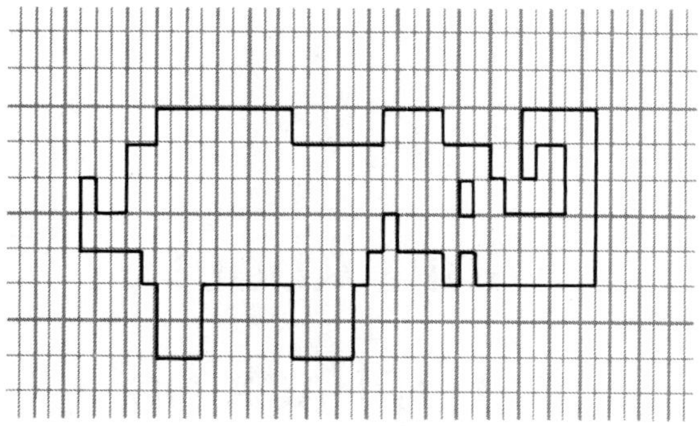

**FIGURE 7-1** Worksheet Elephant figure for Project 7-1

but it is the control section that determines *when* and *where* the available images are drawn.

The following program is built around a single, simple graphic figure—that of a little elephant. See Fig. 7-1. With such a simple figure, it follows that the string-packing, DATA listings, and drawing sections of the program will be quite short and simple. The real burden of the programming in this case rests with the control section—the section that determines what is to be done with the simple figure.

## PROJECT 7-1

Listing 7-1 represents a simple program that is intended to help youngsters learn to count objects. Each time the routine is executed, a random number of ELEPHANT figures (between 1 and 9 of them) appear on the screen. The user responds by entering his or her notion of HOW MANY ELEPHANTS ARE HERE? The program then offers a response that is appropriate to the answer that is given.

```
10 REM ** PROJECT 7-1
15 REM          COUNT THE ELEPHANTS
20 CLEAR 256:DEFSTR F
25 CLS:PRINT STRING$(8,13);STRING$(20,32);"** COUNT THE ELEPHANTS **"
30 GOSUB 1000
35 FOR T=0 TO 1000:NEXT T
100 REM  ** CONTROL  ROUTINE
105 CLS
110 CLS:N=RND(9):V=0:S=0
115 FOR C=0 TO N-1
120 IF C>0 AND C/3=INT(C/3) THEN V=V+193
125 D=V+C*21:GOSUB 505
130 NEXT C
135 GOSUB 530:GOSUB 535
140 INPUT S
145 IF S<>N THEN 160
150 IF N=1 THEN GOSUB 540 ELSE GOSUB 545
155 GOTO 165
```

```
160 IF N=1 THEN GOSUB 550 ELSE GOSUB 555
165 INPUT S$:GOTO 110
500 REM ** DRAWING SUBROUTINE
505 PRINT @ D,F1;
510 PRINT @ D+64,F2;
515 PRINT @ D+130,F3;
520 RETURN
525 REM          MESSAGES
530 PRINT @ 832,STRING$(128,32);:RETURN
535 PRINT @ 832,"HOW MANY ELEPHANTS ARE HERE";:RETURN
540 PRINT @ 832,"YOU ARE RIGHT!!  THERE IS 1 ELEPHANT HERE.":GOTO 560
545 PRINT @ 832,"YOU ARE RIGHT!!  THERE ARE"S"ELEPHANTS HERE.":GOTO 560
550 PRINT @ 832,"SORRY, THERE IS JUST 1 ELEPHANT HERE, NOT"S"OF THEM."
552 GOTO 560
555 PRINT @ 832,"SORRY, THERE ARE"N"ELEPHANTS HERE, NOT"S"OF THEM."
560 PRINT "STRIKE THE 'ENTER' KEY FOR YOUR NEXT TURN...":RETURN
1000 REM ** STRING PACKING SUBROUTINE
1005 P=17:GOSUB 1500:F1=F
1010 P=17:GOSUB 1500:F2=F
1015 P=5:GOSUB 1500:F3=F
1020 RETURN
1500 F="":FOR N=1 TO P:READ A:F=F+CHR$(A):NEXT N:RETURN
2000 REM ** DATA LISTS
2005 DATA 144,168,190,191,191,191,191,188,188,188,191,191,156
2007 DATA 180,138,131,191
2010 DATA 131,131,175,191,143,143,143,191,191,135,130,131,135
2012 DATA 143,143,143,143
2015 DATA 130,131,195,131,131
```

**LISTING 7-1** Programming for Count the Elephants in Project 7-1

This string-packed graphics program can be analyzed this way:
Initialization routine (lines 20–35)

- CLEAR 256 bytes for string variables.
- Define any variable beginning with F as a string variable.
- Clear the screen and print a title.
- Call the string-packing subroutine.

String-packing subroutine (lines 1005–1500)

- Pack the three lines of the figure as variables F1, F2, and F3.

DATA listing (lines 2005–2015)

- Define the character codes for the image in Fig. 7-1.

Drawing subroutines (lines 505–560)

- Draw the graphic by calling the subroutine at line 505. Use a displacement value of D and string variables F1, F2, and F3.

- Print a message. Lines 530 through 560 include a series of messages that are called at the appropriate times from the control section of the program.

Control routine (lines 105–165)

- Clear the screen.
- Select a random number between 1 and 9.
- Plot that number of ELEPHANT figures in an orderly pattern on the screen.
- Erase any old messages (GOSUB 530) and print a request for an answer (GOSUB 535).
- INPUT the user's answer (line 140).
- Check the answer and make an appropriate text response (lines 145–160).
- Wait for the user to strike the ENTER key, then display another set of ELEPHANT figures.

As far as the graphics are concerned, this program is a simple variation of the image-duplicating procedure described in the previous chapter. The ELEPHANT figures are all identical, and they are drawn from the same set of string-packed variables, F1 through F3.

Generally speaking, a string-packed image is drawn from the control routine by first setting a displacement value and then calling an appropriate drawing subroutine. That is the case here, but the matter of setting the displacement value is a bit tricky. The problem is to set the displacement values for some number of figures in such a way that the ELEPHANT figures line up in an orderly pattern on the screen, making certain that no part of an image is broken off at the right side of the screen and folded over to the left side. The purpose of the mathematics in lines 120 and 125 is to come up with a different displacement value for each figure that is to be drawn.

Recall that one of the drawbacks of using string-packed graphics is the initial time delay required for packing the string variables. A clever way to cover for this delay is by printing a title message just before calling the string-packing subroutine. The user thus gets the impression that you've taken the trouble to show a title message when, in fact, you are using it to gloss over the necessary initial delay in activity.

In this particular program, the image is so simple that its string-packing operation takes less than two seconds. That's a tolerable delay in any event, but the title message specified in line 25 is used anyway for illustrative purposes. In fact the string-packing delay is so short that it seemed to be a good idea to add a bit more delay, and that is the purpose of the routine in line 35.

As an exercise, see if you can sort out the graphics portions of the program from everything else. Doing that, you ought to realize that the graphics routines are essentially the same as those used in the previous chapter. They are simply dressed up with other kinds of programming routines that transform a simple graphics demonstration into a useful program.

## MULTIPLE-IMAGE SEQUENCES

Once some images are committed to string variables, they can be drawn fairly rapidly on the screen, and that brings up the possibility of creating programs that display sequences of images. The idea is to string-pack and make up drawing subroutines for two or more figures, then devise a control routine that draws the figures individually.

## PROJECT 7–2

Use the AIRCRAFT picture from Fig. 4–3 and the RACE CAR figure shown in Fig. 7–2 to create a program that sequentially shows only the RACE CAR, only the AIRCRAFT, and both the RACE CAR and AIRCRAFT. See the suggested program in Listing 7–2.

```
10 REM ** PROJECT 7-2
15 REM          MULTIPLE FRAME DEMO
20 CLEAR 1024:DEFSTR F,L,M
25 CLS:PRINT STRING$(8,13);STRING$(21,32);"** MULTI-FRAME DEMO **"
30 GOSUB 1000
100 REM ** CONTROL ROUTINE
105 CLS
110 D=148:GOSUB 510:GOSUB 125
115 D=150:GOSUB 535:GOSUB 125
120 D=136:GOSUB 510:D=172:GOSUB 535:GOSUB 125:GOTO 110
125 PRINT @ 896,"'ENTER' FOR NEXT FRAME"
130 S$=INKEY$:IF S$="" THEN 130 ELSE CLS:RETURN
500 REM  ** DRAWING SUBROUTINES
505 REM         RACE CAR
510 PRINT @ D,F1(1);:PRINT @ D+64,F1(2);
515 PRINT @ D+133,F1(3);:PRINT @ D+198,F1(4);
520 PRINT @ D+258,F1(5);:PRINT @ D+322,F1(6);
525 PRINT @ D+386,F1(7);:RETURN
530 REM         AIRCRAFT
535 PRINT @ D+7,F2(1);:PRINT @ D+71,F2(2);
540 PRINT @ D+136,F2(3);:PRINT @ D+199,F2(4);
545 PRINT @ D+259,F2(5);:PRINT @ D+320,F2(6);
550 PRINT @ D+384,F2(7);:PRINT @ D+448,F2(8);
555 RETURN
1000 REM ** STRING-PACKING SUBROUTINES
1005 REM        RACE CAR
1010 P=21:GOSUB 1500:F1(1)=L:P=23:GOSUB 1500:F1(2)=L
1015 P=13:GOSUB 1500:F1(3)=L:P=11:GOSUB 1500:F1(4)=L
```

*(cont.)*

```
1020 P=17:GOSUB 1500:F1(5)=L:P=19:GOSUB 1500:F1(6)=L
1025 P=19:GOSUB 1500:F1(7)=L
1030 REM        AIRCRAFT
1035 P=4:GOSUB 1500:F2(1)=L:P=4:GOSUB 1500:F2(2)=L
1040 P=2:GOSUB 1500:F2(3)=L:P=4:GOSUB 1500:F2(4)=L
1045 P=12:GOSUB 1500:F2(5)=L:P=18:GOSUB 1500:F2(6)=L
1050 P=18:GOSUB 1500:F2(7)=L:P=18:GOSUB 1500:F2(8)=L
1055 RETURN
1500 L="":FOR  N=1 TO P:READ A:L=L+CHR$(A):NEXT N:RETURN
2000 REM ** DATA LISTS
2005            RACE CAR
2010 DATA 168,188,188,194,188,188,188,176,184,183,179
2012 DATA 187,180,176,188,188,188,194,188,188,148
2015 DATA 170,191,191,131,131,191,191,149,191,191,151,191
2017 DATA 171,191,191,170,191,191,131,131,191,191,149
2020 DATA 171,151,191,191,189,189,191,190,190,191,191,171,151
2025 DATA 149,191,191,159,129,128,130,175,191,191,170
2030 DATA 176,176,144,170,149,191,191,181,195
2032 DATA 186,191,191,170,149,160,176,176
2035 DATA 191,191,157,191,189,191,191,191,191,191
2037 DATA 191,191,191,191,190,191,174,191,191
2040 DATA 131,131,129,128,175,191,179,179,179,179
2042 DATA 179,179,179,191,159,128,130,131,131
2050 REM        AIRCRAFT
2055 DATA 160,190,189,144
2060 DATA 191,177,178,191
2065 DATA 191,191
2070 DATA 168,191,191,148
2075 DATA 160,180,160,184,151,191,191,171,180,144,184,144
2080 DATA 160,180,128,186,175,175,191,149,191
2082 DATA 191,170,191,191,175,181,128,184,144
2085 DATA 186,191,191,191,188,184,191,181,191
2087 DATA 191,186,191,189,184,191,191,191,181
2090 DATA 128,130,130,130,130,128,128,128,191
2092 DATA 191,128,128,128,129,129,129,129,128
```

**LISTING 7-2** Programming for Project 7-2

The five-part analysis of this listing is as follows:

Initialization routine (lines 20–30)
Control routine (lines 105–130)
Drawing subroutines (lines 510–555)
String-packing subroutine (lines 1010–1055)
DATA listings (lines 2010–2092)

As far as the RACE CAR picture is concerned, it is packed by the routines in program lines 1010 through 1025. The seven lines in the picture are assigned to string variables F1(1) through F1(7), and the character data is read from lines 2010 through 2042. The RACE CAR is then drawn on the screen by setting its displacement value and calling its drawing routine at line 510.

The AIRCRAFT picture is string-packed at lines 1035 through 1055,

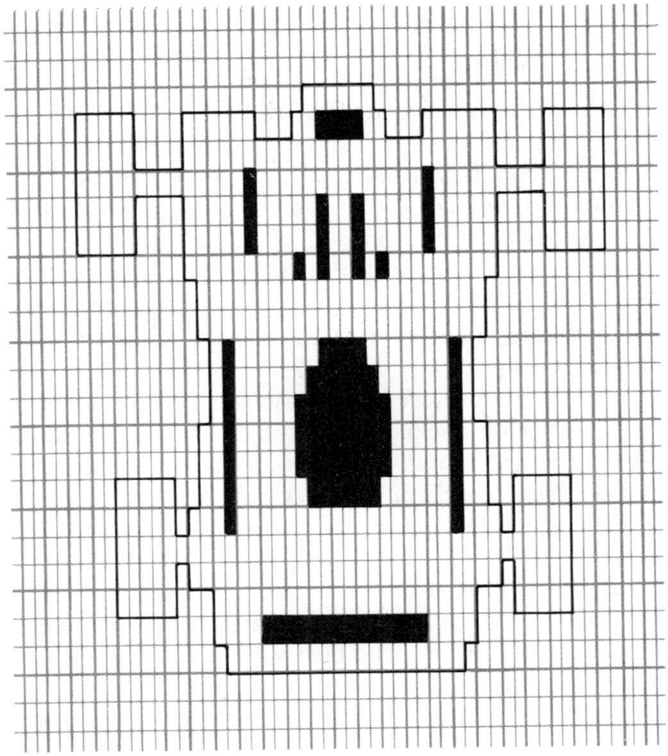

FIGURE 7-2 Worksheet Race Car figure for Project 7-2

and its lines of characters are assigned to string variables F2(1) through F2(8). The DATA is taken from lines 2055 through 2092, and the AIRCRAFT image is drawn by calling its drawing subroutine at line 535.

Once the strings are packed for both images, the control routine manages their presentation on the screen. The instructions in line 110 set the RACE CAR image at screen location 148, call the appropriate drawing subroutine, and then send control to another subroutine that begins at line 125.

The subroutine at line 125 simply prints a prompting message, 'ENTER' FOR NEXT FRAME, and then waits for the user to strike the ENTER key. After that, control returns to the next printing operation.

Line 115 sets the position of the AIRCRAFT figure to location 150, calls the appropriate drawing subroutine, and then calls the ENTER routine again.

Line 120 is responsible for drawing both figures on the screen. First, it positions the RACE CAR and calls its drawing subroutine, then it positions the AIRCRAFT figure and calls its drawing routine.

When line 110 is executed, the RACE CAR appears near the middle of the screen. Executing line 115 causes the AIRCRAFT to appear near the middle of the screen. And when line 120 is executed, both pictures appear at the same time, the RACE CAR near the left side of the screen and the AIRCRAFT near the right side.

The presentation of these three different frames of graphics is separated by an ENTER key input. It is a cycling program that shows the three kinds of displays in succession. Ending the program is a matter of striking the BREAK key.

The purpose of the project is to demonstrate how a control routine can use a couple of string-packed images to create a sequence of pictures on the screen. The job could be done without using string-packed variables (as described in earlier chapters), but the relatively long drawing time would create an unpleasant visual effect. Here, the images are drawn almost instantly.

Incidentally, note the use of a title message in line 25 that is intended to cover for the delay that is necessary for packing the strings. There is no way to avoid that initial delay. The best we can do is dress up things to make the delay seem intentional.

The next project at least suggests a more practical application of multiple-image sequences.

## PACKING WITH STRING$ FUNCTIONS

All of the previous string-packing programs do the packing operation by reading character codes, one at a time, from a DATA list and concatenating them into a string variable. The general routine looks like this:

```
READ A
F$ = F$ + CHR$(A)
```

The routine is repeated until the string is packed with one full line of graphic codes. The number of graphic codes to be packed into a variable has been specified by numeric variable P. Thus if a string variable is to be packed with nine codes, the general sequence looks like this:

```
P = 9
F$""
FOR N = 1 TO P
READ A
F$ = F$ + CHR$(A)
NEXT N
```

That routine reads nine successive character codes from a DATA list, concatenating them into string variable F$.

You have probably noticed, however, that some of the DATA lists in previous projects often repeat the same character code some number of times in succession. That situation invites the use of a STRING$ function, but such a function does not fit the CHR$-oriented packing procedure being used at the time.

The next project happens to be one that never uses the same character code less than twice in succession, and sometimes the same character has to be used 20 times in succession. Writing that program with a CHR$-oriented packing routine would make it necessary to type long lines of identical character codes in the DATA listings. A STRING$-packing procedure would be much simpler.

The general procedure for packing a string variable with a STRING$ function looks like this:

```
READ A,B
F$ = F$ + STRING$(A,B)
```

The routine reads two successive items from a DATA list; the first is the number of characters to be printed in succession and the second is the character code itself. It reads pairs of items from the DATA list, as opposed to reading one item at a time, as is the case when CHR$ packing is used.

Therefore, instead of specifying the number of items to be read and packed into a string, the STRING$-packing technique must specify the number of pairs of DATA items to be read. The following routine specifies five pairs of DATA items—five STRING$ functions to be concatenated into the string variable:

```
P = 5
F$ = ""
FOR N = 1 TO P
READ A,B
F$ = F$ + STRING$(A,B)
NEXT N
```

That routine will read ten items (five pairs) from a DATA list. Each pair is fit into a STRING$ function and concatenated with the earlier version of the variable. When the routine is done, string variable F$ will be composed of five concatenated STRING$ functions.

When making up the DATA lists, it is important to enter the items as pairs of numbers: first the number of characters, then the character code. As an example, look ahead at DATA line 2020 in Listing 7–3:

```
9,191,2,143,9,191
```

That is a DATA line for a STRING$-oriented packing routine. Divided into pairs of items, the list looks like this:

9,191
2,143
9,191

That means the string variable being packed at the time will be composed of three STRING$ functions:

STRING$(9,191)
STRING$(2,143)
STRING$(9,191)

What would that DATA line look like if you were forced to use a CHR$-oriented packing procedure? Well, it would have 20 items in it: 9 successive 191s, 2 successive 143s, and 9 more 191s. That's a lot of typing. Clearly, there are advantages to the STRING$-oriented packing idea, especially when characters are repeated.

## PROJECT 7–3

Try the program in Listing 7–3. It uses a STRING$-oriented packing procedure for making up six different die figures as shown in Fig. 7–3; and once the strings are packed, striking the ENTER key causes a pair of randomly selected die images to appear on the screen.

```
10 REM ** PROJECT 7-3
15 REM          GRAPHIC DICE
20 CLEAR 1024:DEFSTR F,L:CLS
25 PRINT @ 473,"** DICE GAME **"
30 GOSUB 1000
100 REM ** CONTROL ROUTINE
105 CLS:PRINT @ 896,"STRIKE A KEY TO ROLL THE DICE"
110 S$=INKEY$:IF S$="" THEN 110
115 D=10:S=RND(6):ON S GOSUB 510,520,530,540,550,560
120 D=35:S=RND(6):ON S GOSUB 510,520,530,540,550,560
125 GOTO 110
500 REM ** DRAWING SUBROUTINE
505 REM         ONE
510 FOR N=1 TO 6:PRINT @ D+64*N-1,F1(N);:NEXT N:RETURN
515 REM         TWO
520 FOR N=1 TO 6:PRINT @ D+64*N-1,F2(N);:NEXT N:RETURN
525 REM         THREE
530 FOR N=1 TO 6:PRINT @ D+64*N-1,F3(N);:NEXT N:RETURN
535 REM         FOUR
540 FOR N=1 TO 6:PRINT @ D+64*N-1,F4(N);:NEXT N:RETURN
545 REM         FIVE
550 FOR N=1 TO 6:PRINT @ D+64*N-1,F5(N);:NEXT N:RETURN
555 REM         SIX
560 FOR N=1 TO 6:PRINT @ D+64*N-1,F6(N);:NEXT N:RETURN
```

```
1000 REM ** STRING-PACKING SUBROUTINE
1005 REM         ONE
1010 P=1:GOSUB 1500:F1(1)=L:P=1:GOSUB 1500:F1(2)=L
1015 P=3:GOSUB 1500:F1(3)=L:P=3:GOSUB 1500:F1(4)=L
1020 P=1:GOSUB 1500:F1(5)=L:P=1:GOSUB 1500:F1(6)=L
1025 REM         TWO
1030 P=1:GOSUB 1500:F2(1)=L:P=3:GOSUB 1500:F2(2)=L
1035 P=1:GOSUB 1500:F2(3)=L:P=1:GOSUB 1500:F2(4)=L
1040 P=3:GOSUB 1500:F2(5)=L:P=1:GOSUB 1500:F2(6)=L
1045 REM         THREE
1050 P=1:GOSUB 1500:F3(1)=L:P=3:GOSUB 1500:F3(2)=L
1055 P=3:GOSUB 1500:F3(3)=L:P=3:GOSUB 1500:F3(4)=L
1060 P=3:GOSUB 1500:F3(5)=L:P=1:GOSUB 1500:F3(6)=L
1065 REM         FOUR
1070 P=1:GOSUB 1500:F4(1)=L:P=5:GOSUB 1500:F4(2)=L
1075 P=1:GOSUB 1500:F4(3)=L:P=1:GOSUB 1500:F4(4)=L
1080 P=5:GOSUB 1500:F4(5)=L:P=1:GOSUB 1500:F4(6)=L
1085 REM         FIVE
1090 P=1:GOSUB 1500:F5(1)=L:P=5:GOSUB 1500:F5(2)=L
1095 P=3:GOSUB 1500:F5(3)=L:P=3:GOSUB 1500:F5(4)=L
1100 P=5:GOSUB 1500:F5(5)=L:P=1:GOSUB 1500:F5(6)=L
1105 REM         SIX
1110 P=1:GOSUB 1500:F6(1)=L:P=5:GOSUB 1500:F6(2)=L
1115 P=5:GOSUB 1500:F6(3)=L:P=5:GOSUB 1500:F6(4)=L
1120 P=5:GOSUB 1500:F6(5)=L:P=1:GOSUB 1500:F6(6)=L
1125 RETURN
1500 L="":FOR N=1 TO P:READ A,B:L=L+STRING$(A,B):NEXT N:RETURN
2000 REM  ** DATA LISTINGS
2005 REM         ONE
2010 DATA 20,188
2015 DATA 20,191
2020 DATA 9,191,2,143,9,191
2025 DATA 9,191,2,188,9,191
2030 DATA 20,191
2035 DATA 20,143
2040 REM         TWO
2045 DATA 20,188
2050 DATA 3,191,2,176,15,191
2055 DATA 20,191
2060 DATA 20,191
2065 DATA 15,191,2,131,3,191
2070 DATA 20,143
2075 REM         THREE
2080 DATA 20,188
2085 DATA 3,191,2,131,15,191
2090 DATA 9,191,2,143,9,191
2095 DATA 9,191,2,188,9,191
2100 DATA 15,191,2,131,3,191
2105 DATA 20,143
2110 REM         FOUR
2115 DATA 20,188
2120 DATA 3,191,2,176,10,191,2,176,3,191
2125 DATA 20,191
2130 DATA 20,191
2135 DATA 3,191,2,131,10,191,2,131,3,191
2140 DATA 20,143
2145 REM         FIVE
2150 DATA 20,188
2155 DATA 3,191,2,176,10,191,2,176,3,191
2160 DATA 9,191,2,143,9,191
```

*(cont.)*

```
2165 DATA 9,191,2,188,9,191
2170 DATA 3,191,2,131,10,191,2,131,3,191
2175 DATA 20,143
2180 REM        SIX
2185 DATA 20,188
2190 DATA 3,191,2,176,10,191,2,176,3,191
2195 DATA 3,191,2,143,10,191,2,143,3,191
2200 DATA 3,191,2,188,10,191,2,188,3,191
2205 DATA 3,191,2,131,10,191,2,131,3,191
2210 DATA 20,143
```

**LISTING 7-3** Programming for the Graphic Dice game in Project 7-3

This STRING$-oriented packing program uses the same five basic sections that are used for the CHR$ versions; what is more, the sections perform the same general functions.
Initialization routine (lines 20–30)

- CLEAR 1024 bytes for the strings.
- Define any variable beginning with F or L as a string variable.
- Clear the screen and print a title message to occupy matters while the strings are being packed.
- Call the string-packing subroutine.

String-packing subroutine (lines 1010–1125)

- Set variable P equal to the number of STRING$ functions to be packed into a given line. (When using CHR$ packing, P is set to the number of CHR$ functions to be packed into a line.)
- Call the one-line packing routine at line 1500. That line has the same general form as the one used in the CHR$ versions; the only difference is that it reads DATA items two at a time and uses them as the elements of concatenated STRING$ functions.
- Set the string variable that indicates the figure number and line number equal to the packed string variable, L, returned from line 1500. In this particular example the string variables take the general form F*s*(*n*), where *s* is the die figure (one dot, two dots, etc.) and *n* is the graphic line number. Thus a variable such as F3(5) can be interpreted as the string variable for plotting the fifth line in a die figure showing a score of 3.

DATA listings (lines 2010–2210)

- Show the pairs of numbers required for the STRING$ functions—number of characters followed by the character code.

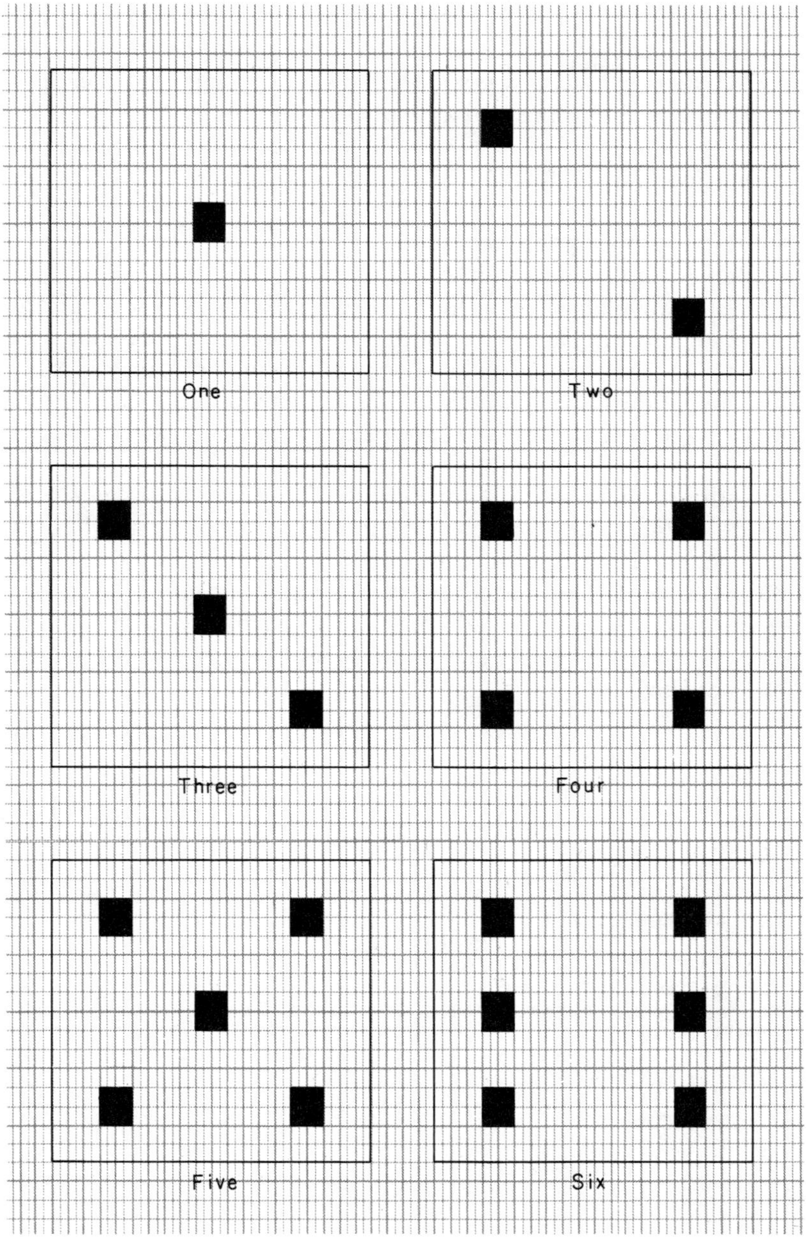
One
Two
Three
Four
Five
Six

Drawing subroutines (lines 510–560)

- Set up a FOR . . . NEXT loop for scanning the six lines used for all of the figures.
- PRINT the lines, using a specified set of string variables for that particular die figure and a displacement value, D.

Control routine (lines 105–125)

- PRINT a prompting message.
- Wait for a keystroke (line 110).
- Set the displacement value for the left-hand die, pick its random value, and call the corresponding drawing subroutine (line 115).
- Set the displacement value for the right-hand die, pick its random value, and call the corresponding drawing subroutine (line 120).
- Loop back up to line 110 to wait for another keystroke.

This program format is appropriate for drawing images and sequences of images that contain a relatively large number of repeated character codes. The program could be simplified a great deal, but the simplification would be based on the simple nature of the figures themselves, and doing so would confuse the purpose of the project—to demonstrate how to set up a general-purpose graphics program that uses STRING$ packing.

## PROJECT 7–4

Use STRING$ packing to draw the FLAMING CANDLE in Fig. 4–2. See the suggested program in Listing 7–4.

```
10 REM ** PROJECT 7-4
15 REM          FLAMING CANDLE, V.2
20 REM ** INITIALIZATION ROUTINE
25 CLEAR 128:DEFSTR F,L:DIM F(12)
30 CLS:PRINT @ 470,"** FLAMING CANDLE **"
35 GOSUB 1000
40 FOR T=1 TO 100:NEXT T
100 REM ** CONTROL ROUTINE
105 CLS
110 D=220:GOSUB 505
115 GOTO 115
500 REM ** DRAWING SUBROUTINE
505 FOR N=1 TO 12:PRINT @ D+64*N,F(N);:NEXT N
510 RETURN
1000 REM ** STRING-PACKING SUBROUTINE
1005 P=2:GOSUB 1500:F(1)=L:P=5:GOSUB 1500:F(2)=L
1010 P=4:GOSUB 1500:F(3)=L:P=2:GOSUB 1500:F(4)=L
1015 P=5:GOSUB 1500:F(5)=L:P=2:GOSUB 1500:F(6)=L
1020 P=2:GOSUB 1500:F(7)=L:P=3:GOSUB 1500:F(8)=L
```

```
1025 P=2:GOSUB 1500:F(9)=L:P=1:GOSUB 1500:F(10)=L
1030 P=1:GOSUB 1500:F(11)=L:P=1:GOSUB 1500:F(12)=L
1035 RETURN
1500 L="":FOR N=1 TO P:READ A,B:L=L+STRING$(A,B):NEXT N:RETURN
2000 REM ** DATA LISTINGS
2005 DATA 1,196,1,176
2010 DATA 1,128,1,184,1,190,2,191,1,148
2015 DATA 1,128,1,175,3,191,1,133
2020 DATA 1,195,1,147
2025 DATA 1,191,1,188,1,176,1,177,1,144
2030 DATA 6,191,1,149
2035 DATA 7,191,1,149
2040 DATA 6,191,1,159,1,149
2050 DATA 6,191,1,133
2055 DATA 6,191
2060 DATA 6,191
2065 DATA 6,191
```

**LISTING 7-4** Programming for a STRING$-packing version of Flaming Candle, Project 7-4

The figure uses a number of 191s in succession, thus lending itself to STRING$-packing operations. Note the instances where a character appears just one time; the general expression in that case is STRING$(1,*c*), where *c* is the character code.

Wouldn't it be nice if there were a string-packing program that could deal with both CHR$ and STRING$ functions in an effective fashion? Well, go on to the next section of this chapter.

## STRING-PACKING COMBINATIONS OF CHR$ AND STRING$ FUNCTIONS

It is possible to write programs that pack strings by means of concatenating CHR$ functions or STRING$ functions. Unfortunately, neither method is wholly appropriate to a vast majority of figures you will ever want to draw. In reality, most figures call for using combinations of CHR$ and STRING$ packing. The next set of projects demonstrates how this can be done.

Recall that a DATA listing for a CHR$ packing routine is composed of elements that represent nothing but the series of character codes. There is a one-for-one correspondence between the number of elements in the DATA list and the number of characters printed onto the screen. When the STRING$-packing routines are used, the DATA listings are organized into pairs of numbers; the first indicates how many characters, are to be printed in succession and the second specifies the character to be printed.

The key to writing a program that can handle both CHR$ and STRING$ packing is a flag, or special symbol, that can be inserted into the DATA listings to indicate whether a CHR$ or STRING$ function is to be applied. For our purposes, the function-indicating flag will be a minus sign inserted in front of the first of the two elements of a STRING$ function. Thus, this combination of elements in a DATA listing:

```
-6,191
```

indicates the application of a STRING$(6,191) function—six graphic 191s in succession.

The following program structure shows how the system can distinguish the application of a STRING$ function from a CHR$ function during the course of the string-packing operation:

```
READ ELEMENT A
IF  A >0 THEN
          READ ELEMENT B
          L$ = L$ + STRING$(ABS(A),B)
ELSE      L$ = L$ + CHR$(A)
```

Literally, the structure says this: Read an element in the DATA list, assigning its value to variable A. If A is negative, then read the next element in the DATA list and assign it to variable B. Concatenate the string variable being packed with STRING$(ABS(A),B). (It is necessary to use the ABS function to get rid of the minus sign, something a STRING$ function cannot handle.) However, if value A is not negative, concatenate the string being packed with CHR$(A).

Thus a DATA listing that uses both STRING$ and CHR$ functions will include both negative and positive numbers. The negative numbers indicate:

1. That a STRING$ function is to be used.
2. That the absolute value of the negative number represents the number of characters to be printed in succession.
3. That the number following the negative number is the character code for the STRING$ function.

All of the string-packing subroutines cited thus far use a variable P to indicate the number of CHR$ or STRING$ functions to be included in a given string variable. You, the programmer, set the value of P, based on the number of elements or pairs of elements in the corresponding DATA list. That matter of counting things in the DATA list in order to set the value of P becomes rather tricky when you are using combinations of CHR$ and STRING$ functions, so it is necessary to introduce an entirely different technique for keeping track of how many DATA items ought to be included in a given string variable.

Eliminating the need for counting DATA items yourself is a matter of introducing two additional flag items: one that indicates the end of a string that is being packed, and another that indicates the end of the last string to be packed. Here we use a zero to mark the end of a string and numeral 1 to indicate the end of the last string in the figure.

Consider the following examples from a DATA listing:

```
DATA  -2,176,191,148,0
DATA  144,-6,191,1
```

The first data line ends with a zero. That zero indicates the end of a given line in a figure but not the end of the last line. In that particular case, the line packs a string variable with STRING$(2,176) CHR$(191) CHR$(148). The second DATA line ends with a 1. That indicates the end of the last string variable in the program, a string composed of CHR$(144) STRING$(6,191).

Look ahead to the string-packing subroutine (lines 1005 through 1035) in Listing 7-5 to see how this packing scheme works.

Variable L in line 1005 is set to 1. That numeric variable is used as a line counter: when the routine is done, it will indicate the number of lines in the figure. Then see how the line being packed is set to the null string in program line 1010.

Line 1015 in the program reads a DATA element, assigning it to variable A. After that, the routine goes through a series of numerical magnitude comparisons:

- If A is greater than 1, the DATA item is treated as a character code that is to be packed as a CHR$ function.
- If A is less than zero (a negative number), the program reads the next item in the DATA list, assigns it to variable B, and packs the string with a STRING$ function.
- If A is equal to zero, it is time to end the string that is currently being packed and start a new one. Note in program line 1030 that the line counter, L, is incremented and program control is returned to line 1010, where the next line-string is nulled.
- If A is equal to 1, it means the packing job is done. Program line 1035 responds to that situation by returning program control to the control routine—to line 40 in this case.

The DATA listings in this case are altered with a negative number to indicate the application of the STRING$ function, with a zero to indicate

## PROJECT 7–5

Rewrite the FLAMING CANDLE program to take advantage of the ability to pack both CHR$ and STRING$ functions. See the suggested result in Listing 7–5.

```
10 REM ** PROJECT 7-5
15 REM          FLAMING CANDLE, V.3
20 REM ** INITIALIZATION ROUTINE
25 CLEAR 128:DEFSTR F:DIM F(12)
30 CLS:PRINT @ 470,"** FLAMING CANDLE **"
35 GOSUB 1000
40 FOR T=1 TO 100:NEXT T
100 REM ** CONTROL ROUTINE
105 CLS
110 D=220:GOSUB 505
115 GOTO 115
500 REM ** DRAWING SUBROUTINE
505 FOR N=1 TO 12:PRINT @ D+64*N,F(N);:NEXT N
510 RETURN
1000 REM ** STRING-PACKING SUBROUTINE
1005 L=1
1010 F(L)=""
1015 READ A
1020 IF A>1 THEN F(L)=F(L)+CHR$(A):GOTO 1015
1025 IF A<0 THEN READ B:F(L)=F(L)+STRING$(ABS(A),B):GOTO 1015
1030 IF A=0 THEN L=L+1:GOTO 1010
1035 IF A=1 THEN RETURN
2000 REM ** DATA LISTINGS
2005 DATA 196,176,0
2010 DATA 128,184,190,-2,191,148,0
2015 DATA 128,175,-3,191,133,0
2020 DATA 195,147,0
2025 DATA 191,188,176,177,144,0
2030 DATA -6,191,149,0
2035 DATA -7,191,149,0
2040 DATA -6,191,159,149,0
2045 DATA -6,191,133,0
2050 DATA -6,191,0
2055 DATA -6,191,0
2060 DATA -6,191,1
```

**LISTING 7-5** Programming for Flaming Candle, using a combination of CHR$ and STRING$ packing, Project 7-5

the end of a line string, and with a numeral 1 to indicate the end of the last line of the picture.

The string-packing subroutine is also modified to interpret the data as it is presented in this sort of DATA listing.

The initialization routine, control routine, and drawing subroutines do not have to be significantly changed in order to use the combinations of CHR$ and STRING$ functions.

The main advantage of the scheme is that it reduces the amount of data in the DATA listings. You can see some benefit by comparing this DATA listing with the one for the same figure in Listing 7–4. More extensive drawings would reflect a much greater reduction in size of the DATA listings. If nothing else, this saves you some programming time.

## PROJECT 7–6

Listing 7–6 represents a rather extensive graphic routine that uses combined CHR$ and STRING$ functions for packing a full screen of string-packed variables. The image is that of a cartoon black cat on a white background. Give it a try; I think you will be pleased with the results and I hope it will challenge you to do some imaginative work of this sort.

```
10 REM ** PROJECT 7-6
15 CLEAR 2048:DEFSTR F:DIM F(15)
20 CLS:PRINT @ 537,"** KRAZY KAT **"
25 GOSUB 1000
100 REM ** CONTROL ROUTINE
105 CLS
110 GOSUB 505
115 GOTO 115
500 REM ** DRAWING SUBROUTINE
505 FOR N=1 TO L:PRINT F(N);:NEXT N:RETURN
1000 REM ** STRING-PACKING SUBROUTINE
1005 L=1
1010 F(L)=""
1015 READ A
1020 IF A>1 THEN F(L)=F(L)+CHR$(A):GOTO 1015
1025 IF A<0 THEN READ B:F(L)=F(L)+STRING$(ABS(A),B):GOTO 1015
1030 IF A=0 THEN L=L+1:GOTO 1010
1035 IF A=1 THEN RETURN
2000 REM ** DATA LISTS
2005 REM       LINE 1
2010 DATA -64,191,0
2015 REM       LINE 2
2020 DATA -64,191,0
2025 REM       LINE 3
2030 DATA -18,191,135,182,175,-19,191,159,135,188,155,-20,191,0
2035 REM       LINE 4
2040 DATA -17,191,133,170,191,189,180,131,143,191,178,175,159,186
2045 DATA -6,191,153,191,167,191,135,184,-2,191,149,-20,191,0
2050 REM       LINE 5
2055 DATA -17,191,144,170,-3,191,148,194,179,-2,178,147,-6,131
2060 DATA 179,144,131,129,136,-3,191,149,-20,191,0
2065 REM       LINE 6
2070 DATA -17,191,149,138,135,129,128,160,190,-5,191
2075 DATA 189,194,160,190,-4,191,180,194,191,143,169,-20,191,0
2080 REM       LINE 7
2085 DATA -7,191,159,-8,191,159,129,196,-4,191,159,143
2090 DATA -2,191,194,191,143,175,-4,191,149,196,171,-9,191
2095 DATA 143,167,185,-7,191,0
2100 REM       LINE 8
2105 DATA -8,191,182,179,-2,143,175,-2,191,189,198,130,143,175
2110 DATA 145,128,129,138,129,194,129,130,128,186,159,-2,143
2115 DATA 197,190,-2,191,143,167,179,185,-3,188,-10,191,0
2120 REM       LINE 9
```

(cont.)

```
2125 DATA -12,191,189,188,156,132,203,168,-4,191,189,203
2130 DATA 131,128,140,-17,191,0
2135 REM       LINE 10
2140 DATA -4,191,143,-3,179,-5,188,148,202,160,195
2145 DATA 139,-2,143,135,129,194,144,203,168,188,-4,179,-3,143
2150 DATA 171,-7,191,0
2155 REM       LINE 11
2160 DATA -3,191,189,-9,191,181,202,160,133,200,150,204,186,-16,191,0
2170 REM       LINE 12
2175 DATA -10,191,143,167,179,-3,188,-5,176,194,152,129
2180 DATA 128,184,188,167,191,159,131,194,130,164,199
2185 DATA -2,176,191,182,179,143,175,-14,191,0
2190 REM       LINE 13
2195 DATA -6,191,159,179,185,188,-13,191,188,180,142,143
2200 DATA 142,143,185,-5,188,190,-13,191,189,188,179,175
2205 DATA -11,191,0
2210 REM       LINE 14
2215 DATA -64,191,0
2220 REM       LINE 15
2225 DATA -64,191,1
```

**LISTING 7-6** Programming for Krazy Kat, Project 7-6

# 8 Customized Character Sets

The TRS–80 includes two character sets: the alphanumerics and the special graphics symbols. There are times, though, when a programmer wishes there were some alternatives available. How about a character set for playing-card games? Or one that generates oversized, black-on-white alphanumerics? Or one that generates a foreign alphabet such as the Russian, Hebrew, Greek, or Chinese?

The techniques already described in this book are adequate for producing one-of-a-kind arrangements of special characters and symbols. You can, for example, create a computerized sign that offers a message composed of oversized English letters, numerals, and punctuation marks. That is a simple matter of laying out the message on a video worksheet, doing a line-by-line character analysis, and then writing a string-packing program that draws the message on the screen for you. If you wish, you can use sequences of these full-screen, custom messages to create the effect of flipping panels of titles and messages.

That isn't the subject of this chapter, however. Rather, it is to create an entire character set, assign some sort of coding to each character, then write control routines that let you select and arrange the characters that you have made available. In effect, the idea is to add a customized character generator to your TRS–80 system.

The emphasis of the discussion is on constructing the character sets and their codes. You will find three different examples of custom character sets and applications offered here, but in general, it is up to you to invent your own applications of these character sets and, better yet, devise your own character sets to suit a wide range of applications.

## A CHARACTER SET FOR CARD GAMES

Fig. 8–1 shows the original worksheet version of a customized character set that can be used for card games. The 5 × 2 graphics format makes it possible to create reasonable facsimiles of face values 2 through A plus the four standard suit symbols. Using a larger graphics format would make it possible to design even clearer and more attractive symbols, but then there would be the problem of fitting a useful number of them onto the screen at one time.

At any rate, the procedure is to decide on a reasonable character size, lay out all the characters onto a video worksheet, and do a character-by-

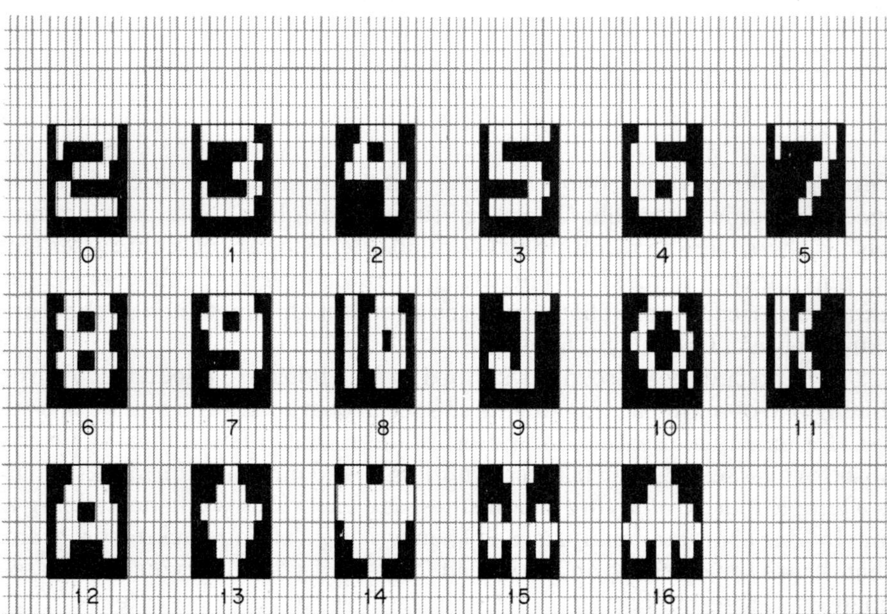


**FIGURE 8–1** Worksheet version of a playing-card character set

character, line-by-line analysis of the pixel graphics needed for each custom character.

The next step is to create a DATA listing for all of those custom characters.

## PROJECT 8-1

Create a DATA list for the custom card-playing characters shown in Fig. 8-1. Use a zero to indicate the end of a line and a 1 to indicate the end of the DATA listing. See the suggested routine in Listing 8-1.

```
10 REM ** PROJECT 8-1
15 REM         PLAYING-CARD GRAPHICS SET
20 T=0
25 READ A:T=T+A
30 IF A<>1 THEN 25
35 IF T=23971 THEN PRINT "OK":DELETE 10-40
40 PRINT "DATA ERROR":END
5000 REM ** DATA LISTINGS
5002 DATA 138,163,179,187,133,0,138,141,-2,140,132,0
5003 DATA 138,-2,131,187,132,0,138,-2,140,142,129,0
5004 DATA 160,190,179,191,144,0,-3,128,143,128,0
5005 DATA 170,183,-2,179,129,0,136,-2,140,142,129,0
5006 DATA 168,191,-2,179,128,0,130,143,140,143,129,0
5007 DATA 138,-2,131,187,133,0,-2,128,142,129,128,0
5008 DATA 136,183,179,187,132,0,130,141,140,142,129,0
5009 DATA 136,191,179,191,148,0,128,-2,140,143,129,0
5010 DATA 170,149,190,175,148,0,138,133,139,143,129,0
5011 DATA 128,130,171,151,129,0,130,143,142,133,128,0
5012 DATA 160,158,131,173,144,0,128,139,140,135,132,0
5013 DATA 170,181,158,129,128,0,138,133,139,132,128,0
5014 DATA 160,190,143,189,144,0,138,135,131,139,133,0
5015 DATA 160,184,191,180,144,0,128,139,191,135,128,0
5016 DATA 190,191,188,191,189,0,130,143,191,143,129,0
5017 DATA 160,146,191,161,144,0,139,135,191,139,135,0
5018 DATA 160,184,191,180,144,0,139,135,191,139,135,0
5019 DATA 1
```

**LISTING 8-1** DATA listing and checksum routine for the playing-card set in Project 8-1

The DATA listing in this case begins at line 5000. In order to maintain a reasonable level of consistency, I have used the last two digits in the DATA line numbers to indicate which character is represented. Line 5002, for example, carries the graphic codes for face value 2, 5010 has the codes for face value 10, and lines 5015 through 5018 hold the graphics for the suit values diamond, heart, club and spade, respectively.

Exactly how this data is packed and applied isn't important at this time. The idea here is to get the character information into the computer. Applying that information is a matter that is left for later consideration.

In the event any reader might want to use this particular character set, I have included a short checksum routine at program lines 20 through

40. The purpose of that routine is to make sure you have made no typing errors while entering the DATA listings. There are a lot of boring numbers in that list, and the chances of making an error are quite high.

After you have entered Listing 8–1 into your system, do a RUN. If there is an error in your DATA listing, you will get the message from program line 40: DATA ERROR. That being the case, you should carefully double-check the listing against your own, making the necessary corrections. But if you have entered the DATA as it is shown here, line 35 will print an OK message and immediately delete the checksum routine, leaving just lines 5000 through 5019 intact.

How does that checksum routine work? It's simple, really. When I set up the characters and viewed them on the screen, I made a couple of modifications and then wrote a short program that summed all the DATA elements. In this case, the sum happens to be 23971; that's the checksum that is compared with variable T in line 35. If you make any typing errors while entering that DATA listing into your computer, the chances of having the numbers add up to 23971 are astronomically small. However, if you have done a perfect job (or have corrected any errors in your own listing), the numbers will match perfectly. The checksum routine, you see, adds up the values of the DATA items in your version of the listing and compares the results with my own version.

When you are putting together your own character sets, a checksum routine isn't very meaningful. It is included here only for the benefit of those who might want to use this particular one for the next couple of projects and, indeed, card games of their own design.

The point is to create a DATA listing that can stand alone. At this time, nothing can or should be done with it. It is supposed to be a separate entity that can be used in any number of ways at some later time.

To simplify matters later on, it is necessary to save the raw DATA listing on cassette tape or disk. So when you need the characters for a particular program, you can begin the programming by loading the character DATA first, then writing all the other programming around it. If, for instance, you plan to work out Projects 8–2 and 8–3, you should run Listing 8–1 until it comes out OK, then save the DATA listing on tape or disk.

When preparing a custom character set, you must double-check the appearance of the characters and the accuracy of the DATA listings by viewing those characters on the screen.

## PROJECT 8–2

With the DATA listings from Listing 8–1 loaded into the computer, expand the program to include a string-packing, initialization, and control routine that lets you view the characters on the screen. See Listing 8–2.

```
10 REM ** PROJECT 8-2
15 REM           VIEW THE CARD CHARACTERS
20 CLEAR 1024:DEFSTR C
25 DIM C(18,2)
30 CLS:PRINT "NOW PACKING ...":GOSUB 4000
100 REM ** CONTROL ROUTINE
105 CLS: PRINT @ 896,"STRIKE A KEY TO SEE THE CHARACTERS"
110 FOR N=0 TO 16
115 C=INKEY$:IF C="" THEN 115
120 D=415:GOSUB 1000
125 NEXT N:GOTO 110
1000 REM  ** DRAWING SUBROUTINES
1005 PRINT @ D,C(N,0);:PRINT @ D+64,C(N,1);
1010 RETURN
4000 REM ** STRING-PACKING SUBROUTINE
4005 N=0
4010 L=0
4015 C(N,L)=""
4020 READ A
4025 IF A>1 THEN C(N,L)=C(N,L)+CHR$(A):GOTO 4020
4030 IF A=0 AND L=0 THEN L=1:GOTO 4015
4035 IF A=0 AND L=1 THEN N=N+1:GOTO 4010
4040 IF A<0 THEN READ B:C(N,L)=C(N,L)+STRING$(ABS(A),B):GOTO 4020
4045 RETURN
5000 REM ** DATA LISTINGS
5002 DATA 138,163,179,187,133,0,138,141,-2,140,132,0
5003 DATA 138,-2,131,187,132,0,138,-2,140,142,129,0
5004 DATA 160,190,179,191,144,0,-3,128,143,128,0
5005 DATA 170,183,-2,179,129,0,136,-2,140,142,129,0
5006 DATA 168,191,-2,179,128,0,130,143,140,143,129,0
5007 DATA 138,-2,131,187,133,0,-2,128,142,129,128,0
5008 DATA 136,183,179,187,132,0,130,141,140,142,129,0
5009 DATA 136,191,179,191,148,0,128,-2,140,143,129,0
5010 DATA 170,149,190,175,148,0,138,133,139,143,129,0
5011 DATA 128,130,171,151,129,0,130,143,142,133,128,0
5012 DATA 160,158,131,173,144,0,128,139,140,135,132,0
5013 DATA 170,181,158,129,128,0,138,133,139,132,128,0
5014 DATA 160,190,143,189,144,0,138,135,131,139,133,0
5015 DATA 160,184,191,180,144,0,128,139,191,135,128,0
5016 DATA 190,191,188,191,189,0,130,143,191,143,129,0
5017 DATA 160,146,191,161,144,0,139,135,191,139,135,0
5018 DATA 160,184,191,180,144,0,139,135,191,139,135,0
5019 DATA 1
```

**LISTING 8-2** Programming for viewing the playing-card characters, Project 8-2

If the DATA listing from Listing 8-1 is already resident in your computer, or if you have saved that listing and can load it from tape or disk, the expanded listing won't be as difficult to enter as it might appear. The hard part has already been done.

In this case, the string-packing subroutine (program lines 4000 through 4045) pack the special card-playing characters into string arrays C(O,*L*) through C(16,*L*), where *L* is the two line numbers—0 and 1—for the characters. The custom characters and their string variables are summarized in Table 8-1.

The initialization routine in program lines 20-30 sets aside a

**TABLE 8-1**

STRING-VARIABLE ASSIGNMENTS FOR THE PLAYING-CARD CHARACTER SET

| *Character* | *Variable* | *Line* |
|---|---|---|
| 2 | C(0,0) | 0 |
| | C(0,1) | 1 |
| 3 | C(1,0) | 0 |
| | C(1,1) | 1 |
| 4 | C(2,0) | 0 |
| | C(2,1) | 1 |
| 5 | C(3,0) | 0 |
| | C(3,1) | 1 |
| 6 | C(4,0) | 0 |
| | C(4,1) | 1 |
| 7 | C(5,0) | 0 |
| | C(5,1) | 1 |
| 8 | C(6,0) | 0 |
| | C(6,1) | 1 |
| 9 | C(7,0) | 0 |
| | C(7,1) | 1 |
| 10 | C(8,0) | 0 |
| | C(8,1) | 1 |
| J | C(9,0) | 0 |
| | C(9,1) | 1 |
| Q | C(10,0) | 0 |
| | C(10,1) | 1 |
| K | C(11,0) | 0 |
| | C(11,1) | 1 |
| A | C(12,0) | 0 |
| | C(12,1) | 1 |
| diamond | C(13,0) | 0 |
| | C(13,1) | 1 |
| heart | C(14,0) | 0 |
| | C(14,1) | 1 |
| club | C(15,0) | 0 |
| | C(15,1) | 1 |
| spade | C(16,0) | 0 |
| | C(16,1) | 1 |

generous amount of string space, defines any variable beginning with C as a string variable, and dimensions the character arrays.

The control routine (lines 100 through 125) lets you view each of the special characters, one at a time, by striking any key on the keyboard. Line 120 is responsible for setting a displacement value that situates the characters near the middle of the screen and for calling the drawing subroutine. The control routine cycles through all 16 characters endlessly, so the best way to terminate is with the BREAK key.

When the program finally calls the drawing subroutine (program lines 1005 and 1010), the character to be drawn has already been selected and positioned. The drawing subroutine does little more than print the two strings that define the selected character.

Through the process of entering Listing 8-2 into the computer, you have, in effect, appended a general-purpose string-packing and drawing subroutine to the custom character codes. You will thus find it helpful in the long run to save lines 1000 through the end of the program on tape or disk for future use. As suggested in earlier chapters, the application of string graphics is most often determined by the nature of the control routine; the drawing and string-packing subroutines and the DATA listings remain unchanged through a wide spectrum of possible control applications. Thus by saving lines 1000 through the DATA listing, you have the foundation for constructing any card game you wish; it's a matter of using those sections in conjunction with an appropriate control and initialization routine. The next project is a case in point.

## PROJECT 8–3

Use the custom card-playing character set to write a simple two-player, five-card poker game. Listing 8–3 is one example.

```
10 REM ** PROJECT 8-3
15 REM          POKER HANDS
20 CLEAR 1024:DEFSTR C
25 DIM C(18,2):DIM SC(12,16)
30 CLS:PRINT @ 408,"** POKER HANDS **":GOSUB 4000
35 CLS
40 INPUT "ENTER FIRST PLAYER'S NAME";P1$
45 IF LEN(P1$)>12 THEN PRINT "NAME IS TOO LONG ... TRY AGAIN":
   PRINT:GOTO 40
50 CLS
55 INPUT "ENTER SECOND PLAYER'S NAME";P2$
60 IF LEN(P2$)>12 THEN PRINT "NAME IS TOO LONG ... TRY AGAIN":
   PRINT:GOTO 55
100 REM ** CONTROL ROUTINE
105 CLS
110 PRINT "DEALER IS SHUFFLING":FOR T=0 TO 1000:NEXT T:CLS
115 FOR NC=0 TO 4:FOR PN=0 TO 1:SC(NC,PN)=0:NEXT PN,NC
120 PRINT @ 192,P1$:PRINT @ 704,P2$:PRINT @ 448,STRING$(64,140)
125 FOR NC=0 TO 4:FOR PN=0 TO 1
130 NV=RND(13)-1:FV=RND(4)+12:IF SC(NV,FV)=1 THEN 130
135 SC(NV,FV)=1
140 N=NV:D=79+10*NC+512*PN:GOSUB 1000
145 N=FV:D=D+192:GOSUB 1000
150 NEXT PN,NC
155 PRINT @ 960,"STRIKE 'ENTER' TO SHUFFLE AND DEAL AGAIN ...";
160 C=INKEY$:IF C="" THEN  160 ELSE 105
1000 REM  ** DRAWING SUBROUTINES
1005 PRINT @ D,C(N,0);:PRINT @ D+64,C(N,1);
1010 RETURN
4000 REM ** STRING-PACKING SUBROUTINE
4005 N=0
```

(cont.)

```
4010 L=0
4015 C(N,L)=""
4020 READ A
4025 IF A>1 THEN C(N,L)=C(N,L)+CHR$(A):GOTO 4020
4030 IF A=0 AND L=0 THEN L=1:GOTO 4015
4035 IF A=0 AND L=1 THEN N=N+1:GOTO 4010
4040 IF A<0 THEN READ B:C(N,L)=C(N,L)+STRING$(ABS(A),B):GOTO 4020
4045 RETURN
5000 REM ** DATA LISTINGS
5002 DATA 138,163,179,187,133,0,138,141,-2,140,132,0
5003 DATA 138,-2,131,187,132,0,138,-2,140,142,129,0
5004 DATA 160,190,179,191,144,0,-3,128,143,128,0
5005 DATA 170,183,-2,179,129,0,136,-2,140,142,129,0
5006 DATA 168,191,-2,179,128,0,130,143,140,143,129,0
5007 DATA 138,-2,131,187,133,0,-2,128,142,129,128,0
5008 DATA 136,183,179,187,132,0,130,141,140,142,129,0
5009 DATA 136,191,179,191,148,0,128,-2,140,143,129,0
5010 DATA 170,149,190,175,148,0,138,133,139,143,129,0
5011 DATA 128,130,171,151,129,0,130,143,142,133,128,0
5012 DATA 160,158,131,173,144,0,128,139,140,135,132,0
5013 DATA 170,181,158,129,128,0,138,133,139,132,128,0
5014 DATA 160,190,143,189,144,0,138,135,131,139,133,0
5015 DATA 160,184,191,180,144,0,128,139,191,135,128,0
5016 DATA 190,191,188,191,189,0,130,143,191,143,129,0
5017 DATA 160,146,191,161,144,0,139,135,191,139,135,0
5018 DATA 160,184,191,180,144,0,139,135,191,139,135,0
5019 DATA 1
```

**LISTING 8-3** Programming for poker hands, Project 8-3

First notice that the drawing subroutine, string-packing subroutine, and DATA listings are identical to those used in the previous project. Furthermore, the DATA listing, beginning at line 5000, is identical to the original one devised as part of Project 8-1. The configuration of the special card-playing symbols, the technique for packing them into string variables, and the procedure for drawing them onto the screen remain unchanged. Only the initialization and control routines have to be revised in order to suit the needs of a particular kind of card game.

This is a simple card game. It deals five cards to two different players. The player with the best poker hand is the winner. That's all. The purpose of the project is to illustrate the application of the custom card-playing graphics set, not to put together a razzle-dazzle computerized card game. That's up to you.

Run the program for a while to see how it works. After doing that, you will be in a better position to figure out how the control routine does its task.

## A DOUBLE-SIZED ALPHANUMERIC SET

Fig. 8-2 shows the worksheet drawings for a complete, 59-character family of keyboard alphanumerics. They fit a 5 × 6 character-space format and are thus about twice the size of the same characters from the

## PROJECT 8–4

Type in the ALPHANUMERIC CHARACTER SET shown in Listing 8–4, run it, and troubleshoot it if necessary. Save the results on tape or disk for future use.

```
10 REM ** PROJECT 8-4
15 REM          ALPHANUMERIC CHARACTER SET
20 T=0
25 READ A:T=T+A
30 IF A<>1 THEN 25
35 IF T=64800 THEN PRINT "OK":DELETE 10-40
40 PRINT "DATA ERROR":END
5000 DATA -4,191,0,-4,191,0
5001 DATA 191,149,170,191,0,191,183,187,191,0
5002 DATA 189,190,189,190,0,-4,191,0
5003 DATA 179,162,145,179,0,188,184,180,188,0
5004 DATA 128,140,136,140,0,-2,179,178,176,0
5005 DATA 188,159,163,188,0,179,188,191,179,0
5006 DATA 153,140,187,175,0,182,179,180,191,0
5007 DATA 191,189,186,191,0,-4,191,0
5008 DATA 131,184,190,191,0,188,178,187,191,0
5009 DATA 191,189,180,131,0,191,183,177,188,0
5010 DATA 134,129,130,137,0,185,180,184,182,0
5011 DATA 143,133,138,143,0,191,181,186,191,0
5012 DATA -4,191,0,180,-3,191,0
5013 DATA -4,143,0,-4,191,0
5014 DATA -4,191,0,179,-3,191,0
5015 DATA 191,159,185,190,0,179,190,-2,191,0
5016 DATA 167,-2,188,155,0,189,-2,179,190,0
5017 DATA 183,188,128,191,0,183,179,176,179,0
5018 DATA 184,-2,140,176,0,176,-3,179,0
5019 DATA 184,-2,140,160,0,178,-2,179,176,0
5020 DATA 128,143,128,143,0,-2,191,176,191,0
5021 DATA 128,-2,140,174,0,-3,179,184,0
5022 DATA 128,-3,143,0,180,178,179,176,0
5023 DATA 184,188,156,160,0,191,183,184,191,0
5024 DATA 145,-2,140,162,0,180,-2,179,184,0
5025 DATA 145,-2,140,134,0,-3,191,176,0
5026 DATA 191,183,187,191,0,191,189,190,191,0
5027 DATA 191,183,187,191,0,191,189,186,191,0
5028 DATA 143,179,188,191,0,191,188,179,191,0
5029 DATA -4,179,0,-4,188,0
5030 DATA 191,188,179,143,0,191,179,188,191,0
5031 DATA 185,188,140,178,0,-2,191,179,191,0
5032 DATA 185,140,188,155,0,189,179,182,190,0
5033 DATA 135,177,178,139,0,176,-2,188,176,0
5034 DATA 128,-2,140,162,0,176,-2,179,184,0
5035 DATA 129,-2,188,180,0,180,-2,179,177,0
5036 DATA 128,188,180,139,0,176,179,177,190,0
5037 DATA 128,-2,140,188,0,176,-3,179,0
5038 DATA 128,-2,140,188,0,176,-3,191,0
5039 DATA 129,156,140,172,0,180,-2,179,184,0
5040 DATA 128,-2,143,128,0,176,-2,191,176,0
5041 DATA 191,149,170,191,0,191,181,186,191,0
5042 DATA -3,191,128,0,180,-2,179,184,0
5043 DATA 128,143,179,188,0,176,191,188,179,0
5044 DATA 128,-3,191,0,176,-3,179,0
5045 DATA 128,155,167,128,0,176,-2,191,176,0
```

(*cont.*)

```
5046 DATA 128,148,175,128,0,176,191,178,176,0
5047 DATA 129,-2,188,130,0,180,-2,179,184,0
5048 DATA 128,-2,140,162,0,176,-3,191,0
5049 DATA 167,-2,188,155,0,189,-2,179,182,0
5050 DATA 128,-2,140,162,0,176,191,180,187,0
5051 DATA 129,-2,140,172,0,-3,179,184,0
5052 DATA 188,148,168,188,0,191,181,186,191,0
5053 DATA 128,-2,191,128,0,180,-2,179,184,0
5054 DATA 128,-2,191,128,0,189,182,185,190,0
5055 DATA 128,-2,191,128,0,176,185,182,176,0
5056 DATA 180,155,167,184,0,177,190,189,178,0
5057 DATA 180,155,167,184,0,191,181,186,191,0
5058 DATA 188,-2,140,176,0,176,-3,179,0
5059 DATA 1
```

**LISTING 8-4** DATA listing and checksum routine for the double-sized alphanumerics, Project 8-4

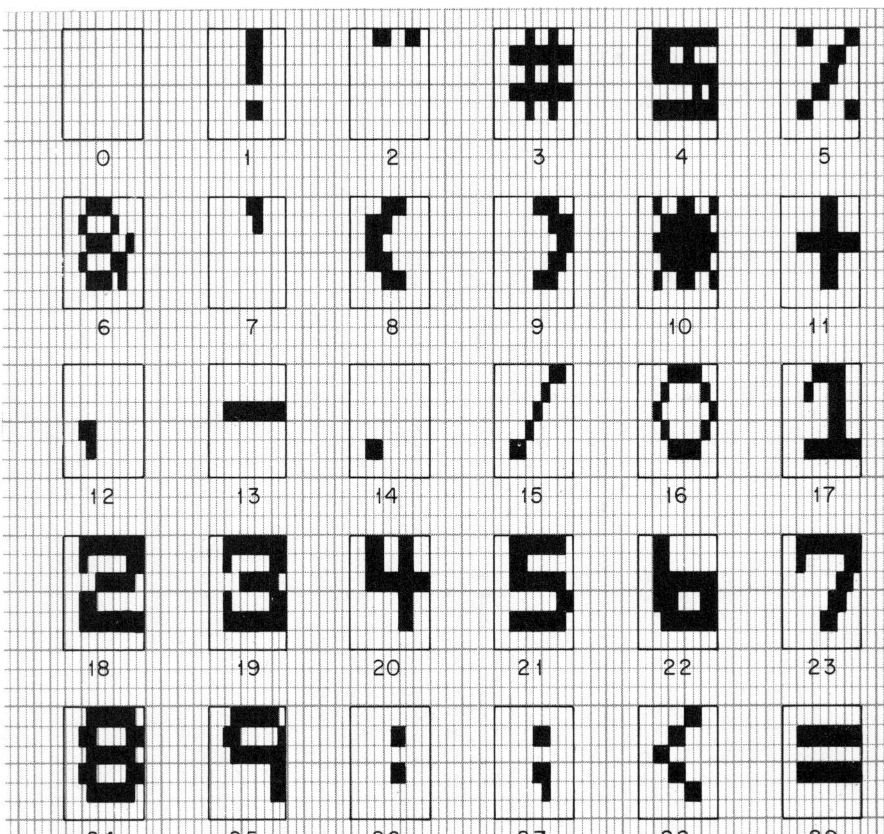


**FIGURE 8-2** Worksheet version of a double-sized, black-on-white alphanumeric character set

TRS-80's built-in character generator. They are also developed as black-on-white characters, but as was suggested in Chapter 2, they can be reversed to show white characters on a black background.

Since each of the characters occupies two screen lines of five characters each, the DATA listing for all 59 of them is a rather extensive one. The DATA listing is shown in Listing 8-4; once you enter all that data and execute the checksum routine successfully, you won't have to worry about typing all that data again.

The line numbers for the DATA listings (program lines 5000 through 5059) are selected so that their last two digits correspond to the customized codes that are assigned to the worksheet characters in Fig. 8-2. Program line 5017, for instance, is the data for character 17—numeral 1. If

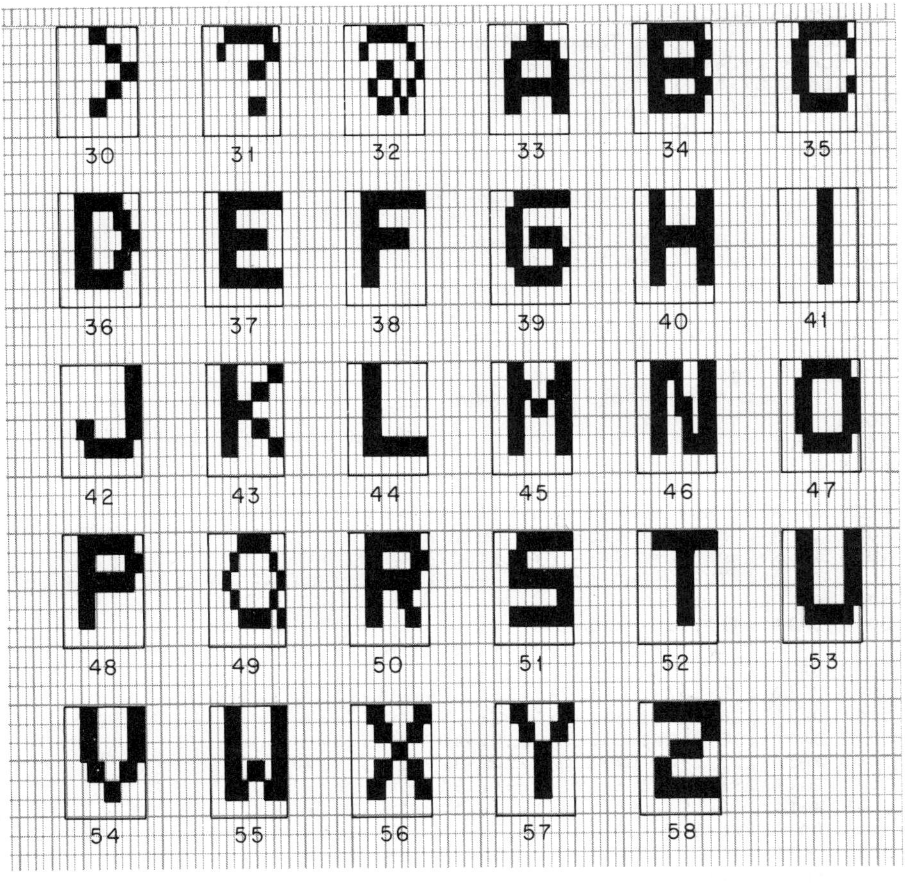

you want to find the DATA list for the letter X—code number 56—just look at DATA line 5056. That line-numbering format allows you to locate the DATA listing for any of the characters, and you might want to do that in order to modify their appearance later in this discussion.

The next project lets you view the individual characters, one at a time, on the screen.

## PROJECT 8–5

Assuming you have entered and successfully executed Listing 8–4, load the resulting alphanumeric DATA listings and extend the program to include standard string-packing and initialization routines. Then add a simple control routine that lets you select a character to be viewed by striking its key on the system keyboard. See Listing 8–5.

```
10 REM ** PROJECT 8-5
15 REM          VIEW THE ALPHANUMERICS
20 CLEAR 1024:DEFSTR C
25 DIM C(59,1)
30 CLS:PRINT "PACKING ...":GOSUB 4000
100 REM ** CONTROL ROUTINE
105 CLS
110 FOR N=0 TO 2
115 PRINT @ 128+N*64,STRING$(10,191);
120 NEXT N
125 PRINT @ 896,"TYPE THE CHARACTERS YOU WANT TO SEE ..."
130 C=INKEY$:IF C="" THEN 130
135 IF ASC(C)<32 OR ASC(C)>90 THEN 130
140 FOR L=0 TO 1
145 PRINT @ 195+L*64,C(ASC(C)-32,L);
150 NEXT L
155 GOTO 130
4000 REM ** STRING-PACKING SUBROUTINE
4005 N=0
4010 L=0
4015 C(N,L)=CHR$(191)
4020 READ A
4025 IF A>1 THEN C(N,L)=C(N,L)+CHR$(A):GOTO 4020
4030 IF A=0 AND L=0 THEN L=1:GOTO 4015
4035 IF A=0 AND L=1 THEN N=N+1:GOTO 4010
4040 IF A<0 THEN READ B:C(N,L)=C(N,L)+STRING$(ABS(A),B):GOTO 4020
4045 RETURN
5000 DATA -4,191,0,-4,191,0
5001 DATA 191,149,170,191,0,191,183,187,191,0
5002 DATA 189,190,189,190,0,-4,191,0
5003 DATA 179,162,145,179,0,188,184,180,188,0
5004 DATA 128,140,136,140,0,-2,179,178,176,0
5005 DATA 188,159,163,188,0,179,188,191,179,0
5006 DATA 153,140,187,175,0,182,179,180,191,0
5007 DATA 191,189,186,191,0,-4,191,0
5008 DATA 131,184,190,191,0,188,178,187,191,0
5009 DATA 191,189,180,131,0,191,183,177,188,0
5010 DATA 134,129,130,137,0,185,180,184,182,0
5011 DATA 143,133,138,143,0,191,181,186,191,0
5012 DATA -4,191,0,180,-3,191,0
5013 DATA -4,143,0,-4,191,0
```

```
5014 DATA -4,191,0,179,-3,191,0
5015 DATA 191,159,185,190,0,179,190,-2,191,0
5016 DATA 167,-2,188,155,0,189,-2,179,190,0
5017 DATA 183,188,128,191,0,183,179,176,179,0
5018 DATA 184,-2,140,176,0,176,-3,179,0
5019 DATA 184,-2,140,160,0,178,-2,179,176,0
5020 DATA 128,143,128,143,0,-2,191,176,191,0
5021 DATA 128,-2,140,174,0,-3,179,184,0
5022 DATA 128,-3,143,0,180,178,179,176,0
5023 DATA 184,188,156,160,0,191,183,184,191,0
5024 DATA 145,-2,140,162,0,180,-2,179,184,0
5025 DATA 145,-2,140,134,0,-3,191,176,0
5026 DATA 191,183,187,191,0,191,189,190,191,0
5027 DATA 191,183,187,191,0,191,189,186,191,0
5028 DATA 143,179,188,191,0,191,188,179,191,0
5029 DATA -4,179,0,-4,188,0
5030 DATA 191,188,179,143,0,191,179,188,191,0
5031 DATA 185,188,140,178,0,-2,191,179,191,0
5032 DATA 185,140,188,155,0,189,179,182,190,0
5033 DATA 135,177,178,139,0,176,-2,188,176,0
5034 DATA 128,-2,140,162,0,176,-2,179,184,0
5035 DATA 129,-2,188,180,0,180,-2,179,177,0
5036 DATA 128,188,180,139,0,176,179,177,190,0
5037 DATA 128,-2,140,188,0,176,-3,179,0
5038 DATA 128,-2,140,188,0,176,-3,191,0
5039 DATA 129,156,140,172,0,180,-2,179,184,0
5040 DATA 128,-2,143,128,0,176,-2,191,176,0
5041 DATA 191,149,170,191,0,191,181,186,191,0
5042 DATA -3,191,128,0,180,-2,179,184,0
5043 DATA 128,143,179,188,0,176,191,188,179,0
5044 DATA 128,-3,191,0,176,-3,179,0
5045 DATA 128,155,167,128,0,176,-2,191,176,0
5046 DATA 128,148,175,128,0,176,191,178,176,0
5047 DATA 129,-2,188,130,0,180,-2,179,184,0
5048 DATA 128,-2,140,162,0,176,-3,191,0
5049 DATA 167,-2,188,155,0,189,-2,179,182,0
5050 DATA 128,-2,140,162,0,176,191,180,187,0
5051 DATA 129,-2,140,172,0,-3,179,184,0
5052 DATA 188,148,168,188,0,191,181,186,191,0
5053 DATA 128,-2,191,128,0,180,-2,179,184,0
5054 DATA 128,-2,191,128,0,189,182,185,190,0
5055 DATA 128,-2,191,128,0,176,185,182,176,0
5056 DATA 180,155,167,184,0,177,190,189,178,0
5057 DATA 180,155,167,184,0,191,181,186,191,0
5058 DATA 188,-2,140,176,0,176,-3,179,0
5059 DATA 1
```

**LISTING 8-5** A routine for viewing the black-on-white alphanumerics, Project 8-5

It doesn't take long to get Listing 8-5 up and running if you have saved the DATA listing on tape or disk as recommended in the previous project. Strike a key or two. If all is going well, you should see a double-sized, black-on-white version of the character near the upper-left part of the screen. Check them all. If you don't happen to like the appearance of one of them, just work out your own worksheet version of it and modify the corresponding DATA line accordingly.

The string-packing subroutine resides in lines 4000 through 4045. It is tailored for a DATA format that uses zeros to mark the end of each of the two lines in each character symbol. A numeral 1 in the DATA (line 5059) marks the end of the packing operation. A negative number indicates the application of a STRING$ function, where the absolute value of the number represents the number of identical characters to be drawn in succession, and DATA item following that negative number indicates the character code. Thus a sequence such as −4,191 sets up the function STRING$(4,191). DATA items that are greater than 1 call for a CHR$ function.

The special character images are packed into a string array of the form C(N,L), where N is the character code number (0 through 59) and L is the line number for that particular character (0 or 1). Notice, however, that the string array is initialized in line 4015 to a value of CHR$(191) as opposed to the usual null value. The purpose in this case is to insert a graphic 191 at the beginning of each line in each of the alphanumeric characters. Doing the insertion at this point saves you from having to type in a lot of 191s through the DATA listings—118 of them.

The control routine (program lines 100 through 155) first plots a white background area, then waits for the user to strike a key. Line 135 makes sure that none of the special control keys has any effect on the operation of the program. Only alphanumeric characters and standard punctuation marks are allowed in this case.

Lines 140–150 are the program's printing operations. The selected character, assigned to variable C, is originally an ASCII code number. The ASC(C)−32 expression in line 145, however, converts it to our special character code number.

### converting to white-on-black

Perhaps you would like to see that same character set printed with its blacks and whites reversed. That would produce the more customary white character on a black background.

As described in Chapter 2, any of the TRS–80's special graphic symbols can be complemented by subtracting the given code number from 319. That simple arithmetic operation reverses the blacks and whites.

Rather than retyping the whole DATA listing for the customized character set, reversing the blacks and whites can be a simple matter of altering the string-packing subroutine so that it packs the complements of the existing DATA listing.

The important lines, as far as the current subject is concerned, are program lines 4015, 4025, and 4040. Compare them with the versions in Listing 8–5.

## PROJECT 8–6

Using the custom alphanumeric DATA listing introduced in Listing 8–4, rewrite the string-packing routine so that the program draws white characters on a black background. See the result in Listing 8–6.

```
10 REM ** PROJECT 8-6
15 REM           WHITE-ON-BLACK CHARACTERS
20 CLEAR 1024:DEFSTR C
25 DIM C(59,1)
30 CLS:PRINT "PACKING ...":GOSUB 4000
100 REM ** CONTROL ROUTINE
105 CLS
125 PRINT @ 896,"TYPE THE CHARACTERS YOU WANT TO SEE ..."
130 C=INKEY$:IF C="" THEN 130
135 IF ASC(C)<32 OR ASC(C)>90 THEN 130
140 FOR L=0 TO 1
145 PRINT @ 195+L*64,C(ASC(C)-32,L);
150 NEXT L
155 GOTO 130
4000 REM ** STRING-PACKING SUBROUTINE
4005 N=0
4010 L=0
4015 C(N,L)=CHR$(128)
4020 READ A
4025 IF A>1 THEN C(N,L)=C(N,L)+CHR$(319-A):GOTO 4020
4030 IF A=0 AND L=0 THEN L=1:GOTO 4015
4035 IF A=0 AND L=1 THEN N=N+1:GOTO 4010
4040 IF A<0 THEN READ B:C(N,L)=C(N,L)+STRING$(ABS(A),319-B):GOTO 4020
4045 RETURN
5000 DATA -4,191,0,-4,191,0
5001 DATA 191,149,170,191,0,191,183,187,191,0
5002 DATA 189,190,189,190,0,-4,191,0
5003 DATA 179,162,145,179,0,188,184,180,188,0
5004 DATA 128,140,136,140,0,-2,179,178,176,0
5005 DATA 188,159,163,188,0,179,188,191,179,0
5006 DATA 153,140,187,175,0,182,179,180,191,0
5007 DATA 191,189,186,191,0,-4,191,0
5008 DATA 131,184,190,191,0,188,178,187,191,0
5009 DATA 191,189,180,131,0,191,183,177,188,0
5010 DATA 134,129,130,137,0,185,180,184,182,0
5011 DATA 143,133,138,143,0,191,181,186,191,0
5012 DATA -4,191,0,180,-3,191,0
5013 DATA -4,143,0,-4,191,0
5014 DATA -4,191,0,179,-3,191,0
5015 DATA 191,159,185,190,0,179,190,-2,191,0
5016 DATA 167,-2,188,155,0,189,-2,179,190,0
5017 DATA 183,188,128,191,0,183,179,176,179,0
5018 DATA 184,-2,140,176,0,176,-3,179,0
5019 DATA 184,-2,140,160,0,178,-2,179,176,0
5020 DATA 128,143,128,143,0,-2,191,176,191,0
5021 DATA 128,-2,140,174,0,-3,179,184,0
5022 DATA 128,-3,143,0,180,178,179,176,0
5023 DATA 184,188,156,160,0,191,183,184,191,0
5024 DATA 145,-2,140,162,0,180,-2,179,184,0
5025 DATA 145,-2,140,134,0,-3,191,176,0
5026 DATA 191,183,187,191,0,191,189,190,191,0
```

(cont.)

```
5027 DATA 191,183,187,191,0,191,189,186,191,0
5028 DATA 143,179,188,191,0,191,188,179,191,0
5029 DATA -4,179,0,-4,188,0
5030 DATA 191,188,179,143,0,191,179,188,191,0
5031 DATA 185,188,140,178,0,-2,191,179,191,0
5032 DATA 185,140,188,155,0,189,179,182,190,0
5033 DATA 135,177,178,139,0,176,-2,188,176,0
5034 DATA 128,-2,140,162,0,176,-2,179,184,0
5035 DATA 129,-2,188,180,0,180,-2,179,177,0
5036 DATA 128,188,180,139,0,176,179,177,190,0
5037 DATA 128,-2,140,188,0,176,-3,179,0
5038 DATA 128,-2,140,188,0,176,-3,191,0
5039 DATA 129,156,140,172,0,180,-2,179,184,0
5040 DATA 128,-2,143,128,0,176,-2,191,176,0
5041 DATA 191,149,170,191,0,191,181,186,191,0
5042 DATA -3,191,128,0,180,-2,179,184,0
5043 DATA 128,143,179,188,0,176,191,188,179,0
5044 DATA 128,-3,191,0,176,-3,179,0
5045 DATA 128,155,167,128,0,176,-2,191,176,0
5046 DATA 128,148,175,128,0,176,191,178,176,0
5047 DATA 129,-2,188,130,0,180,-2,179,184,0
5048 DATA 128,-2,140,162,0,176,-3,191,0
5049 DATA 167,-2,188,155,0,189,-2,179,182,0
5050 DATA 128,-2,140,162,0,176,191,180,187,0
5051 DATA 129,-2,140,172,0,-3,179,184,0
5052 DATA 188,148,168,188,0,191,181,186,191,0
5053 DATA 128,-2,191,128,0,180,-2,179,184,0
5054 DATA 128,-2,191,128,0,189,182,185,190,0
5055 DATA 128,-2,191,128,0,176,185,182,176,0
5056 DATA 180,155,167,184,0,177,190,189,178,0
5057 DATA 180,155,167,184,0,191,181,186,191,0
5058 DATA 188,-2,140,176,0,176,-3,179,0
5059 DATA 1
```

**LISTING 8-6** A routine for converting to white-on-black alphanumerics, Project 8-6

Line 4015 now begins each character line with a black space instead of a white one. In line 4025, a string is packed with a CHR$(319 – A) function so that the original DATA item is complemented. The same sort of operation is found in the STRING$ function of line 4040.

The important idea is that the DATA listing is left unchanged. The blacks and whites are reversed from the DATA specifications in the string-packing part of the program.

In a manner of speaking, a DATA listing is generally regarded as sacred. Once it is generated and debugged, programmers are reluctant to make any changes in it. Any desired modifications are handled elsewhere in the programming.

Incidentally, if you are preparing Listing 8-6 by simply modifying Listing 8-5, notice that the revision omits control routine lines 110-120. Those lines were responsible for drawing a white background for the black characters. In this program, the white background is inappropriate, so its drawing routine is deleted.

### selecting black or white characters

This alphanumeric character set has a lot of potential applications, and it would be nice if you had a chance to select the black or white characters without having to use a separate program for each of them. The next project combines Listings 8–5 and 8–6 into one program.

## PROJECT 8–7

Modify the character-printing routine so that you can select either white-on-black or black-on-white characters. The result appears in Listing 8–7.

```
10 REM ** PROJECT 8-7
15 REM           SELECT BLACK AND WHITE
20 CLEAR 1024:DEFSTR C
25 DIM C(59,1)
30 CLS:PRINT "WHICH COMBINATION (1 OR 2):"
35 PRINT TAB(5);"1 -- BLACK ON WHITE"
40 PRINT TAB(5);"2 -- WHITE ON BLACK"
45 PRINT
50 INPUT T:IF T=1 OR T=2 THEN 55 ELSE 50
55 T=T-1:CLS:PRINT "NOW PACKING ...":GOSUB 4000
100 REM ** CONTROL ROUTINE
105 IF T=1 THEN 125
110 FOR N=0 TO 2
115 PRINT @ 128+N*64,STRING$(10,191);
120 NEXT N
125 PRINT @ 896,"TYPE THE CHARACTERS YOU WANT TO SEE ..."
130 C=INKEY$:IF C="" THEN 130
135 IF ASC(C)<32 OR ASC(C)>90 THEN 130
140 FOR L=0 TO 1
145 PRINT @ 195+L*64,C(ASC(C)-32,L);
150 NEXT L
155 GOTO 130
4000 REM ** STRING-PACKING SUBROUTINE
4005 N=0
4010 L=0
4015 C(N,L)=CHR$(191-T*63)
4020 READ A
4025 IF A>1 THEN C(N,L)=C(N,L)+CHR$(A+T*(319-2*A)):GOTO 4020
4030 IF A=0 AND L=0 THEN L=1:GOTO 4015
4035 IF A=0 AND L=1 THEN N=N+1:GOTO 4010
4040 IF A<0 THEN READ B:C(N,L)=C(N,L)+STRING$(ABS(A),B+T*(319-2*B)):
    GOTO 4020
4045 RETURN
5000 DATA -4,191,0,-4,191,0
5001 DATA 191,149,170,191,0,191,183,187,191,0
5002 DATA 189,190,189,190,0,-4,191,0
5003 DATA 179,162,145,179,0,188,184,180,188,0
5004 DATA 128,140,136,140,0,-2,179,178,176,0
5005 DATA 188,159,163,188,0,179,188,191,179,0
5006 DATA 153,140,187,175,0,182,179,180,191,0
5007 DATA 191,189,186,191,0,-4,191,0
5008 DATA 131,184,190,191,0,188,178,187,191,0
```

```
5009 DATA 191,189,180,131,0,191,183,177,188,0
5010 DATA 134,129,130,137,0,185,180,184,182,0
5011 DATA 143,133,138,143,0,191,181,186,191,0
5012 DATA -4,191,0,180,-3,191,0
5013 DATA -4,143,0,-4,191,0
5014 DATA -4,191,0,179,-3,191,0
5015 DATA 191,159,185,190,0,179,190,-2,191,0
5016 DATA 167,-2,188,155,0,189,-2,179,190,0
5017 DATA 183,188,128,191,0,183,179,176,179,0
5018 DATA 184,-2,140,176,0,176,-3,179,0
5019 DATA 184,-2,140,160,0,178,-2,179,176,0
5020 DATA 128,143,128,143,0,-2,191,176,191,0
5021 DATA 128,-2,140,174,0,-3,179,184,0
5022 DATA 128,-3,143,0,180,178,179,176,0
5023 DATA 184,188,156,160,0,191,183,184,191,0
5024 DATA 145,-2,140,162,0,180,-2,179,184,0
5025 DATA 145,-2,140,134,0,-3,191,176,0
5026 DATA 191,183,187,191,0,191,189,190,191,0
5027 DATA 191,183,187,191,0,191,189,186,191,0
5028 DATA 143,179,188,191,0,191,188,179,191,0
5029 DATA -4,179,0,-4,188,0
5030 DATA 191,188,179,143,0,191,179,188,191,0
5031 DATA 185,188,140,178,0,-2,191,179,191,0
5032 DATA 185,140,188,155,0,189,179,182,190,0
5033 DATA 135,177,178,139,0,176,-2,188,176,0
5034 DATA 128,-2,140,162,0,176,-2,179,184,0
5035 DATA 129,-2,188,180,0,180,-2,179,177,0
5036 DATA 128,188,180,139,0,176,179,177,190,0
5037 DATA 128,-2,140,188,0,176,-3,179,0
5038 DATA 128,-2,140,188,0,176,-3,191,0
5039 DATA 129,156,140,172,0,180,-2,179,184,0
5040 DATA 128,-2,143,128,0,176,-2,191,176,0
5041 DATA 191,149,170,191,0,191,181,186,191,0
5042 DATA -3,191,128,0,180,-2,179,184,0
5043 DATA 128,143,179,188,0,176,191,188,179,0
5044 DATA 128,-3,191,0,176,-3,179,0
5045 DATA 128,155,167,128,0,176,-2,191,176,0
5046 DATA 128,148,175,128,0,176,191,178,176,0
5047 DATA 129,-2,188,130,0,180,-2,179,184,0
5048 DATA 128,-2,140,162,0,176,-3,191,0
5049 DATA 167,-2,188,155,0,189,-2,179,182,0
5050 DATA 128,-2,140,162,0,176,191,180,187,0
5051 DATA 129,-2,140,172,0,-3,179,184,0
5052 DATA 188,148,168,188,0,191,181,186,191,0
5053 DATA 128,-2,191,128,0,180,-2,179,184,0
5054 DATA 128,-2,191,128,0,189,182,185,190,0
5055 DATA 128,-2,191,128,0,176,185,182,176,0
5056 DATA 180,155,167,184,0,177,190,189,178,0
5057 DATA 180,155,167,184,0,191,181,186,191,0
5058 DATA 188,-2,140,176,0,176,-3,179,0
5059 DATA 1
```

**LISTING 8-7** Programming for selecting the white and black areas for Project 8-7

Again, there is no tampering with the original DATA listings, program lines 5000 through 5059. That information can be loaded into the computer by loading Listing 8-4 from tape or disk and doing a RUN to get a checksum and delete the checksum routine.

The initialization routine, program lines 15 through 55, includes a section that lets the user select the character contrast BLACK ON WHITE or WHITE ON BLACK. The response is assigned to variable T; by the time the program gets to the control routine, T is set to zero if the characters are to be black on a white background, or set to 1 if they are to be white characters on a black background. Therefore, if T=1 at program line 105, operations skip down to line 125, bypassing a short routine that draws a white background for black characters. That white background is drawn, however, when T=0.

The remaining lines in the control routine make no further reference to variable T. Whether the characters are white or black has no further relevance at that point.

The value of T is critical through the execution of the string-packing subroutine, however. Line 4015, for instance, inserts either a graphic 191 or graphic 128 at the beginning of both lines in each character. It inserts a 191 if T is equal to zero (black characters) or a graphic 128 if T is equal to 1 (white characters).

What about the CHR$ expression in line 4025? Follow through the arithmetic in that function, and you will find it is equal to CHR$(A) whenever T is equal to zero. In that case, the program packs the values exactly as they are formatted in the DATA listing—as black-on-white characters. But if T is equal to 1, the function turns out to be CHR$(319 – A), thus yielding the complement of the original DATA item. The same mathematical trick is applied to the STRING$ function in line 4040.

## a large-character typing routine

There are many occasions when TRS-80 users want to prepare a full-screen message that is made up of double-sized alphanumerics. Often that means setting up a worksheet analysis and writing a custom program for every sort of message one wants to present. But why go to all that trouble when the special alphanumeric character set offered here is available? Why not just type in the message you want to present?

This program allows you to type in a full screen of oversized alphanumerics just as you would type in the usual TRS-80 characters. The editing features are a bit weak, but with some planning and practice, it is possible to set up some nice full-screen messages.

While typing in a line of characters, you can backspace and erase by striking the left-arrow key. The program does not allow you to backspace from the first position on one line to the last character position on the previous line, however.

If you make a mess of things, start over by holding down the SHIFT key and striking the *C* key. The SHIFT–C operation clears the screen and

## PROJECT 8–8

Load the custom alphanumeric DATA listing from Listing 8–4, then patch in lines 10 through 4045 as shown in Listing 8–8. Do a RUN, reply to the opening request for a choice of black or white characters, wait for the string packing to be done, and then begin typing on the keyboard.

```
10 REM ** PROJECT 8-8
15 REM          ALPHA TYPING
20 CLEAR 1024:DEFSTR C
25 DIM C(59,1)
30 CLS:PRINT "WHICH COMBINATION (1 OR 2):"
35 PRINT TAB(5);"1 -- BLACK ON WHITE"
40 PRINT TAB(5);"2 -- WHITE ON BLACK"
45 PRINT
50 INPUT T:IF T=1 OR T=2 THEN 55 ELSE 50
55 T=T-1
60 CLS:PRINT @ 400,"** ALPHA TYPING ROUTINE **"
65 GOSUB 4000
100 REM ** CONTROL ROUTINE
105 CLS
110 IF T=0 THEN PRINT @ 0,STRING$(64,191);
115 P=64
120 C=INKEY$:IF C="" THEN 120
125 IF ASC(C)=99 THEN 105
130 IF NOT(ASC(C)=8 AND POS(X)>=5) THEN 145
135 P=P-5
140 FOR L=0 TO 1:PRINT @ P+64*L,STRING$(9,128);:NEXT L
145 IF ASC(C)<32 OR ASC(C)>90 THEN 120
150 FOR L=0 TO 1
155 PRINT @ P+64*L,C(ASC(C)-32,L);
160 NEXT L
165 P=P+5
170 IF POS(X)<60 THEN 120
175 IF T=1 THEN 185
180 FOR L=0 TO 1:PRINT @ P+L*64,STRING$(4,191);:NEXT L
185 P=P+68
190 IF P<=959 THEN 120
195 P=64:GOTO 120
4000 REM ** STRING-PACKING SUBROUTINE
4005 N=0
4010 L=0
4015 C(N,L)=CHR$(191-T*63)
4020 READ A
4025 IF A>1 THEN C(N,L)=C(N,L)+CHR$(A+T*(319-2*A)):GOTO 4020
4030 IF A=0 AND L=0 THEN L=1:GOTO 4015
4035 IF A=0 AND L=1 THEN N=N+1:GOTO 4010
4040 IF A<0 THEN READ B:C(N,L)=C(N,L)+STRING$(ABS(A),B+T*(319-2*B)):
   GOTO 4020
4045 RETURN
5000 DATA -4,191,0,-4,191,0
5001 DATA 191,149,170,191,0,191,183,187,191,0
5002 DATA 189,190,189,190,0,-4,191,0
5003 DATA 179,162,145,179,0,188,184,180,188,0
5004 DATA 128,140,136,140,0,-2,179,178,176,0
5005 DATA 188,159,163,188,0,179,188,191,179,0
5006 DATA 153,140,187,175,0,182,179,180,191,0
5007 DATA 191,189,186,191,0,-4,191,0
5008 DATA 131,184,190,191,0,188,178,187,191,0
```

```
5009 DATA 191,189,180,131,0,191,183,177,188,0
5010 DATA 134,129,130,137,0,185,180,184,182,0
5011 DATA 143,133,138,143,0,191,181,186,191,0
5012 DATA -4,191,0,180,-3,191,0
5013 DATA -4,143,0,-4,191,0
5014 DATA -4,191,0,179,-3,191,0
5015 DATA 191,159,185,190,0,179,190,-2,191,0
5016 DATA 167,-2,188,155,0,189,-2,179,190,0
5017 DATA 183,188,128,191,0,183,179,176,179,0
5018 DATA 184,-2,140,176,0,176,-3,179,0
5019 DATA 184,-2,140,160,0,178,-2,179,176,0
5020 DATA 128,143,128,143,0,-2,191,176,191,0
5021 DATA 128,-2,140,174,0,-3,179,184,0
5022 DATA 128,-3,143,0,180,178,179,176,0
5023 DATA 184,188,156,160,0,191,183,184,191,0
5024 DATA 145,-2,140,162,0,180,-2,179,184,0
5025 DATA 145,-2,140,134,0,-3,191,176,0
5026 DATA 191,183,187,191,0,191,189,190,191,0
5027 DATA 191,183,187,191,0,191,189,186,191,0
5028 DATA 143,179,188,191,0,191,188,179,191,0
5029 DATA -4,179,0,-4,188,0
5030 DATA 191,188,179,143,0,191,179,188,191,0
5031 DATA 185,188,140,178,0,-2,191,179,191,0
5032 DATA 185,140,188,155,0,189,179,182,190,0
5033 DATA 135,177,178,139,0,176,-2,188,176,0
5034 DATA 128,-2,140,162,0,176,-2,179,184,0
5035 DATA 129,-2,188,180,0,180,-2,179,177,0
5036 DATA 128,188,180,139,0,176,179,177,190,0
5037 DATA 128,-2,140,188,0,176,-3,179,0
5038 DATA 128,-2,140,188,0,176,-3,191,0
5039 DATA 129,156,140,172,0,180,-2,179,184,0
5040 DATA 128,-2,143,128,0,176,-2,191,176,0
5041 DATA 191,149,170,191,0,191,181,186,191,0
5042 DATA -3,191,128,0,180,-2,179,184,0
5043 DATA 128,143,179,188,0,176,191,188,179,0
5044 DATA 128,-3,191,0,176,-3,179,0
5045 DATA 128,155,167,128,0,176,-2,191,176,0
5046 DATA 128,148,175,128,0,176,191,178,176,0
5047 DATA 129,-2,188,130,0,180,-2,179,184,0
5048 DATA 128,-2,140,162,0,176,-3,191,0
5049 DATA 167,-2,188,155,0,189,-2,179,182,0
5050 DATA 128,-2,140,162,0,176,191,180,187,0
5051 DATA 129,-2,140,172,0,-3,179,184,0
5052 DATA 188,148,168,188,0,191,181,186,191,0
5053 DATA 128,-2,191,128,0,180,-2,179,184,0
5054 DATA 128,-2,191,128,0,189,182,185,190,0
5055 DATA 128,-2,191,128,0,176,185,182,176,0
5056 DATA 180,155,167,184,0,177,190,189,178,0
5057 DATA 180,155,167,184,0,191,181,186,191,0
5058 DATA 188,-2,140,176,0,176,-3,179,0
5059 DATA 1
```

**LISTING 8-8** Programming for typing the double-sized alphanumerics, Project 8-8

homes the invisible cursor, forcing the next-typed character to appear near the upper-left corner of the screen.

Whenever the screen becomes completely filled with characters, the "cursor" is automatically sent to the beginning of the first line. There is no scrolling feature built into this particular control routine.

The editing features do leave a lot to be desired, but the project makes its point: it clearly illustrates how a rather extensive array of string-packed images can be manipulated in an on-line, interactive fashion.

## A RUSSIAN CHARACTER SET

Fig. 8–3 shows a Russian alphanumeric character set. Like the two previous examples of character sets, this one uses a 5 × 6 worksheet format. The Russian alphabet is somewhat more complicated than the English alphabet in terms of fine detail required for some of the characters. It is possible to generate a tolerable facsimile of the characters in this 5 × 6 format, but if there were much more relevant detail in some of the characters, it would be necessary to expand the characters to a larger pixel format. That, indeed, would be the case for Greek, Arabic, and Hebrew character sets.

The first major phase of the job is to:

- Sketch the characters onto a video worksheet, maintaining a uniform set of dimensions and conforming to the limitations of the TRS–80 pixel format.
- Assign numeric codes to all of the characters, using some sort of rational numbering system.
- Make up a program DATA listing.

Normally, you will not include the checksum routine that is in lines 20–40. That is inserted here to make certain you copy this particular version of the DATA listing properly. Just type in Listing 8–9 from scratch, then do a RUN. If you have copied the listing perfectly, you will soon see an OK message and the READY comment. Do a LIST at that point, and you will see that the checksum routine has been deleted. If there are any typing errors in the DATA listing, you will get a DATA ERROR message. The checksum routine will not be deleted, so you will have an opportunity to double-check the listing and RUN it again. When making up your own character sets, you won't know what the checksum number will be; the only way to check the accuracy of the DATA listing is to write a routine that lets you view the characters on the screen.

Now the program is a full-feature string-packing and drawing program. The DATA listing (lines 5000 through 5043) is the one that was developed earlier. If you saved it on tape or disk, there has been no need to type in all that data again.

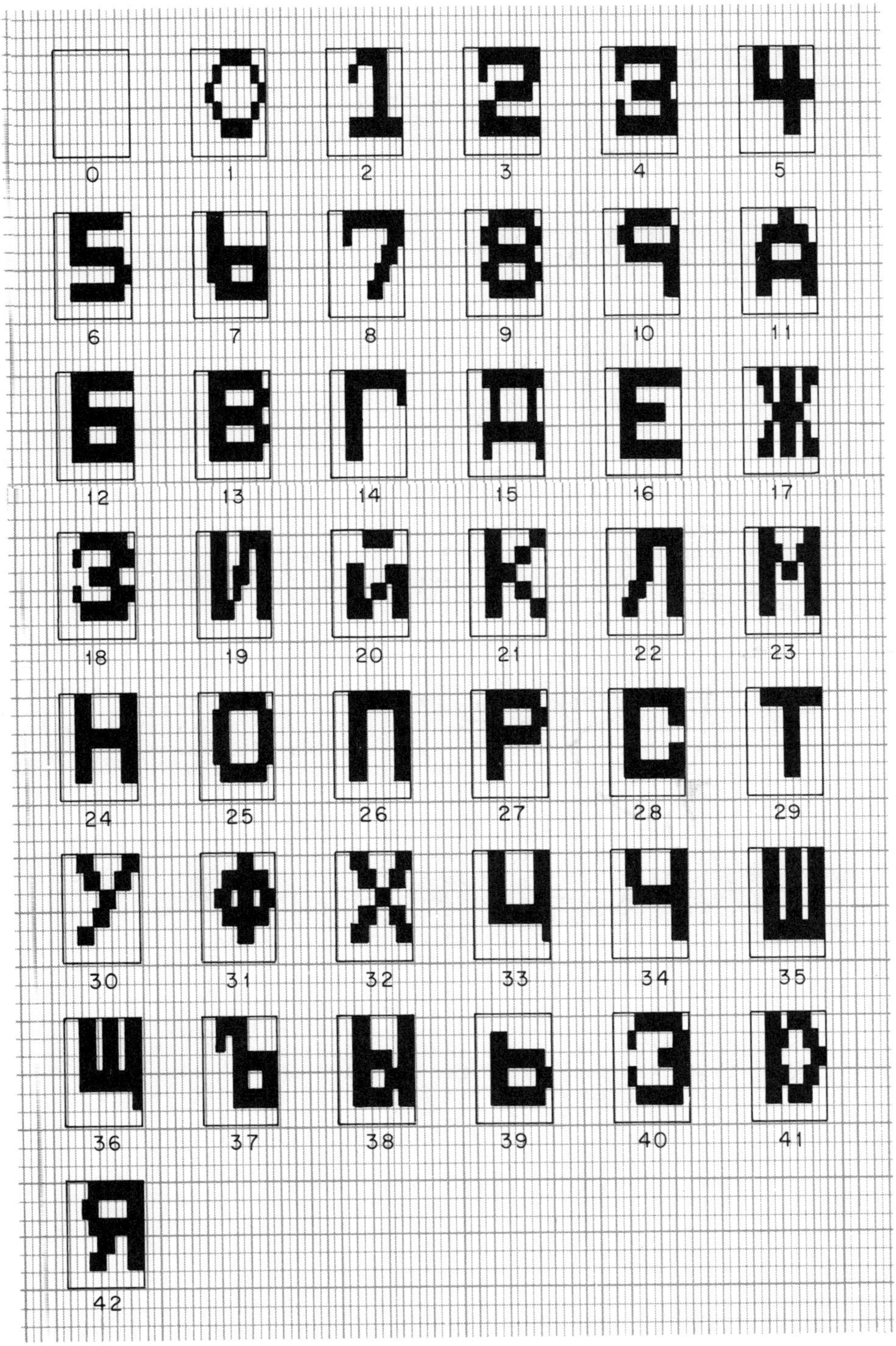

**FIGURE 8-3** Worksheet version of a Russian character set

## PROJECT 8–9

Perform the three steps just described, using the Russian character set in Fig. 8–3. See the DATA listings in Listing 8–9.

```
10 REM ** PROJECT 8-9
15 REM          RUSSIAN CHARACTERS DATA
20 CLS:T=0
25 READ A:T=T+A
30 IF A<>1 THEN 25
35 IF T=46762 THEN PRINT "OK":DELETE 10-40
40 PRINT "DATA ERROR":END
5000 DATA -4,191,0,-4,191,0
5001 DATA 167,-2,188,155,0,189,-2,179,190,0
5002 DATA 183,188,128,191,0,183,179,176,179,0
5003 DATA 184,-2,140,176,0,176,-3,179,0
5004 DATA 184,-2,140,160,0,178,-2,179,176,0
5005 DATA 128,143,128,143,0,-2,191,176,191,0
5006 DATA 128,-2,140,174,0,-3,179,184,0
5007 DATA 128,-3,143,0,180,178,179,176,0
5008 DATA 184,188,156,160,0,191,183,184,191,0
5009 DATA 145,-2,140,162,0,180,-2,179,184,0
5010 DATA 145,-2,140,134,0,-3,191,176,0
5011 DATA 135,177,178,139,0,176,-2,188,176,0
5012 DATA 128,-3,140,0,176,-2,179,176,0
5013 DATA 128,-2,140,162,0,176,-2,179,184,0
5014 DATA 128,-2,188,180,0,176,-3,191,0
5015 DATA 148,-2,188,168,0,184,-2,188,180,0
5016 DATA 128,-2,140,188,0,176,-3,179,0
5017 DATA 180,133,138,184,0,177,181,186,178,0
5018 DATA 185,140,132,178,0,178,179,177,184,0
5019 DATA 128,159,168,128,0,176,185,191,176,0
5020 DATA 143,188,156,143,0,176,185,190,176,0
5021 DATA 128,143,179,188,0,176,191,188,179,0
5022 DATA 191,128,188,128,0,177,190,191,176,0
5023 DATA 128,155,167,128,0,176,-2,191,176,0
5024 DATA 128,-2,143,128,0,176,-2,191,176,0
5025 DATA 129,-2,188,130,0,180,-2,179,184,0
5026 DATA 128,-2,188,128,0,176,-2,191,176,0
5027 DATA 128,-2,140,162,0,176,-3,191,0
5028 DATA 128,-2,188,176,0,176,-2,179,176,0
5029 DATA 188,148,168,188,0,191,181,186,191,0
5030 DATA 180,155,167,184,0,179,188,-2,191,0
5031 DATA 135,145,162,139,0,189,180,184,190,0
5032 DATA 180,155,167,184,0,177,190,189,178,0
5033 DATA 128,-2,191,128,0,-3,188,180,0
5034 DATA 144,-2,143,128,0,-3,191,176,0
5035 DATA 128,149,170,128,0,176,177,178,176,0
5036 DATA 128,149,170,128,0,-3,188,180,0
5037 DATA 184,128,-2,143,0,191,176,179,176,0
5038 DATA 128,143,175,128,0,176,179,184,176,0
5039 DATA 131,-2,143,175,0,176,-2,179,184,0
5040 DATA 185,188,140,130,0,182,-2,179,184,0
5041 DATA 128,185,180,139,0,176,182,177,190,0
5042 DATA 145,-2,140,128,0,183,184,191,176,0
5043 DATA 1
```

**LISTING 8-9** DATA listing and checksum routine for the Russian character set, Project 8-9

## PROJECT 8–10

Write a program that draws white-on-black versions of all the Russian alphanumerics in the DATA listing from Project 8–9. See Listing 8–10.

```
10 REM  ** PROJECT 8-10
15 REM           VIEW RUSSIAN CHARACTERS
20 CLEAR 1024:DEFSTR C
25 DIM C(43,1)
30 CLS:PRINT "NOW PACKING ...":GOSUB 4000
100 REM ** CONTROL ROUTINE
105 CLS:D=0:N=0:S=0
110 FOR L=0 TO 1:PRINT @ D+S+64*L,C(N,L);:NEXT L
115 N=N+1:IF N>42 THEN END
120 S=S+5:IF S>=55 THEN S=0:D=D+128
125 GOTO 110
4000 REM ** STRING-PACKING SUBROUTINE
4005 N=0
4010 L=0
4015 C(N,L)=CHR$(128)
4020 READ A
4025 IF A>1 THEN C(N,L)=C(N,L)+CHR$(319-A):GOTO 4020
4030 IF A=0 AND L=0 THEN L=1:GOTO 4015
4035 IF A=0 AND L=1 THEN N=N+1:GOTO 4010
4040 IF A<0 THEN READ B:C(N,L)=C(N,L)+STRING$(ABS(A),319-B):GOTO 4020
4045 RETURN
5000 DATA -4,191,0,-4,191,0
5001 DATA 167,-2,188,155,0,189,-2,179,190,0
5002 DATA 183,188,128,191,0,183,179,176,179,0
5003 DATA 184,-2,140,176,0,176,-3,179,0
5004 DATA 184,-2,140,160,0,178,-2,179,176,0
5005 DATA 128,143,128,143,0,-2,191,176,191,0
5006 DATA 128,-2,140,174,0,-3,179,184,0
5007 DATA 128,-3,143,0,180,178,179,176,0
5008 DATA 184,188,156,160,0,191,183,184,191,0
5009 DATA 145,-2,140,162,0,180,-2,179,184,0
5010 DATA 145,-2,140,134,0,-3,191,176,0
5011 DATA 135,177,178,139,0,176,-2,188,176,0
5012 DATA 128,-3,140,0,176,-2,179,176,0
5013 DATA 128,-2,140,162,0,176,-2,179,184,0
5014 DATA 128,-2,188,180,0,176,-3,191,0
5015 DATA 148,-2,188,168,0,184,-2,188,180,0
5016 DATA 128,-2,140,188,0,176,-3,179,0
5017 DATA 180,133,138,184,0,177,181,186,178,0
5018 DATA 185,140,132,178,0,178,179,177,184,0
5019 DATA 128,159,168,128,0,176,185,191,176,0
5020 DATA 143,188,156,143,0,176,185,190,176,0
5021 DATA 128,143,179,188,0,176,191,188,179,0
5022 DATA 191,128,188,128,0,177,190,191,176,0
5023 DATA 128,155,167,128,0,176,-2,191,176,0
5024 DATA 128,-2,143,128,0,176,-2,191,176,0
5025 DATA 129,-2,188,130,0,180,-2,179,184,0
5026 DATA 128,-2,188,128,0,176,-2,191,176,0
5027 DATA 128,-2,140,162,0,176,-3,191,0
5028 DATA 128,-2,188,176,0,176,-2,179,176,0
5029 DATA 188,148,168,188,0,191,181,186,191,0
5030 DATA 180,155,167,184,0,179,188,-2,191,0
```

*(cont.)*

```
5031 DATA 135,145,162,139,0,189,180,184,190,0
5032 DATA 180,155,167,184,0,177,190,189,178,0
5033 DATA 128,-2,191,128,0,-3,188,180,0
5034 DATA 144,-2,143,128,0,-3,191,176,0
5035 DATA 128,149,170,128,0,176,177,178,176,0
5036 DATA 128,149,170,128,0,-3,188,180,0
5037 DATA 184,128,-2,143,0,191,176,179,176,0
5038 DATA 128,143,175,128,0,176,179,184,176,0
5039 DATA 131,-2,143,175,0,176,-2,179,184,0
5040 DATA 185,188,140,130,0,182,-2,179,184,0
5041 DATA 128,185,180,139,0,176,182,177,190,0
5042 DATA 145,-2,140,128,0,183,184,191,176,0
5043 DATA 1
```

**LISTING 8-10** Routine for viewing the Russian data set as white-on-black characters, Project 8-10

The string-packing subroutine begins at line 4000. It is tailored to the DATA format (zero marking the ends of lines, negative numbers indicating STRING$ functions, and a 1 marking the end of the current listing), and the 319 − A and 319 − B operations indicate a reversal of blacks and whites. The original data were generated in such a way that they specify a black character on a white background. The string-packing routine in this example reverses that situation for each character being packed into the strings.

The control routine (program lines 100 through 125) positions and draws the characters in rows of 12 across the screen. When the routine is done, you can see the entire character set filling the upper half of the CRT.

If you were working on a custom character set of your own, this would be the time to double-check the appearance of the characters, modifying the DATA listings wherever any changes are necessary. You can do that now, in fact, if you don't agree with the way I configured some of these Russian characters; if you do that, though, bear in mind that the checksum constant appearing in the original listing will no longer apply.

The final phase of the operation is to devise a control and drawing routine that manipulates the available characters in some meaningful fashion. In any event, it is a good idea to save the main DATA listings on tape or disk so that they are readily available for any sort of program you might want to write at a later time.

# 9 A First Look at TRS-80 Animation

The general idea of animation is to create the illusion of motion, or at least to impart a sense of vitality to an otherwise inanimate graphic display. Animation can be as simple as making a small square of light blink on and off, or it can be as complicated as making a couple of complex figures stroll across the screen.

The basic principle of computer animation is identical to that of film animation: the illusion of motion is created by presentation of a series of drawings in rapid succession. Beyond that, however, the differences between film and computer animation are more striking than their similarities.

The biggest differences between film and computer animation are dictated by the time a computer requires for generating character elements on the screen. The larger the number of changes in a drawing from one frame to the next, the longer it takes to generate the image on the CRT—and that always brings up the risk of an unsatisfactory visual impression. With film animation the transition time from one frame to the next is virtually zero, and there is no relationship between the transition time and the complexity of the changes taking place in the drawing.

Computer drawing time thus pervades the thinking of a computer animator. It is an eternal struggle that can be minimized with know-how and experience, but never completely eliminated.

Of course computer animation has some peculiar advantages over film animation. One is the tremendous flexibility with regard to planning, implementing, and editing an animation sequence. Along that same line, there is no need to go through the agony of drawing hundreds of nearly identical frames by hand. Above all, however, the notion of computer animation brings the possibility of creating animated sequences to anyone equipped with nothing more elaborate than a home computer system; film animation is the exclusive domain of well-equipped professionals or exceptionally talented and fortunate amateurs.

For all practical purposes, computer animation is divided sharply into two levels of complexity: those situations that call for moving an image from one place to another on the screen, and those that do not. It is possible to generate some rather exciting and sophisticated animation sequences without actually moving the figure from place to place. One can, for example, create a figure that dances a jig—the legs and feet moving up and down, the arms flying about, the eyes blinking, and the mouth alternating smiling and frowning—all without really moving the figure from its original position on the screen. That is the simpler of the two kinds of computer animation, and it will be implemented here through a special technique called *limited-segment framing.*

Moving an animated figure—even a fairly simple one—from one place to another on the screen is a far more difficult situation. It is simple in principle but difficult in practice because every incremental change in screen position demands a two-step operation: erasing critical elements of the existing figure, and redrawing the entire figure in its new position. Both steps require some computer time, and the overall visual impression of motion can be something far less than satisfying. The obvious solution to the problem is to find a way to erase and generate the image in a faster way—specifically, using machine-language drawing and control routines. That solution offers some problems of its own, and much of the closing portion of this book is devoted to machine-language graphics and control.

## AN INTRODUCTORY APPLICATION OF LIMITED-SEGMENT FRAMING

Fig. 9-1 shows a framing sequence for a little robot figure that blinks its eyes and turns its head to the left, right, and straight ahead. Those six frames roughly resemble the frames a film animator might design for that

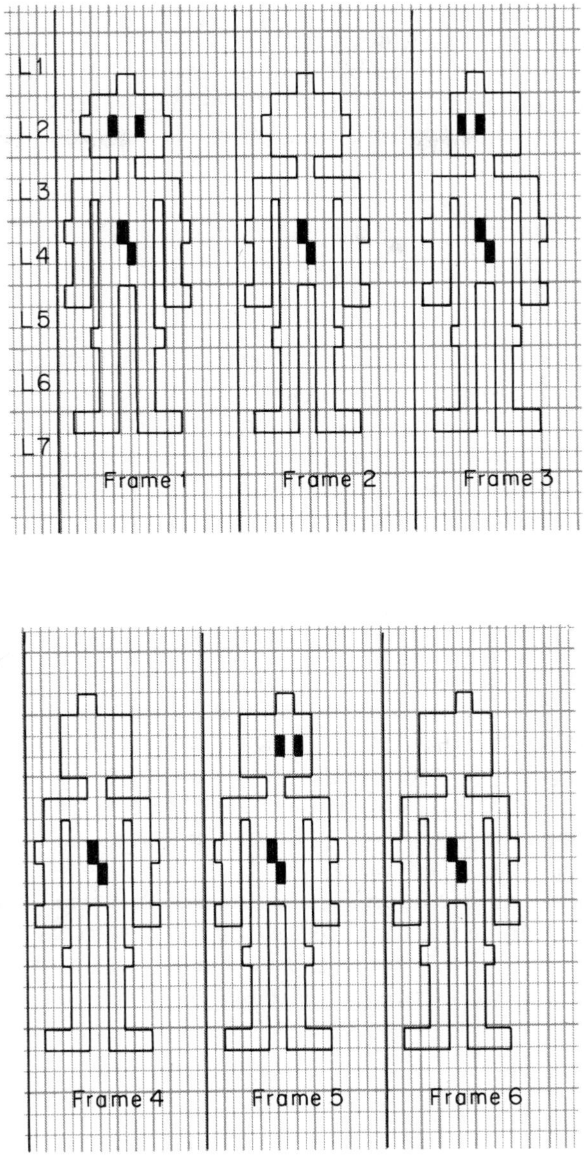


**FIGURE 9-1** Framing sequence for Project 9-1—Blinking robot

particular task. The flexibility of the computer system, however, allows us to create longer and more complicated head-turning and eye-blinking sequences than a six-frame drawing might suggest.

Frame 1, for instance, shows the robot figure looking straight ahead, whereas Frame 2 shows the robot in the same position, but with the eyes missing. Frame 2 is to be used in conjunction with Frame 1 to create the impression that the robot is blinking its eyes. Whenever you want to animate the figure so that it seems to be looking straight ahead and blinking its eyes from time to time, an appropriate drawing sequence might look like this:

1. Draw Frame 1 on the screen; do a 10-second time delay.
2. Draw Frame 2 on the screen; do a 0.5-second time delay, and then return to step 1.

The figure would stare at you from the screen, blinking its eyes for a very brief moment at 10-second intervals.

Before taking a firsthand look at a program that uses Frames 1 and 2 to create the blinking robot, it is important to introduce the notion of limited-segment framing. Limited-segment framing isn't absolutely necessary in this case because the figure and its animation are relatively simple. But there is no harm in using the technique from the very beginning of this discussion.

Looking at Frame 1 (and any of the others, for that matter), you can see that the robot figure is composed of seven lines, L1 through L7. Comparing Frames 1 and 2, you can see that only the characters in line 2 are different; the character configuration of line 1 and lines 3 through 7 are identical. One can thus save some programming time, memory space, and total drawing time by changing only the content of line 2 in the figure. That is the essence of limited-segment framing. Wherever possible, redraw only the lines (or portions of lines) of a figure that are affected by a change from one frame to another.

Thus once the robot figure is drawn as it is shown in Frame 1, getting to Frame 2 is a simple matter of redrawing line 2 with the eye characters absent. Getting back to Frame 1 from Frame 2 is a simple matter of redrawing line 2 with the eyes in place again.

## PROJECT 9–1

Write an animation sequence for a robot figure, using limited-segment framing as it applies to Frames 1 and 2 in Fig. 9–1. See Listing 9–1.

```
×10 REM ** PROJECT 9-1
15 REM          BLINKING ROBOT
20 CLEAR 512:DEFSTR F
25 CLS:PRINT @ 404,"BLINKING ROBOT ANIMATION"
30 GOSUB 4000
100 REM ** CONTROL ROUTINE
105 CLS
110 D=284
115 GOSUB 1000
```

```
120 T=1000:GOSUB 950
125 GOSUB 1022
130 T=25:GOSUB 950
135 GOSUB 1012
140 GOTO 120
950 FOR TD=0 TO T:NEXT TD:RETURN
1000 REM ** DRAWING SUBROUTINES
1001 FOR L=1 TO 7:PRINT @ D+64*(L-1),F(1,L);:NEXT L:RETURN
1012 PRINT @ D+64,F(1,2);:RETURN
1022 PRINT @ D+64,F(2,2);:RETURN
4000 REM ** STRING-PACKING SUBROUTINE
4001 L=1
4002 GOSUB 4500:F(1,L)=F:IF A=0 THEN L=L+1:GOTO 4002
4022 GOSUB 4500:F(2,2)=F
4499 RETURN
4500 F=""
4505 READ A:IF A=0 OR A=1 THEN RETURN
4510 IF A>0 THEN F=F+CHR$(A):GOTO 4505
4515 READ B:F=F+STRING$(ABS(A),B):GOTO 4505
5000 REM ** DATA LISTINGS
5011 DATA 195,160,144,195,0
5012 DATA 193,136,191,187,183,191,132,193,0
5013 DATA 193,188,172,190,189,156,188,193,0
5014 DATA 130,191,170,189,187,149,191,129,0
5015 DATA 130,131,186,149,170,181,131,129,0
5016 DATA 194,170,149,170,149,0
5017 DATA 193,-2,131,129,130,-2,131,0
5018 DATA 1
5022 DATA 193,136,-4,191,132,193,1
```

**LISTING 9-1** Programming for Project 9-1

Type the listing into your computer and give it a try. When you are satisfied that the little robot figure is staring at you and blinking its eyes every once in a while, save the results on tape or disk. Subsequent projects will be easier to load if you have this program as a starting point.

The listing doesn't appear to be much different from any of the string-packing programs described for static figures. Looking through the program, you should be able to identify:

The initialization routine (lines 10–30)

The control routine (lines 100–950)

The drawing subroutines (lines 1000–1022)

The string-packing subroutine (lines 4000–4515)

The DATA listings (lines 5000–5022)

The initialization routine sets up the system for doing the string-oriented program and calls the string-packing subroutine. The string-packing subroutine reads the DATA listing and packs the string variables. Finally, the working portion of the program is underway as the control routine calls the appropriate drawing subroutines and times their presentation on the screen.

It is only the way the strings are defined and the way they are called and drawn from the control routine that makes this program run as an animation sequence instead of a static-figure drawing routine.

Table 9–1 summarizes the definitions of the string variables. The convention used here, and through most of the other animation routines in this book, specifies a frame number and a line number by means of a two-dimensional string array. Line 2 of Frame 1, for instance, is defined as F(1,2); Line 2 of Frame 2 is packed into variable F(2,2). The first numeral in the array expression specifies the frame number, and the second numeral specifies the line number within that frame.

Thus the entire Frame 1—all seven lines—are packed into string arrays F(1,1) through F(1,7) at program lines 4001 and 4002. Those strings are packed from the DATA listings in lines 5011 through 5018.

Frame 2 differs from Frame 1 only by the appearance of Line 2. Thus there is no need to pack variables for all seven lines in Frame 2; packing F(2,2) is sufficient. That variable is packed by means of program line 4022, and it uses the DATA in line 5022.

There are three drawing subroutines: one for drawing all seven lines of Frame 1, one for drawing Line 2 of Frame 2, and one for drawing just Line 2 of Frame 1. See program lines 1001, 1012, and 1022 respectively.

Up to this point in the analysis of the program, you have seen how the relevant string variables are defined, packed, and drawn. All that remains is to design an appropriate control routine.

The animation portion of the control routine is shown as a flowchart in Fig. 9–2. Obviously, the routine must begin by drawing the full robot figure. In this particular instance, that means drawing all of Frame 1. A relatively long time delay then creates the impression that the figure is staring straight out of the screen. See if you can follow these two operations as they are implemented in program lines 115 and 120.

Then it is time to make the robot figure blink its eyes. The general

**TABLE 9–1**

DEFINITIONS OF STRING-PACKED VARIABLES FOR PROJECT 9–1

| *Variable Name* | *Definition* |
|---|---|
| F(1,1) | Frame 1, Line 1 |
| F(1,2) | Frame 1, Line 2 |
| F(1,3) | Frame 1, Line 3 |
| F(1,4) | Frame 1, Line 4 |
| F(1,5) | Frame 1, Line 5 |
| F(1,6) | Frame 1, Line 6 |
| F(1,7) | Frame 1, Line 7 |
| F(2,2) | Frame 2, Line 2 |

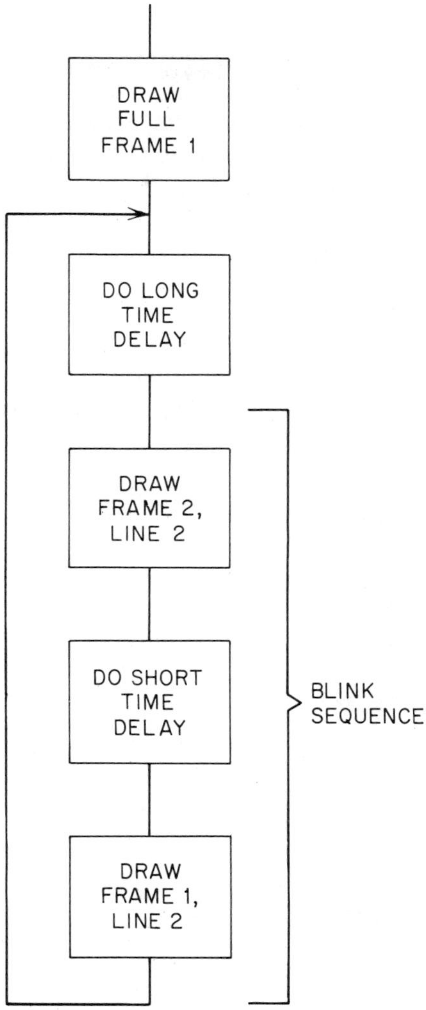


**FIGURE 9-2** Flowchart form of an animation sequence

idea is to call the routine that draws Line 2 of Frame 2, do a brief time delay, and then "reopen" the robot's eyes by calling the routine that draws Line 2 of Frame 1. Compare the BLINK SEQUENCE in the flowchart with the operations designated in lines 125–135 in the program. At the conclusion of the BLINK SEQUENCE, program line 140 loops operations back to line 120 to do the long time delay again.

It is important to note that the full Frame 1 is drawn just one time, at program line 115. After that, the animation effect is achieved by your tampering with just Line 2 in Frames 1 and 2. That is the essence of limited-segment animation. As mentioned earlier in this discussion, the technique of limited-segment animation isn't really critical to the satisfactory operation of this particular animation sequence; one could write the control routine so that program line 135 was a GOTO 115. That way, the robot's eyes would be reopened by virtue of the fact that the entire Frame 1 is redrawn. I have demonstrated the operation of limited-segment operation from the very start, so the control routine is written so that the eyes are reopened by your drawing only Line 2 of Frame 1.

Perhaps you find the timing of the blinking-robot animation a bit too regular. In that case, simply rewrite program line 115 to read:

```
115 T=RND(1000):GOSUB 950
```

That way, the intervals between blinks is randomly selected; if there is such a thing as a realistic robot blink, this comes closer to achieving that impression.

## PROJECT 9–2

Implement all six frames in Fig. 9–1 to create an animation sequence that shows the robot turning its head in both directions and blinking its eyes. See a suggested routine in Listing 9–2.

```
10 REM ** PROJECT 9-2
15 REM          BLINKING, HEAD-TURNING ROBOT
20 CLEAR 512:DEFSTR F
25 CLS:PRINT @ 396,"BLINKING AND HEAD-TURNING ROBOT ANIMATION"
30 GOSUB 4000
100 REM ** CONTROL ROUTINE
105 CLS
110 D=284
115 GOSUB 1000
120 T=RND(1000):GOSUB 950
125 GOSUB 1022:T=25:GOSUB 950:GOSUB 1012
130 T=RND(1000):GOSUB 950
135 GOSUB 1031:GOSUB 1032
140 T=RND(1000):GOSUB 950
145 GOSUB 1042:T=25:GOSUB 950:GOSUB 1032
150 T=RND(1000):GOSUB 950
155 GOSUB 1011:GOSUB 1012:GOSUB 1051:GOSUB 1052
160 T=RND(1000):GOSUB 950
165 GOSUB 1062:T=25:GOSUB 950:GOSUB 1052
170 T=RND(1000):GOSUB 950
175 GOSUB 1011:GOSUB 1012
180 GOTO 120
950 FOR TD=0 TO T:NEXT TD:RETURN
1000 REM ** DRAWING SUBROUTINES
1001 FOR L=1 TO 7:PRINT @ D+64*(L-1),F(1,L);:NEXT L:RETURN
1011 PRINT @ D,F(1,1);:RETURN
1012 PRINT @ D+64,F(1,2);:RETURN
1022 PRINT @ D+64,F(2,2);:RETURN
1031 PRINT @ D,F(3,1);:RETURN
1032 PRINT @ D+64,F(3,2);:RETURN
1042 PRINT @ D+64,F(4,2);:RETURN
1051 PRINT @ D, F(5,1);:RETURN
```

```
1052 PRINT @ D+64,F(5,2);:RETURN
1062 PRINT @ D+64,F(6,2);:RETURN
4000 REM ** STRING-PACKING SUBROUTINE
4001 L=1
4002 GOSUB 4500:F(1,L)=F:IF A=0 THEN L=L+1:GOTO 4002
4022 GOSUB 4500:F(2,2)=F
4031 GOSUB 4500:F(3,1)=F
4032 GOSUB 4500:F(3,2)=F
4042 GOSUB 4500:F(4,2)=F
4051 GOSUB 4500:F(5,1)=F
4052 GOSUB 4500:F(5,2)=F
4062 GOSUB 4500:F(6,2)=F
4499 RETURN
4500 F=""
4505 READ A:IF A=0 OR A=1 THEN RETURN
4510 IF A>0 THEN F=F+CHR$(A):GOTO 4505
4515 READ B:F=F+STRING$(ABS(A),B):GOTO 4505
5000 REM ** DATA LISTINGS
5011 DATA 195,160,144,195,0
5012 DATA 193,136,191,187,183,191,132,193,0
5013 DATA 193,188,172,190,189,156,188,193,0
5014 DATA 130,191,170,189,187,149,191,129,0
5015 DATA 130,131,186,149,170,181,131,129,0
5016 DATA 194,170,149,170,149,0
5017 DATA 193,-2,131,129,130,-2,131,0
5018 DATA 1
5022 DATA 193,136,-4,191,132,193,1
5031 DATA 195,176,196,1
5032 DATA 194,-2,183,-2,191,194,1
5042 DATA 194,-4,191,194,1
5051 DATA 196,176,195,1
5052 DATA 194,-2,191,-2,187,194,1
5062 DATA 194,-4,191,194,1
```

**LISTING 9-2** Programming for Project 9-2

The sequence of operations in the control routine and, indeed, the overall design of the animation program are structured around a general plan of what the robot is to do and when it is to do it. Basically, the overall sequence of events evolves from this preliminary outline:

1. Draw full Frame 1.
2. Look straight ahead for a while.
3. Blink eyes while looking straight ahead.
4. Continue looking straight ahead for a while.
5. Look to the left.
6. Continue looking to the left for a while.
7. Blink eyes while looking to the left.
8. Continue looking to the left for a while.
9. Look ahead.
10. Look to the right.
11. Continue looking to the right for a while.
12. Blink eyes while looking to the right.
13. Continue looking to the right for a while.

14. Look straight ahead.
15. Repeat the sequence from Step 2 above.

Such a list of events represents the first major step in planning the program—assuming, of course, that the frames have been completely defined as in Fig. 9-1.

The next step is to expand on that working outline, spelling out specific frame numbers and providing more details concerning timing:

1. Draw full Frame 1.
2. Do a long, random time delay with Frame 1.
3. Blink eyes while doing Frame 1.
   A. Do Frame 2.
   B. Do a short, fixed time delay.
   C. Do Frame 1.
4. Do a long, random time delay with Frame 1.
5. Do Frame 3.
6. Do a long, random time delay with Frame 3.
7. Blink eyes while doing Frame 3.
   A. Do Frame 4.
   B. Do a short, fixed time delay.
   C. Do Frame 3.
8. Do a long, random time delay with Frame 3.
9. Do Frame 1.
10. Do Frame 5.
11. Do a long, random time delay with Frame 5.
12. Blink eyes while doing Frame 5.
    A. Do Frame 6.
    B. Do a short, fixed time delay.
    C. Do Frame 5.
13. Do a long, random time delay with Frame 5.
14. Do Frame 1.
15. Repeat the sequence from Step 2 above.

That expanded version of the animation outline clearly specifies which frames are to be used and where they are to be fit into the sequence of operations. It also designates two kinds of time delays: a long, random delay and a short, fixed delay. In a sense, this outline is the skeleton for the control routine in the BASIC programming.

The process of transforming the outline into a working program would be rather straightforward if we were drawing each frame completely. It is possible to write a BASIC program routine for drawing each of the six frames, then do a GOSUB statement to draw them on the screen. However, here we are illustrating applications of limited-segment animation—drawing only those portions of a frame that change from one frame to the next. Thus, there is another important step in the planning phase of the program: determining which portions of a frame must be redrawn when making a transition from one frame to the next.

Using the previous animation outline as a guide, you can see that the following frame transitions must take place:

- Step 3A. Frame 1 to Frame 2
- Step 3C. Frame 2 to Frame 1
- Step 5. Frame 1 to Frame 3
- Step 7A. Frame 3 to Frame 4
- Step 7C. Frame 4 to Frame 3
- Step 9. Frame 3 to Frame 1
- Step 10. Frame 1 to Frame 5
- Step 12A. Frame 5 to Frame 6
- Step 12C. Frame 6 to Frame 5
- Step 14. Frame 5 to Frame 1

Then compare these sets of frame transitions with the actual drawings in Fig. 9-1. The idea is to determine which lines must be changed in order to alter the frame transition.

- Step 3A. Draw F(2,2)
- Step 3C. Draw F(1,2)
- Step 5. Draw F(3,1), F(3,2)
- Step 7A. Draw F(4,2)
- Step 7C. Draw F(3,1)
- Step 9. Draw F(1,1), F(1,2)
- Step 10. Draw F(5,1), F(5,2)
- Step 12A. Draw F(6,2)
- Step 12C. Draw F(5,2)
- Step 14. Draw F(1,1), F(1,2)

Recall that the first numeral in the parentheses specifies the frame number and the second specifies the line within that frame. Thus *Draw F(5,1)* literally means: Draw Line 1 of Frame 5.

At this point in the analysis, you have a clear idea of what drawing routines you will need for the desired animation sequence. It is an efficient, limited-segment analysis that uses time for drawing only those portions of a figure that change from one frame to the next.

Putting those frame numbers into numerical sequence, one can see what drawing subroutines are required and the names of string variables that have to be packed.

F(1,1), F(1,2), F(2,2), F(3,1), F(3,2), F(4,2), F(5,1), F(5,2), F(6,2)

Lines 3 through 7 never change; thus the Frame-1 version of them applies throughout the program.

Referring back to the program in Listing 9–2, all the lines for Frame 1, including the F(1,1) and F(1,2) variables needed for the special animation sequences, are string-packed in lines 4001 and 4002, using DATA from lines 5011 through 5018. The full-frame drawing subroutine for Frame 1 is located at program line 1001, and it is called by the control routine at line 115.

The remaining seven string variables cited in the list—F(2,2), F(3,1), F(3,2), etc.—are packed separately in program lines 4022 through 4062, and they use DATA lines 5022 through 5062.

The drawing subroutines for all the special strings are found at lines 1011 through 1062, and they are called at the appropriate times from the control routine.

Turning to the control routine, it begins by clearing the screen in line 105 and setting the displacement value for the figure in line 110. After that, the control routine follows the animation analysis:

Line 115: Draw full Frame 1 (Step 1)
Line 120: Do a long, random time delay (Step 2)
Line 125: Blink eyes while doing Frame 1 (Step 3)
Line 130: Do a long, random time delay (Step 4)
Line 135: Do Frame 3 (Step 5)
Line 140: Do a long, random time delay (Step 6)
Line 145: Blink eyes while doing Frame 3 (Step 7)
Line 150: Do a long, random time delay (Step 8)
Line 155: Do Frame 1, followed by Frame 5 (Steps 9 and 10)
Line 160: Do a long, random time delay (Step 11)
Line 165: Blink eyes while doing Frame 5 (Step 12)
Line 170: Do a long, random time delay (Step 13)
Line 175: Do Frame 1 (Step 14)
Line 180: Repeat the sequence from Step 2 (Step 15)

It is quite likely that this procedure for developing an animated sequence appears terribly cumbersome. Broken down into a detailed step-by-step analysis, it probably is a cumbersome process, but it really isn't a very difficult one. In summary, it goes like this:

1. Draw the frames you think you will need to accomplish the animation sequence.
2. Make up a step-by-step listing of the frames to be shown, giving some indication of their timing.
3. Determine the frame transitions—which frames are to follow which.
4. Determine which lines within the frame transitions must be changed.
5. Write a program that packs the required strings and draws them as required.
6. Compose a control program that implements the original animation plan.
7. Try the program, debugging and modifying as necessary and desirable.

## ORGANIZING AND EDITING ANIMATION SEQUENCES

A computer artist must learn to live with some serious constraints that are imposed by the nature of his or her equipment and the principles of computer programming. There is, however, one distinct advantage over traditional artistic and animation techniques—ease of editing. It is far easier to form and compose static images with a computer than to revise drawings and paintings that are committed to paper and canvas. In the context of composing static pictures on the CRT, ease of editing and inline composition was a theme introduced earlier in this book. Now, the same idea of on-line spontaneity applies to the creation of animated sequences.

The general idea is to compose a single animation sequence, get it into the computer, and try it out. When you are satisfied with it, add another sequence and get it working to your satisfaction. Then blend the two together to come up with a choreography of two sequences. Any number of independent animation sequences can be strung together in this way; what's more, individual elements within a sequence can be refined and extended to create some rather elaborate animations.

Doing the animation job on a piecemeal basis, working the individual parts together and experimenting with some of the finer details, offers the possibility of making some interesting and spontaneous ideas that might be lost if the entire system were developed on a worksheet and committed to a program from the very beginning.

As you might imagine, developing such animation sequences in-line and in a piecemeal fashion can result in some cumbersome programs. There is no harm done if the sequences run quickly enough to satisfy you, but a cumbersome, pieced-together program sometimes runs too slowly in places to create the desired effect. In such cases, the resulting program has to be refined a bit; redundancies and time-consuming program statements have to be eliminated or combined in such a way that they run faster.

The following series of projects shows how to develop a series of animation sequences, string them together to produce a more complex performance, and then refine the result to produce a cleaner and more efficient program.

The subject of the examples is the same little robot figure that was used earlier in this chapter. The goal in this instance is to create an animation sequence that shows the figure acting as a traffic policeman. The robot will observe the traffic for a while, turning its head from side to side and blinking its eyes. Then the figure will stroll to the middle of the street, turn its entire body to the left, and hold out an arm with a traffic-stopping gesture. After stopping the traffic for a while, the figure turns its back to the viewer, strolls back to the curb, turns around, and begins observing the traffic again.

Since we are still dealing with single-figure animation, the robot figure will be the only one appearing on the screen; the traffic will remain purely imaginary. The matter of multiple-figure animation must await a later discussion.

Computer animations need not be developed in the exact order they are to appear in the final product. Creating the effect of a walking figure is one of the most challenging animation tasks, so I decided to deal with it first. It will be fit into the proper scene later on.

## PROJECT 9–3

Listing 9–3 uses the frames shown in Fig. 9–3 to create the figure's walking sequence. Type in the program as shown here, give it a try, and if you are satisfied it is working properly, save it on tape or disk for later use.

```
10 REM ** PROJECT 9-3
15 REM          WALKING TO THE MIDDLE OF THE STREET
20 CLEAR 512:DEFSTR F
25 CLS:PRINT @ 405,"ROBOT TRAFFIC CONTROLLER"
30 GOSUB 4000
100 REM ** CONTROL ROUTINE
105 CLS
110 D=284
115 GOSUB 1000
122 GOSUB 1020
123 GOSUB 1000
124 GOSUB 1030
125 GOTO 115
```

```
1000 REM ** DRAWING SUBROUTINES
1001 FOR L=1 TO 7:PRINT @ D+64*(L-1),F(1,L);:NEXT L:RETURN
1020 FOR L=3 TO 7:PRINT  @ D+64*(L-1),F(2,L);:NEXT L:RETURN
1030 FOR L=3 TO 7:PRINT @ D+64*(L-1),F(3,L);:NEXT L:RETURN
4000 REM ** STRING-PACKING SUBROUTINE
4001 L=1
4002 GOSUB 4500:F(1,L)=F:IF A=0 THEN L=L+1:GOTO 4002
4020 L=3
4021 GOSUB 4500:F(2,L)=F:IF A=0 THEN L=L+1:GOTO 4021
4030 L=3
4031 GOSUB 4500:F(3,L)=F:IF A=0 THEN L=L+1:GOTO 4031
4499 RETURN
4500 F=""
4505 READ A:IF A=0 OR A=1 THEN RETURN
4510 IF A>0 THEN F=F+CHR$(A):GOTO 4505
4515 READ B:F=F+STRING$(ABS(A),B):GOTO 4505
5000 REM ** DATA LISTINGS
5011 DATA 197,160,144,197,0
5012 DATA 195,136,191,187,183,191,132,195,0
5013 DATA 195,188,172,190,189,156,188,195,0
5014 DATA 194,130,191,170,189,187,149,191,129,194,0
5015 DATA 194,130,131,186,149,170,181,131,129,194,0
5016 DATA 196,170,149,170,149,196,0
5017 DATA 195,-2,131,129,130,-2,131,195,1
5023 DATA 195,188,172,190,189,156,188,195,0
5024 DATA 194,138,189,170,-2,25,191,129,195,0
5025 DATA 196,186,149,130,191,180,195,0
5026 DATA 196,170,149,128,191,176,144,194,0
5027 DATA 195,-2,131,129,198,1
5033 DATA 195,188,172,190,189,156,188,194,0
5034 DATA 195,130,191,-2,25,149,190,133,128,0
5035 DATA 195,184,191,129,170,181,195,0
5036 DATA 194,160,176,191,128,170,149,195,0
5037 DATA 198,130,-2,131,194,1
```

**LISTING 9-3** Programming for Project 9-3

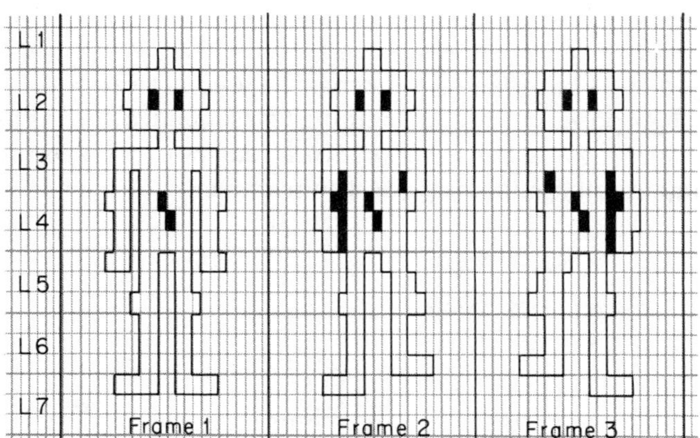


**FIGURE 9-3** Frames 1, 2 and 3—the strolling-forward sequence—for Project 9-3

This is really just a testing program, although it is fun to watch the little robot's rolling gait. The real purposes are to double-check the selection and entry of the DATA elements and to see whether or not the choice of frames is satisfactory.

The framing sequence goes like this:

1. Frame 1
2. Frame 2
3. Frame 1
4. Frame 3
5. Repeat from Step 1

Looking at the program listing, you can see that Frame 1 is string-packed at lines 4001 and 4002, using DATA from lines 5011 through 5017. The seven lines in that frame are assigned to variables F(1,1) through F(1,7). Frame 1 is drawn by calling the subroutine at line 1001.

Since the first two lines in Frames 2 and 3 are identical to their counterparts in Frame 1, there is no need to take up valuable drawing time for those two lines (provided, of course, that Frame 1 is always drawn first). Thus the strings for Frames 2 and 3 are packed and drawn from lines 3 through 7.

Frame 2 is packed at program lines 4020 and 4021, using DATA from lines 5023 through 5027. It is drawn from line 1020.

Frame 3 uses the same general programming format. It is packed at line 4030 and 4031, it uses DATA from lines 5033 through 5037, and it is drawn by calling its drawing subroutine at line 1030.

The walking sequence is choreographed by the control routine, lines 115 through 125.

You are invited to play with the control routine, doing things such as inserting a time delay while showing Frame 1. Try experimenting with short time delays between each frame; the idea is to slow down the walking as much as possible without making the sequence appear jerky. Whatever you decide to do with the control routine, just keep in mind the GOSUB line numbers for drawing the frames:

Frame 1: GOSUB 1000
Frame 2: GOSUB 1020
Frame 3: GOSUB 1030

The matter of getting the robot figure to stroll back to the curb calls for adding just one more frame, Frame 4 in Fig. 9–4. That shows the robot from a rear view. Comparing it with the front-on view in Frame 1, you can see that only lines 2 and 4 are different. Thus the strings for lines 1, 3, and

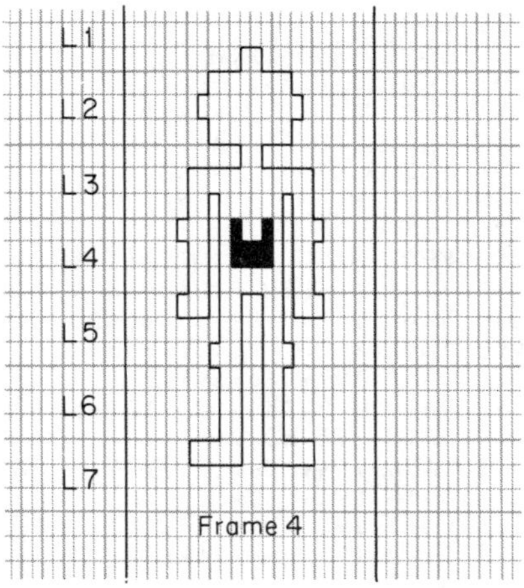


**FIGURE 9–4** Frame 4 required for the strolling-back sequence in Project 9–4

## PROJECT 9–4

The animation we are gradually concocting here calls for having the robot figure stroll to and from the curb. Project 9–3 took care of the strolling-from-curb sequence, and Listing 9–4 shows the program as it is extended to include a strolling-back-to-curb sequence.

```
10 REM ** PROJECT 9-4
15 REM          WALKING TO AND FROM THE CURB
20 CLEAR 512:DEFSTR F
25 CLS:PRINT @ 405,"ROBOT TRAFFIC CONTROLLER"
30 GOSUB 4000
100 REM ** CONTROL ROUTINE
105 CLS
110 D=284
115 FOR N=0 TO 9
120 GOSUB 1000:GOSUB 1020:GOSUB 1000:GOSUB 1030
125 NEXT N
130 GOSUB 1000:T=500:GOSUB 950
135 FOR N=0 TO 9
140 GOSUB 1040:GOSUB 1020:GOSUB 1040:GOSUB 1030
145 NEXT N
150 GOSUB 1040:T=500:GOSUB 950
155 GOTO 115
950 FOR TD=0 TO T:NEXT TD:RETURN
1000 REM ** DRAWING SUBROUTINES
1001 FOR L=1 TO 7:PRINT @ D+64*(L-1),F(1,L);:NEXT L:RETURN
1020 FOR L=3 TO 7:PRINT  @ D+64*(L-1),F(2,L);:NEXT L:RETURN
1030 FOR L=3 TO 7:PRINT @ D+64*(L-1),F(3,L);:NEXT L:RETURN
1040 FOR L=1 TO 7:PRINT @ D+64*(L-1),F(4,L);:NEXT L:RETURN
4000 REM ** STRING-PACKING SUBROUTINE
4001 L=1
4002 GOSUB 4500:F(1,L)=F:IF A=0 THEN L=L+1:GOTO 4002
4020 L=3
4021 GOSUB 4500:F(2,L)=F:IF A=0 THEN L=L+1:GOTO 4021
```

*(cont.)*

```
4030 L=3
4031 GOSUB 4500:F(3,L)=F:IF A=0 THEN L=L+1:GOTO 4031
4040 F(4,1)=F(1,1):F(4,3)=F(1,3)
4041 FOR N=5 TO 7:F(4,N)=F(1,N):NEXT N
4042 GOSUB 4500:F(4,2)=F
4044 GOSUB 4500:F(4,4)=F
4499 RETURN
4500 F=""
4505 READ A:IF A=0 OR A=1 THEN RETURN
4510 IF A>0 THEN F=F+CHR$(A):GOTO 4505
4515 READ B:F=F+STRING$(ABS(A),B):GOTO 4505
5000 REM ** DATA LISTINGS
5011 DATA 197,160,144,197,0
5012 DATA 195,136,191,187,183,191,132,195,0
5013 DATA 195,188,172,190,189,156,188,195,0
5014 DATA 194,130,191,170,189,187,149,191,129,194,0
5015 DATA 194,130,131,186,149,170,181,131,129,194,0
5016 DATA 196,170,149,170,149,196,0
5017 DATA 195,-2,131,129,130,-2,131,195,1
5023 DATA 195,188,172,190,189,156,188,195,0
5024 DATA 194,138,189,170,-2,25,191,129,195,0
5025 DATA 196,186,149,130,191,180,195,0
5026 DATA 196,170,149,128,191,176,144,194,0
5027 DATA 195,-2,131,129,198,1
5033 DATA 195,188,172,190,189,156,188,194,0
5034 DATA 195,130,191,-2,25,149,190,133,128,0
5035 DATA 195,184,191,129,170,181,195,0
5036 DATA 194,160,176,191,128,170,149,195,0
5037 DATA 198,130,-2,131,194,1
5042 DATA 195,136,-4,191,132,195,0
5044 DATA 194,130,191,170,178,177,149,191,129,194,1
```

**LISTING 9-4** Complete programming for Project 9-4

5 through 7 can be packed by equating them with those lines in Frame 1; there is no need to duplicate the DATA listings for those lines. See how the lines are equated in program lines 4040 and 4041.

Lines 2 and 4 in Frame 4 are packed by program lines 4042 and 4044, using the DATA in lines 5042 and 5044.

Frame 4 is drawn by calling the subroutine at program line 1040.

The figure is made to appear walking back to the curb by our taking advantage of the limited-segment nature of Frames 2 and 3. Neither of those frames affects the special elements that distinguish the robot's front and back—the lack of eyes in line 2, and the square-U shape in line 4. The framing sequence for making the robot stroll back to the curb is thus:

1. Frame 4
2. Frame 2
3. Frame 4
4. Frame 3
5. Repeat from Step 1

The control routine is set up to display the two currently available sequences: making the robot stroll toward the viewer and then away from the viewer. Lines 115 through 125 execute the strolling-forward sequence ten times. Line 130 does a brief time delay, and then lines 135 through 146 execute ten cycles of the strolling-away sequence. After that, line 150 causes the figure to stand with its back to the view for a moment, and then line 155 loops the whole program back to line 115 to begin the two sequences all over.

To check your understanding of how the framing works, try inventing a few sequences of your own. Draw the frames by doing the following GOSUBs:

Frame 1: GOSUB 1000
Frame 2: GOSUB 1020
Frame 3: GOSUB 1030
Frame 4: GOSUB 1040

## PROJECT 9–5

Listing 9–5 expands the program to include a third animation sequence that is built around Frames 5, 6, and 7. See Fig. 9–5. The idea is to show the figure turning around to face the left-hand side of the screen.

```
10 REM ** PROJECT 9-5
15 REM          WALKING FORWARD AND TURNING TO LEFT
20 CLEAR 512:DEFSTR F
25 CLS:PRINT @ 405,"ROBOT TRAFFIC CONTROLLER"
30 GOSUB 4000
100 REM ** CONTROL ROUTINE
105 CLS
110 D=284
115 FOR N=0 TO 9
120 GOSUB 1000:GOSUB 1020:GOSUB 1000:GOSUB 1030
125 NEXT N
130 GOSUB 1000:T=500:GOSUB 950
135 GOSUB 1030:GOSUB 1050:GOSUB 1060:GOSUB 1070
140 T=500:GOSUB 950
145 GOSUB 1060:GOSUB 1050:GOSUB 1030:GOSUB 1000
150 GOTO 115
950 FOR TD=0 TO T:NEXT TD:RETURN
1000 REM ** DRAWING SUBROUTINES
1001 FOR L=1 TO 7:PRINT @ D+64*(L-1),F(1,L);:NEXT L:RETURN
1020 FOR L=3 TO 7:PRINT  @ D+64*(L-1),F(2,L);:NEXT L:RETURN
1030 FOR L=3 TO 7:PRINT @ D+64*(L-1),F(3,L);:NEXT L:RETURN
1040 FOR L=1 TO 7:PRINT @ D+64*(L-1),F(4,L);:NEXT L:RETURN
1050 FOR L=1 TO 7:PRINT @ D+64*(L-1),F(5,L);:NEXT L:RETURN
1060 FOR L=1 TO 7:PRINT @ D+64*(L-1),F(6,L);:NEXT L:RETURN
1070 FOR L=1 TO 7:PRINT @ D+64*(L-1),F(7,L);:NEXT L:RETURN
4000 REM ** STRING-PACKING SUBROUTINE
4001 L=1
4002 GOSUB 4500:F(1,L)=F:IF A=0 THEN L=L+1:GOTO 4002
4020 L=3
```

*(cont.)*

```
4021 GOSUB 4500:F(2,L)=F:IF A=0 THEN L=L+1:GOTO 4021
4030 L=3
4031 GOSUB 4500:F(3,L)=F:IF A=0 THEN L=L+1:GOTO 4031
4040 F(4,1)=F(1,1):F(4,3)=F(1,3)
4041 FOR N=5 TO 7:F(4,N)=F(1,N):NEXT N
4042 GOSUB 4500:F(4,2)=F
4044 GOSUB 4500:F(4,4)=F
4050 L=1
4051 GOSUB 4500:F(5,L)=F:IF A=0 THEN L=L+1:GOTO 4051
4060 L=1
4061 GOSUB4500:F(6,L)=F:IF A=0 THEN  L=L+1:GOTO 4061
4070 L=1
4071 GOSUB 4500:F(7,L)=F:IF A=0 THEN L=L+1:GOTO 4071
4499 RETURN
4500 F=""
4505 READ A:IF A=0 OR A=1 THEN RETURN
4510 IF A>0 THEN F=F+CHR$(A):GOTO 4505
4515 READ B:F=F+STRING$(ABS(A),B):GOTO 4505
5000 REM ** DATA LISTINGS
5011 DATA 197,160,144,197,0
5012 DATA 195,136,191,187,183,191,132,195,0
5013 DATA 195,188,172,190,189,156,188,195,0
5014 DATA 194,130,191,170,189,187,149,191,129,194,0
5015 DATA 194,130,131,186,149,170,181,131,129,194,0
5016 DATA 196,170,149,170,149,196,0
5017 DATA 195,-2,131,129,130,-2,131,195,1
5023 DATA 195,188,172,190,189,156,188,195,0
5024 DATA 194,138,189,170,-2,25,191,129,195,0
5025 DATA 196,186,149,130,191,180,195,0
5026 DATA 196,170,149,128,191,176,144,194,0
5027 DATA 195,-2,131,129,198,1
5033 DATA 195,188,172,190,189,156,188,194,0
5034 DATA 195,130,191,-2,25,149,190,133,128,0
5035 DATA 195,184,191,129,170,181,195,0
5036 DATA 194,160,176,191,128,170,149,195,0
5037 DATA 198,130,-2,131,194,1
5042 DATA 195,136,-4,191,132,195,0
5044 DATA 194,130,191,170,178,177,149,191,129,194,1
5051 DATA 197,176,198,0
5052 DATA 196,183,191,187,191,196,0
5053 DATA 195,184,188,190,189,172,180,195,0
5054 DATA 195,175,191,182,191,184,159,129,194,0
5055 DATA 196,170,-2,191,130,131,195,0
5056 DATA 195,160,186,-2,191,197,0
5057 DATA 198,131,129,196,1
5061 DATA 197,176,198,0
5062 DATA 196,191,187,-2,191,196,0
5063 DATA 196,160,190,189,180,196,0
5064 DATA 196,175,-2,191,159,189,144,194,0
5065 DATA 197,186,149,197,0
5066 DATA 197,170,191,180,196,0
5067 DATA 196,-2,131,129,197,1
5071 DATA 197,176,198,0
5072 DATA 196,183,-3,191,196,0
5073 DATA 196,160,190,189,180,196,0
5074 DATA 196,175,-2,191,159,196,0
5075 DATA 197,186,149,197,0
5076 DATA 197,170,149,197,0
5077 DATA 196,-2,131,129,197,1
```

**LISTING 9-5** Complete programming for Project 9-5

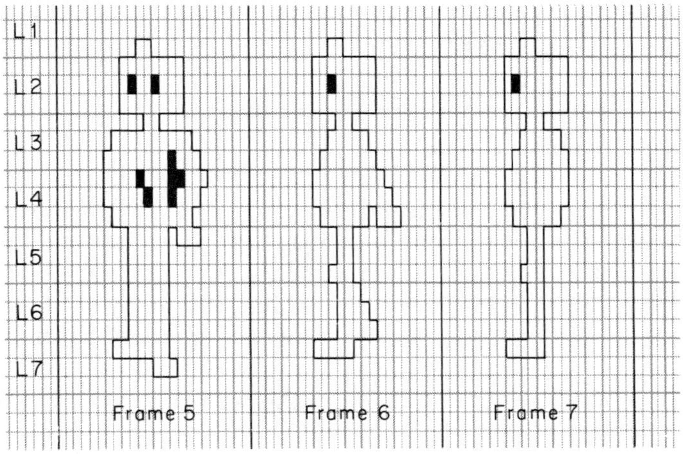


**FIGURE 9-5** Framing sequence for doing a 90-degree turn to face the left side of the screen, Project 9-5

Here is how those frames are packed and drawn:

Frame 5: Packed into string variables F(5,1) through F(5,7) by program lines 4050 and 4051, using DATA in lines 5051 through 5057; drawn by calling the subroutine at line 1050.

Frame 6: Packed into variables F(6,1) through F(6,7) by program lines 4060 and 4061, using DATA in lines 5061 through 5067; drawn by calling the subroutine at line 1060.

Frame 7: Packed into variables F(7,1) through F(7,7) by program lines 4070 and 4071, using DATA in lines 5071 through 5077; drawn by calling the subroutine at line 1070.

The framing sequence for creating the impression that the robot figure is turning 90 degrees to the left takes advantage of the already-available Frame 3 as well as new Frames 5, 6, and 7. Here is a nice framing sequence:

1. Start from Frame 1.
2. Draw Frame 3.
3. Draw Frame 5.
4. Draw Frame 6.
5. Draw Frame 7.

Once that is done, getting the figure to turn 90 degrees to face straight ahead is a matter of running this frame sequence:

1. Start from Frame 7.
2. Draw Frame 6.
3. Draw Frame 5.
4. Draw Frame 3.
5. Draw Frame 1.

The control routine in the current program listing blends these two sequences with the stroll-ahead sequence that was described earlier. The figure begins by stepping about 20 paces straight ahead (lines 115 through 125). Then there is a brief pause (line 130), followed by the turn-to-face-left sequence (line 135). The figure pauses again in that position (line 140), then it turns 90 degrees to face forward again (line 145). After that, the routine simply loops back to begin the scene all over from the beginning.

Notice how we are able to take advantage of a frame that was defined earlier in the development process—Frame 3. Using that frame in conjunction with the new ones creates a smoother and more interesting turning effect, all with no additional programming work.

## PROJECT 9-6

The original scenario calls for having the robot figure stroll to the middle of the street, turn 90 degrees to the left, then raise an arm as though stopping some traffic. The arm-raising (and lowering) frames are shown in Fig. 9–6. An animation program that uses those frames is shown here as Listing 9–6.

NOTE: **Revise line 20 to read as shown here.**

```
10 REM ** PROJECT 9-6
15 REM          WALKING, TURNING, LIFTING ARM
20 CLEAR 1024:DEFSTR F:DIM F(10,7)
25 CLS:PRINT @ 405,"ROBOT TRAFFIC CONTROLLER"
30 GOSUB 4000
100 REM ** CONTROL ROUTINE
105 CLS
110 D=284
115 FOR N=0 TO 9
120 GOSUB 1000:GOSUB 1020:GOSUB 1000:GOSUB 1030
125 NEXT N
130 GOSUB 1000:T=500:GOSUB 950
135 GOSUB 1030:GOSUB 1050:GOSUB 1060:GOSUB 1070
140 T=50:GOSUB 950
145 GOSUB 1080:GOSUB 1090
150 T=500:GOSUB 950:GOSUB 1100:T=25:GOSUB 950:GOSUB 1090
155 T=500:GOSUB 950
200 GOSUB 1080:GOSUB 1070
205 T=100:GOSUB 950
210 GOSUB 1060:GOSUB 1050:GOSUB 1030:GOSUB 1000
215 GOTO 115
950 FOR TD=0 TO T:NEXT TD:RETURN
```

```
1000 REM ** DRAWING SUBROUTINES
1001 FOR L=1 TO 7:PRINT @ D+64*(L-1),F(1,L);:NEXT L:RETURN
1020 FOR L=3 TO 7:PRINT  @ D+64*(L-1),F(2,L);:NEXT L:RETURN
1030 FOR L=3 TO 7:PRINT @ D+64*(L-1),F(3,L);:NEXT L:RETURN
1040 FOR L=1 TO 7:PRINT @ D+64*(L-1),F(4,L);:NEXT L:RETURN
1050 FOR L=1 TO 7:PRINT @ D+64*(L-1),F(5,L);:NEXT L:RETURN
1060 FOR L=1 TO 7:PRINT @ D+64*(L-1),F(6,L);:NEXT L:RETURN
1070 FOR L=1 TO 7:PRINT @ D+64*(L-1),F(7,L);:NEXT L:RETURN
1080 FOR L=3 TO 4:PRINT @ D+64*(L-1),F(8,L);:NEXT L:RETURN
1090 FOR L=2 TO 4:PRINT @ D+64*(L-1),F(9,L);:NEXT L:RETURN
1100 PRINT @ D+64,F(10,2);:RETURN
4000 REM ** STRING-PACKING SUBROUTINE
4001 L=1
4002 GOSUB 4500:F(1,L)=F:IF A=0 THEN L=L+1:GOTO 4002
4020 L=3
4021 GOSUB 4500:F(2,L)=F:IF A=0 THEN L=L+1:GOTO 4021
4030 L=3
4031 GOSUB 4500:F(3,L)=F:IF A=0 THEN L=L+1:GOTO 4031
4040 F(4,1)=F(1,1):F(4,3)=F(1,3)
4041 FOR N=5 TO 7:F(4,N)=F(1,N):NEXT N
4042 GOSUB 4500:F(4,2)=F
4044 GOSUB 4500:F(4,4)=F
4050 L=1
4051 GOSUB 4500:F(5,L)=F:IF A=0 THEN L=L+1:GOTO 4051
4060 L=1
4061 GOSUB4500:F(6,L)=F:IF A=0 THEN  L=L+1:GOTO 4061
4070 L=1
4071 GOSUB 4500:F(7,L)=F:IF A=0 THEN L=L+1:GOTO 4071
4080 L=3
4081 GOSUB 4500:F(8,L)=F:IF A=0 THEN L=L+1:GOTO 4081
4090 L=3
4091 GOSUB 4500:F(9,L)=F:IF A=0 THEN L=L+1:GOTO 4091
4092 F(9,2)=F(7,2)
4100 GOSUB 4500:F(10,2)=F
4499 RETURN
4500 F=""
4505 READ A:IF A=0 OR A=1 THEN RETURN
4510 IF A>0 THEN F=F+CHR$(A):GOTO 4505
4515 READ B:F=F+STRING$(ABS(A),B):GOTO 4505
5000 REM ** DATA LISTINGS
5011 DATA 197,160,144,197,0
5012 DATA 195,136,191,187,183,191,132,195,0
5013 DATA 195,188,172,190,189,156,188,195,0
5014 DATA 194,130,191,170,189,187,149,191,129,194,0
5015 DATA 194,130,131,186,149,170,181,131,129,194,0
5016 DATA 196,170,149,170,149,196,0
5017 DATA 195,-2,131,129,130,-2,131,195,1
5023 DATA 195,188,172,190,189,156,188,195,0
5024 DATA 194,138,189,170,-2,25,191,129,195,0
5025 DATA 196,186,149,130,191,180,195,0
5026 DATA 196,170,149,128,191,176,144,194,0
5027 DATA 195,-2,131,129,198,1
5033 DATA 195,188,172,190,189,156,188,194,0
5034 DATA 195,130,191,-2,25,149,190,133,128,0
5035 DATA 195,184,191,129,170,181,195,0
5036 DATA 194,160,176,191,128,170,149,195,0
5037 DATA 198,130,-2,131,194,1
5042 DATA 195,136,-4,191,132,195,0
5044 DATA 194,130,191,170,178,177,149,191,129,194,1
5051 DATA 197,176,198,0
5052 DATA 196,183,191,187,191,196,0
```

*(cont.)*

```
5053 DATA 195,184,188,190,189,172,180,195,0
5054 DATA 195,175,191,182,191,184,159,129,194,0
5055 DATA 196,170,-2,191,130,131,195,0
5056 DATA 195,160,186,-2,191,197,0
5057 DATA 198,131,129,196,1
5061 DATA 197,176,198,0
5062 DATA 196,191,187,-2,191,196,0
5063 DATA 196,160,190,189,180,196,0
5064 DATA 196,175,-2,191,159,189,144,194,0
5065 DATA 197,186,149,197,0
5066 DATA 197,170,191,180,196,0
5067 DATA 196,-2,131,129,197,1
5071 DATA 197,176,198,0
5072 DATA 196,183,-3,191,196,0
5073 DATA 196,160,190,189,180,196,0
5074 DATA 196,175,-2,191,159,196,0
5075 DATA 197,186,149,197,0
5076 DATA 197,170,149,197,0
5077 DATA 196,-2,131,129,197,1
5083 DATA 195,176,188,0
5084 DATA 128,188,143,129,1
5093 DATA 141,-3,140,172,0
5094 DATA 196,1
5102 DATA 196,-4,191,1
```

**LISTING 9-6** Complete programming for Project 9-6

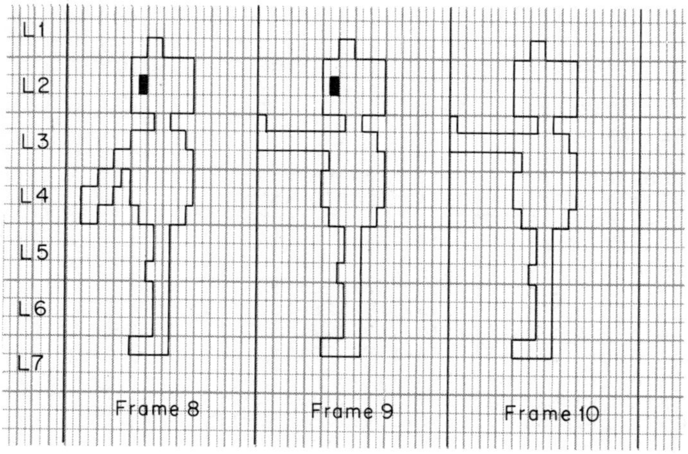


**FIGURE 9-6** Framing sequence for raising an arm, Project 9-6

Frame 8 shows the figure with its arm partly raised, and Frame 9 shows the arm fully extended. Frame 10 is used for creating a blinking effect of the robot's eyes: it will be able to blink while "holding up the traffic."

Since these three frames are always to follow a drawing of Frame 7, they can be generated quite efficiently by using some limited-segment framing techniques. Frame 8, for example, differs from Frame 7 only by the appearance of lines 3 and 4. The two unique lines in Frame 8 are packed at program lines 4080 and 4081, using DATA from lines 5083 and 5084. The elements of Frame 8 are drawn by calling the subroutine at line 1080.

Alternating between Frames 9 and 10 creates the impression that the figure is blinking its eyes while holding up an arm. Thus, Frame 9 must include a string for its Line 2; otherwise the robot's eyes would not open after drawing Frame 10.

A complete traffic-stopping sequence might run this way:

1. Begin by drawing Frame 7.
2. Raise arm.
   A. Draw Frame 8 (GOSUB 1080).
   B. Draw Frame 9 (GOSUB 1090).
3. Do a long time delay.
4. Blink while holding up arm.
   A. Draw Frame 10 (GOSUB 1100).
   B. Do a very short time delay.
   C. Draw Frame 9 (GOSUB 1090).
5. Do a long time delay.
6. Lower arm.
   A. Draw Frame 8 (GOSUB 1080).
   B. Draw Frame 7 (GOSUB 1070).

This particular sequence is blended with walking and turning sequences in the current program listing:

- Take about 20 paces forward (lines 115–125).
- Do a short delay while facing forward (line 130).
- Turn 90 degrees to face the left side of the screen (line 135).
- Do a short delay (line 140).
- Raise the arm (line 145).
- Do a fairly long delay, then blink (line 150).
- Do a fairly long delay (line 155).
- Lower the arm (line 200).
- Do a short delay (line 205).
- Turn 90 degrees to face forward (line 210).
- Go back to the beginning, walking forward again (line 215).

When you have seen this suggested program at work, do take some time to experiment with the control routine. Take advantage of the frames that are now available, and create some animated scenarios of your own.

## PROJECT 9–7

The scenario we are gradually developing here calls for the robot figure to turn its back to the screen and walk to the curb. Then the figure must make a 180-degree turn to face forward again. Listing 9–7 uses two new frames, shown in Fig. 9–7.

NOTE: **Modify the array DIMension as shown in line 20.**

```
10 REM ** PROJECT 9-7
15 REM          FULL TURN-AROUND SEQUENCES
20 CLEAR 1024:DEFSTR F:DIM F(15,7)
25 CLS:PRINT @ 405,"ROBOT TRAFFIC CONTROLLER"
30 GOSUB 4000
100 REM ** CONTROL ROUTINE
105 CLS
110 D=284
115 GOSUB 1010
120 T=500:GOSUB 950
125 FOR N=0 TO 4
130 GOSUB 1020:GOSUB 1010:GOSUB 1030:GOSUB 1010
135 NEXT N
140 T=100:GOSUB 950
145 GOSUB 1050:GOSUB 1060:GOSUB 1070
150 T=100:GOSUB 950
155 GOSUB 1080:GOSUB 1090:GOSUB 1100
160 T=100:GOSUB 950
165 GOSUB 1090:GOSUB 1080:GOSUB 1070
170 T=100:GOSUB 950
175 GOSUB 1070:GOSUB 1110:GOSUB 1120:GOSUB 1040
180 T=100:GOSUB 950
185 FOR N=0 TO 4
190 GOSUB 1020:GOSUB 1040:GOSUB 1030:GOSUB 1040
195 NEXT N
200 T=100:GOSUB 950
205 GOSUB 1120:GOSUB 1110:GOSUB 1060:GOSUB 1070
210 GOSUB 1050:GOSUB 1030:GOSUB 1010
215 GOTO 115
950 FOR TD=0 TO T:NEXT TD:RETURN
1000 REM ** DRAWING SUBROUTINES
1010 FOR L=1 TO 7:PRINT @ D+64*(L-1),F(1,L);:NEXT L:RETURN
1020 FOR L=3 TO 7:PRINT @ D+64*(L-1),F(2,L);:NEXT L:RETURN
1030 FOR L=3 TO 7:PRINT @ D+64*(L-1),F(3,L);:NEXT L:RETURN
1040 FOR L=1 TO 7:PRINT @ D+64*(L-1),F(4,L);:NEXT L:RETURN
1050 FOR L=1 TO 7:PRINT @ D+64*(L-1),F(5,L);:NEXT L:RETURN
1060 FOR L=1 TO 7:PRINT @ D+64*(L-1),F(6,L);:NEXT L:RETURN
1070 FOR L=1 TO 7:PRINT @ D+64*(L-1),F(7,L);:NEXT L:RETURN
1080 FOR L=3 TO 4:PRINT @ D+64*(L-1),F(8,L);:NEXT L:RETURN
1090 FOR L=2 TO 4:PRINT @ D+64*(L-1),F(9,L);:NEXT L:RETURN
1100 PRINT @ D+64,F(10,2);:RETURN
1110 FOR L=1 TO 7:PRINT @ D+64*(L-1),F(11,L);:NEXT L:RETURN
1120 FOR L=1 TO 7:PRINT @ D+64*(L-1),F(12,L);:NEXT L:RETURN
4000 REM ** STRING-PACKING SUBROUTINE
4001 L=1
4002 GOSUB 4500:F(1,L)=F:IF A=0 THEN L=L+1:GOTO 4002
4020 L=3
4021 GOSUB 4500:F(2,L)=F:IF A=0 THEN L=L+1:GOTO 4021
4030 L=3
4031 GOSUB 4500:F(3,L)=F:IF A=0 THEN L=L+1:GOTO 4031
4040 F(4,1)=F(1,1):F(4,3)=F(1,3)
```

```
4041 FOR N=5 TO 7:F(4,N)=F(1,N):NEXT N
4042 GOSUB 4500:F(4,2)=F
4044 GOSUB 4500:F(4,4)=F
4050 L=1
4051 GOSUB 4500:F(5,L)=F:IF A=0 THEN L=L+1:GOTO 4051
4060 L=1
4061 GOSUB4500:F(6,L)=F:IF A=0 THEN  L=L+1:GOTO 4061
4070 L=1
4071 GOSUB 4500:F(7,L)=F:IF A=0 THEN L=L+1:GOTO 4071
4080 L=3
4081 GOSUB 4500:F(8,L)=F:IF A=0 THEN L=L+1:GOTO 4081
4090 L=3
4091 GOSUB 4500:F(9,L)=F:IF A=0 THEN L=L+1:GOTO 4091
4092 F(9,2)=F(7,2)
4100 GOSUB 4500:F(10,2)=F
4110 F(11,1)=F(5,1):F(11,2)=F(10,2):F(11,3)=F(6,3)
4114 GOSUB 4500:F(11,4)=F
4115 FOR N=5 TO 7:F(11,N)=F(6,N):NEXT N
4121 F(12,1)=F(1,1):F(12,2)=F(4,2):F(12,3)=F(2,3)
4124 GOSUB 4500:F(12,4)=F
4125 FOR N=5 TO 7:F(12,N)=F(2,N):NEXT N
4499 RETURN
4500 F=""
4505 READ A:IF A=0 OR A=1 THEN RETURN
4510 IF A>0 THEN F=F+CHR$(A):GOTO 4505
4515 READ B:F=F+STRING$(ABS(A),B):GOTO 4505
5000 REM ** DATA LISTINGS
5011 DATA 197,160,144,197,0
5012 DATA 195,136,191,187,183,191,132,195,0
5013 DATA 195,188,172,190,189,156,188,195,0
5014 DATA 194,130,191,170,189,187,149,191,129,194,0
5015 DATA 194,130,131,186,149,170,181,131,129,194,0
5016 DATA 196,170,149,170,149,196,0
5017 DATA 195,-2,131,129,130,-2,131,195,1
5023 DATA 195,188,172,190,189,156,188,195,0
5024 DATA 194,138,189,170,-2,25,191,129,195,0
5025 DATA 196,186,149,130,191,180,195,0
5026 DATA 196,170,149,128,191,176,144,194,0
5027 DATA 195,-2,131,129,198,1
5033 DATA 195,188,172,190,189,156,188,194,0
5034 DATA 195,130,191,-2,25,149,190,133,128,0
5035 DATA 195,184,191,129,170,181,195,0
5036 DATA 194,160,176,191,128,170,149,195,0
5037 DATA 198,130,-2,131,194,1
5042 DATA 195,136,-4,191,132,195,0
5044 DATA 194,130,191,170,178,177,149,191,129,194,1
5051 DATA 197,176,198,0
5052 DATA 196,183,191,187,191,196,0
5053 DATA 195,184,188,190,189,172,180,195,0
5054 DATA 195,175,191,182,191,184,159,129,194,0
5055 DATA 196,170,-2,191,130,131,195,0
5056 DATA 195,160,186,-2,191,197,0
5057 DATA 198,131,129,196,1
5061 DATA 197,176,198,0
5062 DATA 196,191,187,-2,191,196,0
5063 DATA 196,160,190,189,180,196,0
5064 DATA 196,175,-2,191,159,189,144,194,0
5065 DATA 197,186,149,197,0
5066 DATA 197,170,191,180,196,0
5067 DATA 196,-2,131,129,197,1
5071 DATA 197,176,198,0
```

(cont.)

```
5072 DATA 196,183,-3,191,196,0
5073 DATA 196,160,190,189,180,196,0
5074 DATA 196,175,-2,191,159,196,0
5075 DATA 197,186,149,197,0
5076 DATA 197,170,149,197,0
5077 DATA 196,-2,131,129,197,1
5083 DATA 195,176,188,0
5084 DATA 128,188,143,129,1
5093 DATA 141,-3,140,172,0
5094 DATA 196,1
5102 DATA 196,-4,191,1
5114 DATA 196,175,191,176,155,189,144,194,1
5124 DATA 194,138,189,170,181,177,191,129,195,1
```

**LISTING 9-7** Complete programming for Project 9-7

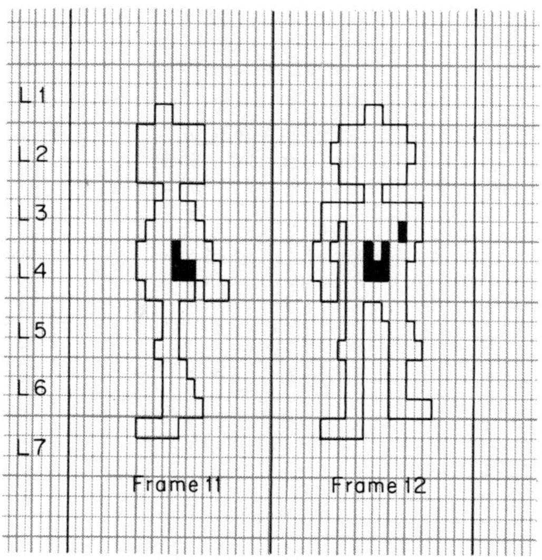


**FIGURE 9-7** Framing that must be added to do a turn to the rear

Frame 11 is packed by means of the instructions in lines 4110 through 4115. That packing operation takes advantage of the fact that Line 1 is the same as Line 1 in Frame 5, Line 2 is identical to Line 2 in Frame 10, Line 3 is the same as Line 3 in Frame 6, and Lines 5 through 7 are the same as those lines in Frame 6. Only Line 4 is unique, and its variable F(11,4) is packed from DATA in line 5114.

Frame 12 also has a number of lines that are common to other frames. See how they are equated in program lines 4121 and 4125. Again, Line 4 is unique; it is packed by program line 4124 and uses DATA from line 5124.

Frame 11 is drawn by calling the subroutine at program line 1110, and Frame 12 is drawn from line 1120.

Listing 9-7 is certainly an imposing piece of BASIC programming; but if you have been evolving the programming and saving the results of each project as suggested earlier, there really isn't much work involved in getting this program underway. Simply add the new drawing subroutines, string-packing lines, and DATA listings for Frames 11 and 12. Then rewrite the control routine as shown here.

The control routine in this case generates the following animation sequence:

1. Begin by drawing Frame 1 (line 115).
2. Take about ten paces forward (lines 125–135).
3. Do a short time delay (line 140).
4. Do a 90-degree turn to face left (line 145).
5. Do a short time delay (line 150).
6. Raise arm (line 155).
7. Do a short time delay (line 160).
8. Lower arm (line 165).
9. Do a short time delay (line 170).
10. Do another 90-degree turn to face curb (line 175).
11. Do a short time delay (line 180).
12. Take about ten paces back to the curb (lines 185–195).
13. Do a short time delay (line 200).
14. Do a 180-degree turn to face forward (lines 205 and 210).
15. Repeat the scenario from Step 1 (line 215).

If you see any flaws in the appearance of the figure as it does the turns in Steps 10 and 14, double-check the drawing subroutines, string-packing lines and DATA elements for Frames 11 and 12.

## PROJECT 9–8

Complete the scenario as shown in Listing 9–8. This includes several new frames for making the figure blink its eyes and look from side to side while facing forward. See those frames as they are partially drawn in Fig. 9–8.

```
10 REM ** PROJECT 9-8
15 REM          A COMPLETE ROBOT SCENARIO
20 CLEAR 1024:DEFSTR F:DIM F(15,7)
25 CLS:PRINT @ 405,"ROBOT TRAFFIC CONTROLLER"
30 GOSUB 4000
100 REM ** CONTROL ROUTINE
```

*(cont.)*

```
105 CLS
110 D=284
115 GOSUB 1010
120 FOR S=1 TO RND(4)
125 T=RND(1000):GOSUB 950
130 GOSUB 1130
135 T=RND(1000):GOSUB 950
140 GOSUB 1010:GOSUB 1150
145 T=RND(1000):GOSUB 950
150 GOSUB 1010
155 T=RND(1000):GOSUB 950
160 GOSUB 1140:T=25:GOSUB 950:GOSUB 1010
165 NEXT S
170 FOR N=0 TO 9
175 GOSUB 1020:GOSUB 1010:GOSUB 1030:GOSUB 1010
180 NEXT N
185 T=250:GOSUB 950
190 GOSUB 1020:GOSUB 1050:GOSUB 1060:GOSUB 1070
195 T=250:GOSUB 950
200 GOSUB 1080:GOSUB 1090
205 FOR S=1 TO RND(4)
210 GOSUB 1090
215 T=RND(500):GOSUB 950
220 GOSUB 1100:T=25:GOSUB 950:GOSUB 1090
225 T=RND(500):GOSUB 950
230 NEXT S
235 GOSUB 1080:GOSUB 1070
240 T=250:GOSUB 950
245 GOSUB 1110:GOSUB 1120:GOSUB 1040
250 T=250:GOSUB 950
255 FOR N=0 TO 9
260 GOSUB 1020:GOSUB 1040:GOSUB 1030:GOSUB 1040
265 NEXT N
270 T=250:GOSUB 950
275 GOSUB 1120:GOSUB 1110:GOSUB 1070
280 GOSUB 1060:GOSUB 1050:GOSUB 1020:GOSUB 1010
285 GOTO 115
950 FOR TD=0 TO T:NEXT TD:RETURN
1000 REM ** DRAWING SUBROUTINES
1010 FOR L=1 TO 7:PRINT @ D+64*(L-1),F(1,L);:NEXT L:RETURN
1020 FOR L=3 TO 7:PRINT @ D+64*(L-1),F(2,L);:NEXT L:RETURN
1030 FOR L=3 TO 7:PRINT @ D+64*(L-1),F(3,L);:NEXT L:RETURN
1040 FOR L=1 TO 7:PRINT @ D+64*(L-1),F(4,L);:NEXT L:RETURN
1050 FOR L=1 TO 7:PRINT @ D+64*(L-1),F(5,L);:NEXT L:RETURN
1060 FOR L=1 TO 7:PRINT @ D+64*(L-1),F(6,L);:NEXT L:RETURN
1070 FOR L=1 TO 7:PRINT @ D+64*(L-1),F(7,L);:NEXT L:RETURN
1080 FOR L=3 TO 4:PRINT @ D+64*(L-1),F(8,L);:NEXT L:RETURN
1090 FOR L=2 TO 4:PRINT @ D+64*(L-1),F(9,L);:NEXT L:RETURN
1100 PRINT @ D+64,F(10,2);:RETURN
1110 FOR L=1 TO 7:PRINT @ D+64*(L-1),F(11,L);:NEXT L:RETURN
1120 FOR L=1 TO 7:PRINT @ D+64*(L-1),F(12,L);:NEXT L:RETURN
1130 FOR L=1 TO 2:PRINT @ D+64*(L-1),F(13,L);:NEXT L:RETURN
1140 FOR L=1 TO 2:PRINT @ D+64*(L-1),F(14,L);:NEXT L:RETURN
1150 FOR L=1 TO 2:PRINT @ D+64*(L-1),F(15,L);:NEXT L:RETURN
4000 REM ** STRING-PACKING SUBROUTINE
4001 L=1
4002 GOSUB 4500:F(1,L)=F:IF A=0 THEN L=L+1:GOTO 4002
4020 L=3
4021 GOSUB 4500:F(2,L)=F:IF A=0 THEN L=L+1:GOTO 4021
4030 L=3
4031 GOSUB 4500:F(3,L)=F:IF A=0 THEN L=L+1:GOTO 4031
4040 F(4,1)=F(1,1):F(4,3)=F(1,3)
4041 FOR N=5 TO 7:F(4,N)=F(1,N):NEXT N
```

```
4042 GOSUB 4500:F(4,2)=F
4044 GOSUB 4500:F(4,4)=F
4050 L=1
4051 GOSUB 4500:F(5,L)=F:IF A=0 THEN L=L+1:GOTO 4051
4060 L=1
4061 GOSUB4500:F(6,L)=F:IF A=0 THEN  L=L+1:GOTO 4061
4070 L=1
4071 GOSUB 4500:F(7,L)=F:IF A=0 THEN L=L+1:GOTO 4071
4080 L=3
4081 GOSUB 4500:F(8,L)=F:IF A=0 THEN L=L+1:GOTO 4081
4090 L=3
4091 GOSUB 4500:F(9,L)=F:IF A=0 THEN L=L+1:GOTO 4091
4092 F(9,2)=F(7,2)
4100 GOSUB 4500:F(10,2)=F
4110 F(11,1)=F(5,1):F(11,2)=F(10,2):F(11,3)=F(6,3)
4114 GOSUB 4500:F(11,4)=F
4115 FOR N=5 TO 7:F(11,N)=F(6,N):NEXT N
4121 F(12,1)=F(1,1):F(12,2)=F(4,2):F(12,3)=F(2,3)
4124 GOSUB 4500:F(12,4)=F
4125 FOR N=5 TO 7:F(12,N)=F(2,N):NEXT N
4130 L=1
4131 GOSUB 4500:F(13,L)=F:IF A=0 THEN L=L+1:GOTO 4131
4140 F(14,1)=F(4,1):F(14,2)=F(4,2)
4150 L=1
4151 GOSUB 4500:F(15,L)=F:IF A=0 THEN L=L+1:GOTO 4151
4499 RETURN
4500 F=""
4505 READ A:IF A=0 OR A=1 THEN RETURN
4510 IF A>0 THEN F=F+CHR$(A):GOTO 4505
4515 READ B:F=F+STRING$(ABS(A),B):GOTO 4505
5000 REM ** DATA LISTINGS
5011 DATA 197,160,144,197,0
5012 DATA 195,136,191,187,183,191,132,195,0
5013 DATA 195,188,172,190,189,156,188,195,0
5014 DATA 194,130,191,170,189,187,149,191,129,194,0
5015 DATA 194,130,131,186,149,170,181,131,129,194,0
5016 DATA 196,170,149,170,149,196,0
5017 DATA 195,-2,131,129,130,-2,131,195,1
5023 DATA 195,188,172,190,189,156,188,195,0
5024 DATA 194,138,189,170,-2,25,191,129,195,0
5025 DATA 196,186,149,130,191,180,195,0
5026 DATA 196,170,149,128,191,176,144,194,0
5027 DATA 195,-2,131,129,198,1
5033 DATA 195,188,172,190,189,156,188,194,0
5034 DATA 195,130,191,-2,25,149,190,133,128,0
5035 DATA 195,184,191,129,170,181,195,0
5036 DATA 194,160,176,191,128,170,149,195,0
5037 DATA 198,130,-2,131,194,1
5042 DATA 195,136,-4,191,132,195,0
5044 DATA 194,130,191,170,178,177,149,191,129,194,1
5051 DATA 197,176,198,0
5052 DATA 196,183,191,187,191,196,0
5053 DATA 195,184,188,190,189,172,180,195,0
5054 DATA 195,175,191,182,191,184,159,129,194,0
5055 DATA 196,170,-2,191,130,131,195,0
5056 DATA 195,160,186,-2,191,197,0
5057 DATA 198,131,129,196,1
5061 DATA 197,176,198,0
5062 DATA 196,191,187,-2,191,196,0
5063 DATA 196,160,190,189,180,196,0
5064 DATA 196,175,-2,191,159,189,144,194,0
```

*(cont.)*

```
5065 DATA 197,186,149,197,0
5066 DATA 197,170,191,180,196,0
5067 DATA 196,-2,131,129,197,1
5071 DATA 197,176,198,0
5072 DATA 196,183,-3,191,196,0
5073 DATA 196,160,190,189,180,196,0
5074 DATA 196,175,-2,191,159,196,0
5075 DATA 197,186,149,197,0
5076 DATA 197,170,149,197,0
5077 DATA 196,-2,131,129,197,1
5083 DATA 195,176,188,0
5084 DATA 128,188,143,129,1
5093 DATA 141,-3,140,172,0
5094 DATA 196,1
5102 DATA 196,-4,191,1
5114 DATA 196,175,191,176,155,189,144,194,1
5124 DATA 194,138,189,170,181,177,191,129,195,1
5131 DATA 197,176,198,0
5132 DATA 196,183,191,187,191,196,1
5151 DATA 198,176,197,0
5152 DATA 196,191,183,191,187,196,1
```

**LISTING 9-8** Complete programming for Project 9-8

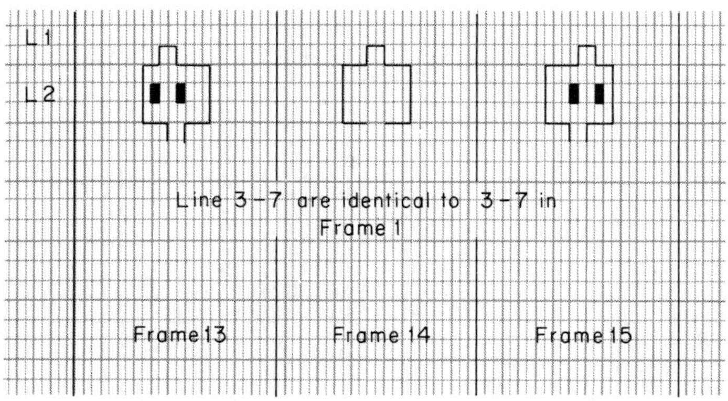


**FIGURE 9-8** Additional limited-segment frames for making the robot figure look left and right and blink its eyes

The new lines in the drawing-subroutines section are 1130, 1140, and 1150; in the string-packing subroutine are new lines 4130, 4131, 4140, 4150, and 4151. New DATA lines are from 5131 through 5152. The control routine is entirely new; it must be entered from scratch.

Here is the outline for the final robot scenario:

1. Draw full Frame 1 (line 115).
2. Do the curb sequence between one and four times.
   A. Do a long, random time delay (line 125).
   B. Look to the left side of the screen (line 130).

   C. Do a long, random time delay (line 135).
   D. Change from left to looking right (line 140).
   E. Do a long, random time delay (line 145).
   F. Look straight ahead (line 150).
   G. Do a long, random time delay (line 155).
   H. Blink eyes while looking forward (line 160).
3. Walk forward about 20 paces (lines 170–180).
4. Do a short, fixed time delay (line 185).
5. Turn 90 degrees to face left side (line 190).
6. Do a short, fixed time delay (line 195).
7. Raise arm (line 200).
8. Do arm-raised sequence between one and four times.
   A. Arm up, eyes open (line 210).
   B. Do medium, random time delay (line 215).
   C. Blink with arm raised (line 220).
   D. Do medium, random time delay (line 225).
9. Lower the arm (235).
10. Do a short, fixed time delay (line 240).
11. Turn another 90 degrees to face backward (line 245).
12. Do a short, fixed time delay (line 250).
13. Take about 20 paces to the rear (lines 255–265).
14. Do a short, fixed time delay (line 270).
15. Turn 180 degrees to face forward again (lines 275 and 280).
16. Repeat the scenario from the beginning (line 285).

Tinker with the time delays and FOR . . . TO . . . NEXT statements to create some interesting and unusual effects of your own. Try extending the scenario as far as your understanding of the animation techniques will allow.

## PROJECT 9–9

Use the string-packed frames available in Listing 9–8 to compose an entirely different scenario—for instance, getting the robot to dance a jig. See if you can add a couple of new frames to create a goose-stepping robot.

# 10 Complex-Figure Animation

The robot figure featured in the previous chapter was a fairly simple one; what's more, the projects demonstrated some fairly simple animation routines. This chapter expands the notion of creating animated figures from packed-string variables, pushing matters about as far as they can go.

The topic of complex-figure animation includes the techniques for generating a complex series of animation sequences for a single figure and working out independent animation sequences for two or more figures. In both instances, the speed of execution of BASIC programs is a most powerful factor in determining how the sequences are designed and run. BASIC, being an interpretive language, is bound to run much slower than a corresponding program written in a machine language. Here we begin running into the speed limits of TRS-80 BASIC. There are, however, some techniques for generating satisfactory complex animation sequences from BASIC, and they are, of course, offered here for your consideration.

These discussions use the string-packing format that has been built up through the last few chapters. There will be nothing new as far as the program formatting is concerned; there will be the familiar initialization and control routines, string-packing subroutines, and drawing subroutines. We will even stay with the same line-numbering format for the program. The only new ideas concern the implementation of those familiar features.

## ANIMATING LARGE, COMPLEX FIGURES

The larger a figure becomes, the more lines it covers and the more characters there are in each line. Also the larger the number of lines, and the larger the number of characters in each line, the longer it takes to draw the figure. Limited-segment framing, a technique introduced in the previous chapter, attempts to create smooth animation effects by drawing the moving parts of a figure in a piecemeal fashion: move a little bit of the figure here, move another little bit over there, and so on. If things are properly coordinated, limited-segment framing can produce some nice animation effects, even on large and complex figures.

In this chapter, limited-segment framing is refined to a higher degree by taking advantage of the TRS–80's ASCII control codes, codes that can be treated as CHR$ or STRING$ characters but that control the position of the cursor rather than printing something on the screen.

### taking advantage of control codes

Three TRS–80 control codes are especially useful for high-performance, limited-segment framing. They are:

| | |
|---|---|
| 24 | Backspace the cursor one character space. |
| 25 | Advance the cursor one character space. |
| 26 | Drop the cursor down one line. |

PRINTing a CHR$(24), for instance, moves the cursor (the next printable character space) one space backward, and it does not delete the character residing there. PRINTing a CHR$(8) will backspace and erase, but CHR$(24) does not. Whenever you have a need to backspace a number of locations in succession, PRINTing a CHR$(*n*,24) will do the job, where *n* is the number of spaces.

Doing a PRINT CHR$(25) advances the cursor, again without disturbing any character that might reside in that new cursor location.

That code works with the STRING$ function to let you advance the cursor some desired number of character locations.

Finally, CHR$(26) drops the cursor down one line from its present position.

These control codes can be concatenated into packed strings just as any of the graphics codes can be packed. Thus a single string variable can both print characters and control the position of the cursor. The notion is relevant to our present topic because it allows for faster adjustment of small, moving segments of an animated figure.

Suppose, for example, you want to redraw the last eight characters in a twelve-character line of graphics. Rather than your redrawing the first four characters, the string variable can start out with a STRING$(4,25) function, followed by the eight graphic codes that are necessary for making the change. Certainly it takes some time for BASIC to execute that STRING$(4,25) function, but it runs faster than a PRINT @ D+8 operation. (The latter idea adjusts the displacement value for printing the portion of the line that is to be redrawn.)

For a specific example, look ahead at program line 5110 in Listing 10-1. The DATA line begins with the sequence −5,25. When it is packed, those two figures are interpreted as a STRING$(5,25) function—skipping the first five character spaces in the line.

Using the control codes really begins paying off in situations where a limited-segment framing situation calls for redrawing several characters over two or more lines in succession. Maybe an animation sequence requires redrawing the characters in a 4 × 2 segment of a complex figure. That's two successive lines of four characters apiece. A single string variable can handle the job by first printing the four characters for the first line, doing a CHR$(26), doing a STRING$(4,24), and then printing the four characters for the next line. CHR$(26)+STRING$(4,24) drops the cursor down one line and then moves it back four character locations, back to the beginning of the second line to be redrawn. Packing this line-control sequence into a single string variable makes things run a lot faster than is possible when you are specifying different PRINT @ locations for the two lines.

Lines 5441 through 5444 in Listing 10-1 use all of these control techniques. All of those data are packed into a single string variable. Line 5441 begins by skipping nine character locations, then it prints some standard graphics, and it ends by dropping down one line and running backward nine character locations. The data in line 5442 is concatenated into that same string, and it also concludes by dropping down a line and skipping back nine spaces to the beginning of the next line. That particular string is completely packed only when the end of line 5444 is reached. The resulting string offsets the start of the drawing by eight character spaces, then fills in a selected area that measures 9 × 4.

## an example: COUNTRY GAL

Fig. 10–1 is a moderately large, complex figure. It is certainly larger and more complex than the robot figure offered in the previous chapter. What is equally important, however, is the need to generate a highly complex series of animation sequences that will make the COUNTRY GAL sing, roll her eyes, tap her foot, slap her knee, and dance a little jig.

The notion of drawing a complete 17 × 10 frame for every little element of animation is an unworkable one. The drawing time for a frame that large is simply too long to achieve a satisfactory result. Specifically, there would be too much flicker; the drawing operation would be obvious each time the frame is altered. The job must be done via the careful selection and coordination of limited-segment framing.

Figs. 10–2 through 10–5 show a number of limited segments. Each, standing alone, makes little sense. They are simply bits and pieces of the overall animation. Figure 10–2A, for instance, shows five different configurations for the gal's mouth, Fig. 10–2B shows four different eye positions, and Fig. 10–2C shows two positions for her foot closest to the left side of the frame. In all of those cases, the figures represent just a part of a single line on the screen: the braids in Line 2 of the main drawing are miss-

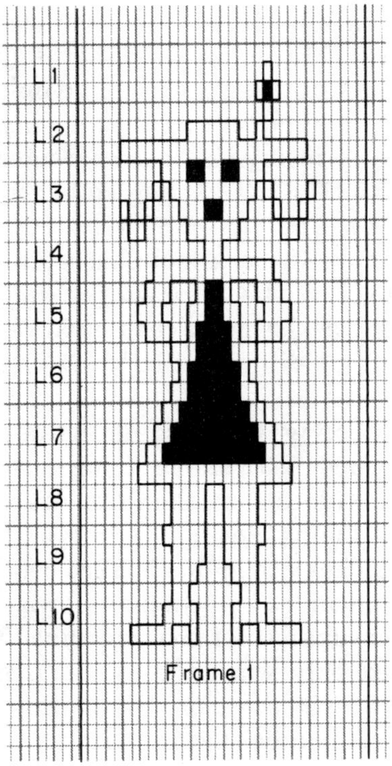


**FIGURE 10–1** Worksheet version of Frame 1 for Country Gal

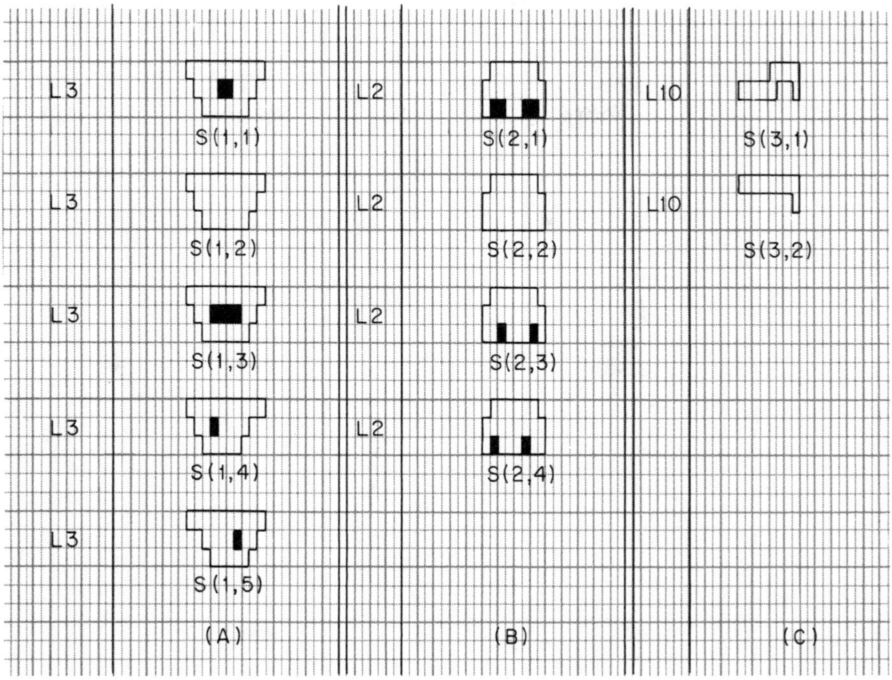


**FIGURE 10-2** Single-line segments for Country Gal animation: (A) mouths; (B) eyes; (C) left-side foot

ing in the segments of the mouth, parts of the girl's hat are missing from the eye segments in Fig. 10–2B, and the right-side foot is missing from the two segments in Fig. 10–2C.

Fig. 10–3 shows leg segments from Lines 7 through 10, Fig. 10–4 shows arm segments for Lines 4 and 5, and Fig. 10–5 shows braid segments for Line 3. All of them are partial lines—segments of the figure—that are to be drawn at the appropriate time in a complex animation sequence.

All of these segments, as well as the main figure in Fig. 10–1, are brought together in Listing 10–1. That program includes the DATA listings, string-packing subroutine, and drawing routines. The idea is to get the information for these animation segments into the computer and packed into strings so that they can be drawn in a coordinated fashion from a control routine.

The main COUNTRY GAL figure, Fig. 10–1, is represented by the DATA items in program lines 5011 through 5020. You will find nothing new there, but you can check your understanding of earlier principles by comparing what you see in Fig. 10–1 with the DATA in those lines.

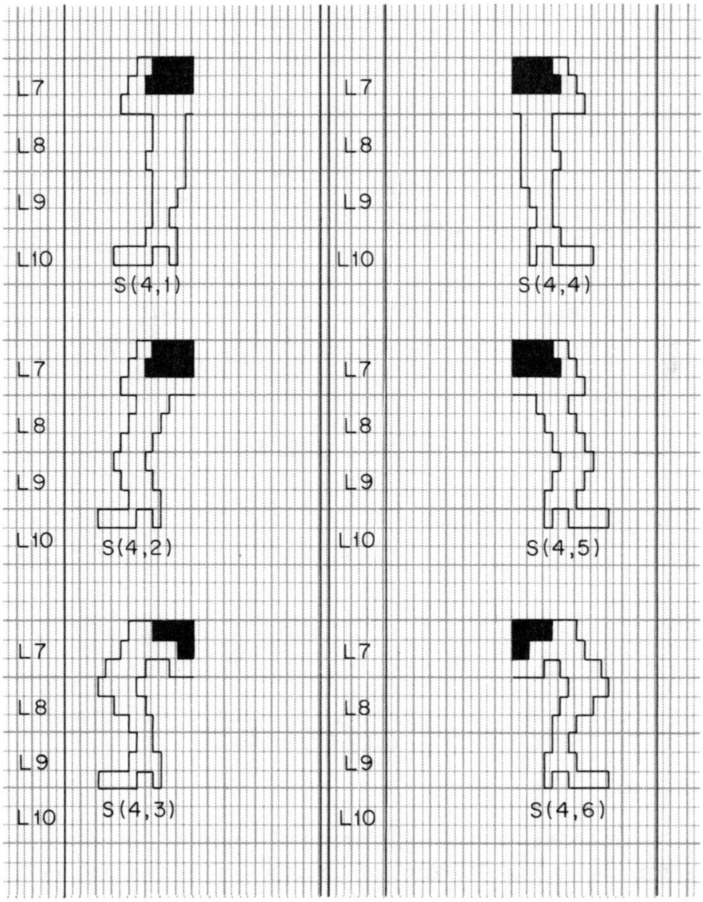


**FIGURE 10-3** Leg segments for Country Gal animation

The DATA for the mouth segments in Fig. 10–2A occupy program lines 5110 through 5150. Notice that each of those lines begins with a −5,25 sequence, a sequence that will pack into a string as STRING$(5,25). That means the mouth segments are drawn from the sixth character space; it means the mouth-drawing operations skip over the girl's left-side braid that also occupies Line 3 of the main drawing.

The eye segments from Fig. 10–2B fill out DATA lines 5210 through 5240. They, too, call for skipping over any characters to the left of the upper-face portion of the drawing, namely the left-hand side of the girl's hat.

The foot segments are handled in the same way by DATA in program lines 5310 and 5320.

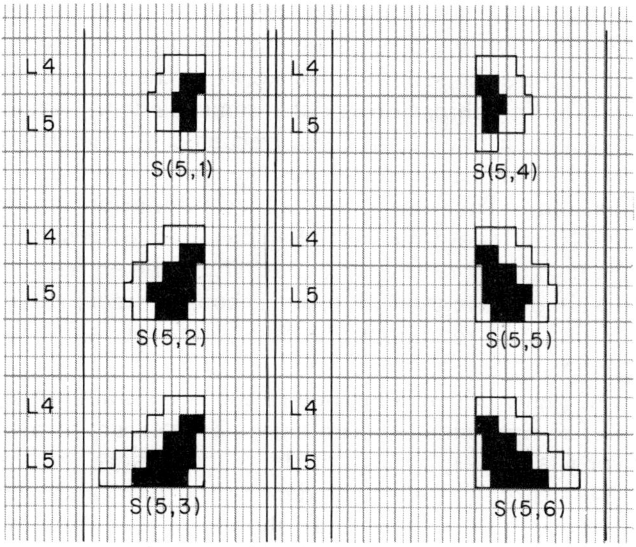


**FIGURE 10-4** Arm segments for Country Gal

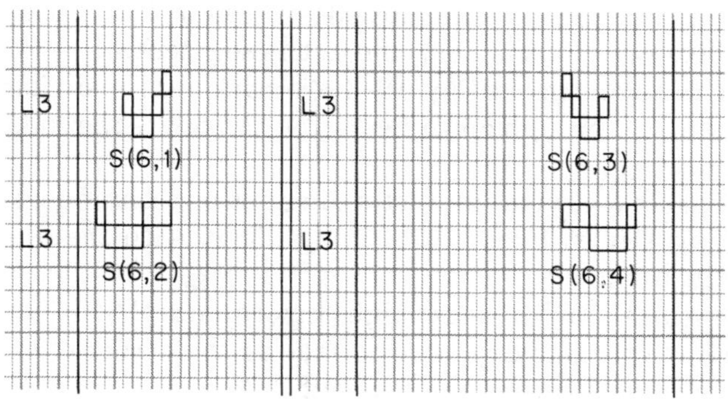


**FIGURE 10-5** Braid segments for Country Gal

All of the DATA lines for the mouth, eye, and foot segments are packed into separate string variables. The fact that each of those lines ends with a 1 character signifies that fact. That is not the case, however, for the more complex leg parts.

Looking at Fig. 10-3, you can see that there are six leg segments: three for the left-side leg and three for the right-side leg. Unlike the segments described thus far, these occupy more than one line in the figure; they occupy four lines to be exact.

The first leg segment, labeled S(4,1), is packed from DATA in lines

5411 through 5414. Although there are four CRT lines in the drawing and four corresponding DATA listings, all of those data are packed as a single string variable. Note the sequence 26, −8,24 at the ends of the first three DATA lines. That combination of data items, as described earlier, effectively starts the next line of graphics. In each case, the 26 is packed into the string of CHR$(26), and that drops the cursor down one line from its present position. Then the −8,24 combination is packed as STRING$(8,24), and that function, when included in the string, moves the cursor to the beginning of the next line. Thus, the entire leg segment is packed into a single string variable, even though it includes four different lines of characters. It runs about as fast as any string-packed series of operations can run.

The same general idea is applied to the five remaining leg segments in Fig. 10-3. The right-side leg segments, however, are printed only after skipping over the left-leg portion of the picture. Note, for instance, program lines 5441 through 5444. The data in those lines are packed as the leg segment labeled S(4,4). Line 5441 shows a −8,25 combination at the beginning, and that is packed as STRING$(8,25); skip over eight character spaces before beginning the drawing. Then the first three of those DATA lines conclude with a −9,24—STRING$(9,24). That function, in combination with the preceding 26 code, is responsible for setting the cursor to the beginning of the next line in the segment.

The arm segments in Fig. 10-4 are packed in a similar way, using DATA lines 5511 through 5562. See if you can relate the codes 24, 25, and 26 to the drawings.

As a final test of your understanding of this technique, try your hand at associating DATA lines 5610 through 5640 with the braid segments shown in Fig. 10-5.

As mentioned earlier, these high-performance BASIC animation programs can have the same general format as the earlier ones. This one is lacking a control routine at the moment, but everything else is there.

The main figure, Fig. 10-1, is packed at lines 4015 and 4020, using DATA items from program lines 5011-5020. It is drawn by calling the drawing subroutine at line 1015 (or 1000, or 1010).

## PROJECT 10-1

Load the program in Listing 10-1 into your system, then RUN it. It includes a checksum routine that is intended to test the accuracy of the DATA listing section. If you have made no errors in that rather extensive DATA listing, you will see an OK printed on the screen. Otherwise, a DATA ERROR message will appear. In the latter case, you will have to double-check the DATA lines and correct any typographical errors you have made.

```
10 REM **       PROJECT 10-1
15 REM          COUNTRY GAL DATA
20 CLEAR 1024:DEFSTR F,S
25 DIM F(1,10),S(6,6)
100 REM ** CHECKSUM ROUTINE
105 T=0
110 READ A
115 ON ERROR GOTO 125
120 T=T+A:GOTO 110
125 IF T<>57166 THEN PRINT "DATA ERROR":END
130 PRINT "OK":END
1000 REM ** DRAWING SUBROUTINES
1010 REM         DRAW FRAME 1
1015 FOR L=1 TO 10:PRINT @ D+64*(L-1),F(1,L);:NEXT L:RETURN
1100 REM         DRAW SEGMENTS 1
1110 PRINT @ D+128,S(1,1);:RETURN
1120 PRINT @ D+128,S(1,2);:RETURN
1130 PRINT @ D+128,S(1,3);:RETURN
1140 PRINT @ D+128,S(1,4);:RETURN
1150 PRINT @ D+128,S(1,5);:RETURN
1200 REM         DRAW SEGMENTS 2
1210 PRINT @ D+64,S(2,1);:RETURN
1220 PRINT @ D+64,S(2,2);:RETURN
1230 PRINT @ D+64,S(2,3);:RETURN
1240 PRINT @ D+64,S(2,4);:RETURN
1300 REM         DRAW SEGMENTS 3
1310 PRINT @ D+576,S(3,1);:RETURN
1320 PRINT @ D+576,S(3,2);:RETURN
1400 REM         DRAW SEGMENTS 4
1410 PRINT @ D+384,S(4,1);:RETURN
1420 PRINT @ D+384,S(4,2);:RETURN
1430 PRINT @ D+384,S(4,3);:RETURN
1440 PRINT @ D+384,S(4,4);:RETURN
1450 PRINT @ D+384,S(4,5);:RETURN
1460 PRINT @ D+384,S(4,6);:RETURN
1500 REM         DRAW SEGMENTS 5
1510 PRINT @ D+192,S(5,1);:RETURN
1520 PRINT @ D+192,S(5,2);:RETURN
1530 PRINT @ D+192,S(5,3);:RETURN
1540 PRINT @ D+192,S(5,4);:RETURN
1550 PRINT @ D+192,S(5,5);:RETURN
1560 PRINT @ D+192,S(5,6);:RETURN
1600 REM         DRAW SEGMENTS 6
1610 PRINT @ D+128,S(6,1);:RETURN
1620 PRINT @ D+128,S(6,2);:RETURN
1630 PRINT @ D+128,S(6,3);:RETURN
1640 PRINT @ D+128,S(6,4);:RETURN
4000 REM ** STRING-PACKING SUBROUTINE
4010 REM         PACK FRAME 1
4015 L=1
4020 GOSUB 4900:F(1,L)=F:IF A=0 THEN L=L+1:GOTO 4020
4100 REM         PACK SEGMENTS 1
4110 FOR N=1 TO 5:GOSUB 4900:S(1,N)=F:NEXT N
4200 REM         PACK SEGMENTS 2
4210 FOR N=1 TO 4:GOSUB 4900:S(2,N)=F:NEXT N
4300 REM         PACK SEGMENTS 3
4310 FOR N=1 TO 2:GOSUB 4900:S(3,N)=F:NEXT N
4400 REM         PACK SEGMENTS 4
4410 FOR N=1 TO 6:GOSUB 4900:S(4,N)=F:NEXT N
4500 REM         PACK SEGMENTS 5
4510 FOR N=1 TO 6:GOSUB 4900:S(5,N)=F:NEXT N
```

*(cont.)*

```
4600 REM        PACK SEGMENTS 6
4610 FOR N=1 TO 4:GOSUB 4900:S(6,N)=F:NEXT N
4895 RETURN
4900 F=""
4905 READ A:IF A=0 OR A=1 THEN RETURN
4910 IF A>0 THEN F=F+CHR$(A):GOTO 4905
4915 READ B:F=F+STRING$(ABS(A),B):GOTO 4905
5000 REM ** DATA LISTINGS
5010 REM      FULL FRAME-1 DATA
5011 DATA 202,136,153,197,0
5012 DATA 194,136,-2,140,188,158,175,159,173,190,-2,140,132,195,0
5013 DATA 194,136,176,134,130,175,183,187,159,129,137,176,132,0
5014 DATA 196,184,156,140,158,173,140,172,180,197,0
5015 DATA 195,130,143,164,186,129,130,181,152,143,129,196,0
5016 DATA 197,184,133,194,138,180,198,0
5017 DATA 195,160,190,177,-4,176,178,189,144,196,0
5018 DATA 197,186,191,149,170,191,181,198,0
5019 DATA 197,170,159,129,130,175,149,198,0
5020 DATA 195,-2,140,135,139,194,135,139,-2,140,196,1
5100 REM        SEGMENTS 1 DATA
5110 DATA -5,25,130,175,183,187,159,129,1
5120 DATA -5,25,130,175,-2,191,159,129,1
5130 DATA -5,25,130,175,-2,179,159,129,1
5140 DATA -5,25,130,175,187,191,135,129,1
5150 DATA -5,25,130,139,191,183,159,129,1
5200 REM        SEGMENTS 2 DATA
5210 DATA -6,25,158,175,159,173,1
5220 DATA -6,25,190,-2,191,189,1
5230 DATA -6,25,190,175,191,173,1
5240 DATA -6,25,158,191,159,189,1
5300 REM        SEGMENTS 3 DATA
5310 DATA -3,25,-2,140,135,139,1
5320 DATA -3,25,-3,131,139,1
5400 REM        SEGMENTS 4 DATA
5411 DATA 195,160,190,177,-2,176,26,-8,24
5412 DATA 197,186,191,149,26,-8,24
5413 DATA 197,170,159,129,26,-8,24
5414 DATA 195,-2,140,135,139,128,1
5421 DATA 195,160,190,177,-2,176,26,-8,24
5422 DATA 195,160,190,159,129,128,26,-8,24
5423 DATA 195,139,191,180,194,26,-8,24
5424 DATA 194,-2,131,129,130,194,1
5431 DATA 194,160,184,191,141,172,176,26,-8,24
5432 DATA 194,131,143,189,144,194,26,-8,24
5433 DATA 194,-2,176,158,173,194,26,-8,24
5434 DATA 200,1
5441 DATA -8,25,-2,176,178,189,144,196,26,-9,24
5442 DATA 170,191,181,198,26,-9,24
5443 DATA 130,175,149,198,26,-9,24
5444 DATA 128,135,139,-2,140,196,1
5451 DATA -8,25,-2,176,178,189,144,196,26,-9,24
5452 DATA 128,130,175,189,144,196,26,-9,24
5453 DATA 194,184,191,135,196,26,-9,24
5454 DATA 194,129,130,-2,131,1
5461 DATA -8,25,176,156,142,191,180,144,195,26,-9,24
5462 DATA 194,160,190,143,131,195,26,-9,24
5463 DATA 194,158,173,-2,176,195,26,-9,24
5464 DATA 201,1
5500 REM        SEGMENTS 5 DATA
5511 DATA 196,184,156,140,26,-7,24
5512 DATA 195,130,143,164,186,1
```

```
5521 DATA 195,160,184,156,140,26,-7,24
5522 DATA 194,174,183,129,128,186,1
5531 DATA 195,160,184,156,140,26,-7,24
5532 DATA 160,184,158,135,129,128,186,1
5541 DATA -9,25,140,172,180,197,26,-8,24
5542 DATA 181,152,143,129,196,1
5551 DATA -9,25,140,172,180,144,196,26,-8,24
5552 DATA 181,128,130,187,157,195,1
5561 DATA -9,25,140,172,180,144,196,26,-8,24
5562 DATA 181,128,130,139,173,180,144,128,1
5600 REM        SEGMENTS 6 DATA
5610 DATA 194,136,176,134,1
5620 DATA 128,137,176,134,131,1
5630 DATA -11,25,137,176,132,195,1
5640 DATA -11,25,131,137,140,134,194,1
```

**LISTING 10-1** Checksum routine, drawing subroutines, string-packing subroutine, and DATA listings for Country Gal Frame 1 and all animation segments; refer to Project 10-1

## PROJECT 10-2

Once you get an OK message in response to running Listing 10-1, *add to it* the control routine in Listing 10-2.

```
10 REM **       PROJECT 10-2
15 REM   SINGING AND DANCING COUNTRY GAL
20 CLEAR 1024:DEFSTR F,S
25 DIM F(1,10),S(6,6)
30 CLS:PRINT @ 408,"SINGIN' & DANCIN'";STRING$(49,32);"COUNTRY GAL"
35 GOSUB 4000
100 REM ** CONTROL ROUTINE
110 D=153:CLS:GOSUB 1010
115 FOR R1=1 TO RND(100)
120 T=25:N=RND(9)
125 ON N GOSUB 1110,1120,1130,1140,1150,1210,1220,1230,1240
130 GOSUB 1310:GOSUB 950:GOSUB 1320:GOSUB 950
135 NEXT R1
140 FOR R2=1 TO RND(50)
145 T=2:N=RND(9)
150 ON N GOSUB 1110,1120,1130,1140,1150,1210,1220,1230,1240
155 FOR M=1 TO 11
160 ON M GOSUB 1410,1510,1420,1520,1430,1530,950,1520,1420,1510,1410
165 NEXT M,R2
170 GOSUB 1210:GOSUB 1520:GOSUB 1550
175 FOR R3=1 TO RND(50)
180 GOSUB 1420:GOSUB 1560:GOSUB 1640:GOSUB 1630:GOSUB 1550:GOSUB 1410
185 GOSUB 1450:GOSUB 1530:GOSUB 1620:GOSUB 1610:GOSUB 1520:GOSUB 1440
190 NEXT R3
200 GOSUB 1510:GOSUB 1540
205 GOTO 115
950 FOR TD=0 TO T:NEXT TD:RETURN
```

**LISTING 10-2** Initialization and control routines to be added to Listing 10-1; see Project 10-2

Tables 10–1 through 10–4 completely summarize the string-variable names and program lines devoted to the picture segments. Every picture segment shown in Figs. 10–2 through 10–5 has a two-dimensional string array, S, assigned to it. Those are all listed on the tables along with the subroutine number that should be called for drawing them, their string-packing line numbers, and their DATA line numbers.

RUN the program to see what it does. If all is going well, the COUNTRY GAL should sing for a little bit, tapping her foot with the "beat." Then she gets a bit carried away, stomping her left-side foot and slapping her waist with one hand. After that, things really get going, and she dances a little jig, with arms, legs, and braids flying about.

**TABLE 10–1**

STRING VARIABLE ASSIGNMENTS AND PROGRAM LINE NUMBERS FOR THE COUNTRY GAL MOUTH, EYES, AND LEFT-SIDE FOOT (see Fig. 10–2)

| *Segment* | *Draw* | *Pack* | *DATA* |
|---|---|---|---|
| S(1,1) | 1110 | 4110 | 5110 |
| S(1,2) | 1120 | 4110 | 5120 |
| S(1,3) | 1130 | 4110 | 5130 |
| S(1,4) | 1140 | 4110 | 5140 |
| S(1,5) | 1150 | 4110 | 5150 |
| S(2,1) | 1210 | 4210 | 5210 |
| S(2,2) | 1220 | 4210 | 5220 |
| S(2,3) | 1230 | 4210 | 5230 |
| S(2,4) | 1240 | 4210 | 5240 |
| S(3,1) | 1310 | 4310 | 5310 |
| S(3,2) | 1320 | 4310 | 5320 |

**TABLE 10–2**

STRING VARIABLE ASSIGNMENTS AND PROGRAM LINE NUMBERS FOR THE COUNTRY GAL LEG SEGMENTS (see Fig. 10–3)

| *Segment* | *Draw* | *Pack* | *DATA* | | | |
|---|---|---|---|---|---|---|
| S(4,1) | 1410 | 4410 | 5411 | 5412 | 5413 | 5414 |
| S(4,2) | 1420 | 4410 | 5421 | 5422 | 5423 | 5424 |
| S(4,3) | 1430 | 4410 | 5431 | 5432 | 5433 | 5434 |
| S(4,4) | 1440 | 4410 | 5441 | 5442 | 5443 | 5444 |
| S(4,5) | 1450 | 4410 | 5451 | 5452 | 5453 | 5454 |
| S(4,6) | 1460 | 4410 | 5461 | 5462 | 5463 | 5464 |

**TABLE 10-3**

STRING VARIABLE ASSIGNMENTS AND PROGRAM LINE NUMBERS FOR THE COUNTRY GAL ARM SEGMENTS (see Fig. 10–4)

| *Segment* | *Draw* | *Pack* | *DATA* |
|---|---|---|---|
| S(5,1) | 1510 | 4510 | 5511 5512 |
| S(5,2) | 1520 | 4510 | 5521 5522 |
| S(5,3) | 1530 | 4510 | 5531 5532 |
| S(5,4) | 1540 | 4510 | 5541 5542 |
| S(5,5) | 1550 | 4510 | 5551 5552 |
| S(5,6) | 1560 | 4510 | 5561 5562 |

**TABLE 10-4**

STRING VARIABLE ASSIGNMENTS AND PROGRAM LINE NUMBERS FOR THE COUNTRY GAL BRAID SEGMENTS (see Fig. 10–5)

| *Segment* | *Draw* | *Pack* | *DATA* |
|---|---|---|---|
| S(6,1) | 1610 | 4610 | 5610 |
| S(6,2) | 1620 | 4610 | 5620 |
| S(6,3) | 1630 | 4610 | 5630 |
| S(6,4) | 1640 | 4610 | 5640 |

That isn't all she can do, of course. There is a lot of flexibility inherent in this limited-segment animation scheme. There are hundreds of permutations available, and it's all done with the control routine.

Given the information in the preceding figures and tables, see if you can see the function of program lines 120 through 130. What does line 160 do? Lines 180 and 185? They call segment-drawing subroutines in some cases and execute sequences of limited-segment drawings in others.

Once all the segments have been defined as in Listing 10–1, it is up to your imagination and skill with BASIC programming to assemble some sort of desired animation sequence. Play with the programming of the control routine for a while. The poor little gal can be made to do some ridiculous things, and there is no end to the possible performances.

Work on some sequences of your own; you'll learn a lot more from your own successes and failures than you can from a dozen additional pages I might write for you.

The program is expandable, and you can add some animation segments of your own. Why not work out some static images that serve as a backdrop or stage for COUNTRY GAL? There is no need for me to show you how.

## SYNCHRONOUS ANIMATION OF TWO OR MORE FIGURES

In principle, animating two or more figures is no different from animating selected segments of a large, complex figure. There is no difference between the thinking involved in animating a single figure that has six moving parts and animating six independent figures that each have one moving part.

Once the basic figures and their respective limited-segment parts are defined and translated into BASIC programs, all that remains is to write a control routine that coordinates the animation of all the figures and their moving segments. The fact that the drawing subroutines apply to several different figures is irrelevant.

The matter of animating more than one independent figure forces a certain problem into the limelight. A microprocessor system, namely your TRS-80 home computer, is capable of carrying out just one task at a time. Everything must be done in a certain sequence, one step at a time. Sometimes one gets the impression that two or more figures are moved simultaneously, but that is an illusion; those things are simply happening in an extremely fast sequence.

Because everything has to take place one step at a time, control routines must move a segment for one figure, then move a segment for another figure, and so on. A faster-acting figure must be addressed more often than a slower-moving one. Ideally, any attention given one figure should not have any appreciable effect on the animation effect of another. That isn't always easy.

Achieving the illusion of simultaneous animation of two or more figures is a topic that occupies the remainder of this chapter. Let's begin with a specific example.

### PROJECT 10–3

Type Listing 10–3 into your system, then do a RUN. If you have copied the DATA listing properly, you will get an OK message. Otherwise you will get a DATA ERROR message and you must double-check the DATA listings and make the necessary corrections.

```
10 REM ** PROJECT 10-3
15 REM          DOG AND CAT DATA
20 CLEAR 512:DEFSTR F,S
25 CLS:PRINT @ 410,"DOG AND CAT"
100 REM ** CHECKSUM ROUTINE
115 T=0
120 READ A
125 ON ERROR GOTO 135
130 T=T+A:GOTO 120
```

```
135 IF T<>12567 THEN PRINT "DATA ERROR":END
140 PRINT "DATA OK":END
1000 REM ** DRAWING SUBROUTINES
1100 REM        DOG -- FRAME 1
1101 FOR L=1 TO 3:PRINT @ D1+64*(L-1),F(1,L);:NEXT L:RETURN
1109 REM        DOG SEGMENTS
1110 PRINT @ D1+64,S(1,1);:RETURN
1120 PRINT @ D1+64,S(1,2);:RETURN
1130 PRINT @ D1,S(1,3);:RETURN
1140 PRINT @ D1,S(1,4);:RETURN
1150 PRINT @ D1,S(1,5);:RETURN
1160 PRINT @ D1,S(1,6);:RETURN
1170 PRINT @ D1,S(1,6);:RETURN
1200 REM        CAT -- FRAME 2
1201 FOR L=1 TO 4:PRINT @ D2+64*(L-1),F(2,L);:NEXT L:RETURN
1209 REM        CAT SEGMENTS
1210 PRINT @ D2+128,S(2,1);:RETURN
1220 PRINT @ D2+128,S(2,2);:RETURN
1230 PRINT @ D2+128,S(2,3);:RETURN
1240 PRINT @ D2+128,S(2,4);:RETURN
1250 PRINT @ D2,S(2,5);:RETURN
1260 PRINT @ D2,S(2,6);:RETURN
1270 PRINT @ D2+192,S(2,7);:RETURN
1280 PRINT @ D2+192,S(2,8);:RETURN
1290 PRINT @ D2+192,S(2,9);:RETURN
4000 REM ** STRING-PACKING SUBROUTINE
4100 REM        DOG -- FRAME 1
4102 L=1
4103 GOSUB 4900:F(1,L)=F:IF A=0 THEN L=L+1:GOTO 4103
4109 REM        DOG SEGMENTS
4110 FOR N=1 TO 6:GOSUB 4900:S(1,N)=F:NEXT N
4200 REM        CAT -- FRAME 2
4202 L=1
4203 GOSUB 4900:F(2,L)=F:IF A=0 THEN L=L+1:GOTO 4203
4209 REM        CAT SEGMENTS
4210 FOR N=1 TO 9:GOSUB 4900:S(2,N)=F:NEXT N
4895 RETURN
4900 F=""
4905 READ A:IF A=0 OR A=1 THEN RETURN
4910 IF A>0 THEN F=F+CHR$(A):GOTO 4905
4915 READ B:F=F+STRING$(ABS(A),B):GOTO 4905
5000 REM ** DATA LISTINGS
5100 REM        DOG -- FRAME 1
5101 DATA 149,199,184,191,172,-2,176,144,0
5102 DATA -8,191,135,-4,143,128,0
5103 DATA 191,176,197,191,176,197,1
5109 REM        DOG SEGMENTS
5110 DATA -9,25,-4,143,128,1
5120 DATA -9,25,143,191,-2,179,128,1
5130 DATA -10,25,172,1
5140 DATA -10,25,188,1
5150 DATA 149,128,1
5160 DATA 152,129,1
5200 REM        CAT -- FRAME 2
5201 DATA 207,0
5202 DATA 128,176,184,176,200,191,131,129,0
5203 DATA 130,143,142,175,189,188,-7,191,194,0
5204 DATA 195,160,191,129,197,187,151,197,1
5209 REM        CAT SEGMENTS
5210 DATA 25,143,1
```

*(cont.)*

```
5220 DATA 25,131,1
5230 DATA -2,25,142,1
5240 DATA -2,25,143,1
5251 DATA -11,25,196,26,-4,24
5252 DATA 128,191,131,129,1
5261 DATA -11,25,-2,188,26,-2,24
5262 DATA -2,191,194,1
5270 DATA 195,160,1
5280 DATA 128,140,135,163,1
5290 DATA 130,-2,131,163,1
```

**LISTING 10-3** Checksum routine, drawing subroutines, string-packing subroutine, and DATA listings for the dog and cat animation; refer to Project 10-3

Save the program on tape or disk; you will need it again later in this section.

The program deals with the two figures shown in Fig. 10-6. The cat and dog are shown in their standard positions. The dog figure, FRAME 1, is packed into string variables F(1,1) through F(1,3) by program lines 4102 and 4103, and it uses DATA from lines 5101 through 5103. That dog frame is drawn by calling the drawing subroutine at program line 1101.

The main cat figure, FRAME 2, is packed into string variables F(2,1) through F(2,4). See the packing instructions in lines 4202 and 4203, and the DATA in lines 5201 through 5204.

The programming equips the dog figure with three moving segments: tail, eye, and mouth. The cat has four moving segments: tail, eye, mouth, and forepaw. Thus the dog can wag its tail, blink its eye, and bark; the cat can blink, puff up its tail, open its mouth, and strike out at the dog with a forepaw. Those individual segments aren't shown on the drawing, but Table 10-5 can help you identify their fairly simple configurations.

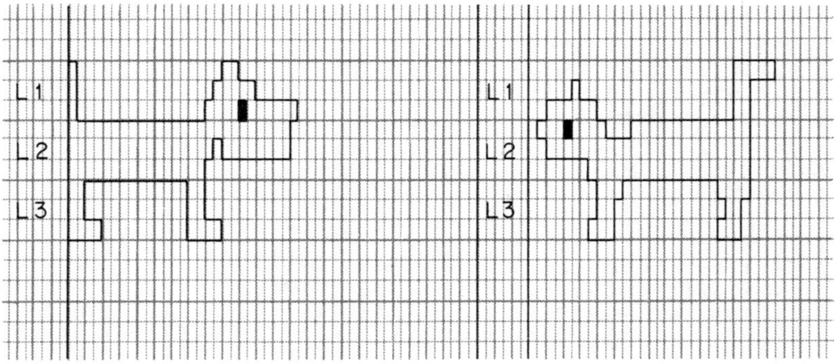


**FIGURE 10-6** Worksheet drawings for independent dog and cat figures

**TABLE 10-5**
SEGMENT FUNCTIONS, VARIABLE ASSIGNMENTS, AND PROGRAM LINE NUMBERS FOR THE DOG AND CAT FIGURES

| *Function* | *Variable* | *Draw* | *Pack* | *DATA* |
|---|---|---|---|---|
| Close dog's mouth | S(1,1) | 1110 | 4110 | 5110 |
| Open dog's mouth | S(1,2) | 1120 | 4110 | 5120 |
| Open dog's eye | S(1,3) | 1130 | 4110 | 5130 |
| Close dog's eye | S(1,4) | 1140 | 4110 | 5140 |
| Straighten dog's tail | S(1,5) | 1150 | 4110 | 5150 |
| Bend dog's tail | S(1,6) | 1160 | 4110 | 5160 |
| Close cat's mouth | S(2,1) | 1210 | 4210 | 5210 |
| Open cat's mouth | S(2,2) | 1220 | 4210 | 5220 |
| Open cat's eye | S(2,3) | 1230 | 4210 | 5230 |
| Close cat's eye | S(2,4) | 1240 | 4210 | 5240 |
| Bend cat's tail | S(2,5) | 1250 | 4210 | 5250 |
| Puff up cat's tail | S(2,6) | 1260 | 4210 | 5260 |
| Lower cat's paw | S(2,7) | 1270 | 4210 | 5270 |
| Medium raise cat's paw | S(2,8) | 1280 | 4210 | 5280 |
| High raise cat's paw | S(2,9) | 1290 | 4210 | 5290 |

According to the table, getting the dog to blink an eye is a matter of calling subroutines 1140 and 1130 in succession. The former subroutine closes the dog's eye, and the latter opens it again. If you want to raise the cat's paw, call subroutines 1280 and 1290. To lower it, call 1280 and 1270 in that order.

Remember that the main topic under discussion here is creating the illusion of simultaneous animation of two (or more) independent figures. Try Project 10-4.

If the program is properly loaded, you should see the dog figure wagging its tail and blinking its eye. The cat is simply standing there blinking its eye. You should have the impression that the two figures are being animated independently—there is no apparent correspondence between the position of the dog's tail and the blinking of the two creatures' eyes. There is, however, an underlying synchronization of the activity; the use of random functions tends to cover it up.

## PROJECT 10–4

Rewrite the initialization and control routines from Listing 10–3 to make them conform to this version. Actually, the instructions in Listing 10–4 are added to the drawing subroutines, string-packing subroutine, and DATA listings of the previous program.

```
10 REM ** PROJECT 10-4
15 REM          DOG AND CAT -- SEQUENCE 1
20 CLEAR 512:DEFSTR F,S
25 CLS:PRINT @ 410,"DOG AND CAT"
30 GOSUB 4000
100 REM ** CONTROL ROUTINE
105 D1=465:D2=421
110 CLS:GOSUB 1100:GOSUB 1200
115 GOSUB 1160
120 BD=RND( 10 ):BC=RND( 10 )
125 IF BD<3 THEN GOSUB 1140
130 T=10:GOSUB 950:GOSUB 1130
135 GOSUB 1150
140 IF BC<3 THEN GOSUB 1240
145 T=10:GOSUB 950:GOSUB 1230
150 GOTO 115
950 FOR TD=0 TO T:NEXT TD:RETURN
```

**LISTING 10-4** Initialization and control routines to be added to Listing 10-3 as described in Project 10-4

A line-by-line analysis of this control routine can be quite instructive at this point.

Line 105: Set the displacement values for the two figures. Here, D1 sets the displacement value, or screen position, for the dog. Variable D2 is the displacement value for the cat figure.

Line 110: Clear the screen and draw the two figures in their standard positions, as they appear in Fig. 10-6.

Line 115: Bend the dog's tail. Doing that GOSUB 1160 bends the tail inward, marking the first of a two-phase tail-wagging sequence.

Line 120: Pick a pair of random numbers that will determine whether or not each creature will blink its eyes during the current operating cycle. Variable BD applies to the dog, and BC applies to the cat.

Line 125: If the value of BD is less than three (out of a possible ten), close the dog's eye.

Line 130: Do a short, fixed time delay, then open the dog's eye.

Line 135: Straighten the dog's tail to complete the two-phase, tail-wagging sequence.

Line 140: If the value of BC is less than three, close the cat's eye.

Line 145: Do a short, fixed time delay, then open the cat's eye.

Line 150: Repeat the sequence from the beginning.

The underlying synchronization of the routine ought to be more apparent now. Consider, for example, the two-phase sequence for making the dog wag its tail. Line 115 bends the tail forward and line 135 straightens it out. Those two program lines are inevitably executed with every operating cycle. Now notice lines 125 and 130, two of the lines tucked in between the tail-wagging sequence. If the dog is to blink its eye, that blinking always takes place between the time the tail is bent and then straightened out. The eye blinking for the dog is tightly synchronized to its tail wagging. Were it not for the random function regarding whether or not the eye should be blinked, you would see the synchronization more clearly—every tail motion would be coupled with an eye blink—but the program is written such that there is only a two-out-of-ten chance that the dog will blink its eye during a given cycle, and that random feature covers the synchronization rather nicely.

Furthermore, the cat blinks its eye only after the dog's tail-wagging cycle is over. Again, if it weren't for the random function regarding whether or not the cat should blink its eye on a given cycle, you would see the cat blink after each one of the dog's tail-wagging cycles.

Thus, the use of random functions goes a long way toward hiding the fact that the two figures and their individual segments are tightly synchronized. Otherwise the whole animation would have an unsatisfactory "mechanical" appearance.

Another important feature of this animation sequence is its timing. The eyes must blink faster than the dog's tail wags. Notice how that is achieved without any apparent interrupting of the animation.

First see how the eyes for both the dog and cat are held closed for a short, fixed interval. The dog's eye, for instance, is closed by the last statement in program line 125. Line 130 then does the short, eye-closed, delay and then opens the dog's eye by the last statement in that same line.

The blinking of the cat's eye is carried out in exactly the same fashion in program lines 140 and 145.

Thus the eye-blinking effect for both figures is timed by a prescribed figure, variable T, but there is no apparent delay inserted for timing the dog's tail wagging—an effect that is supposed to run even more slowly than the eye blinks.

The tail-wagging animation is timed in a more indirect way. The tail is set to one position by the statement in line 115, then it is set to the straight-up position later in the program at line 135. In between those two instructions you will find the eye-blink delay (line 130), which is executed whether the dog's eye is blinking or not. There is thus a built-in delay between lines 115 and 135, a delay that is set not only by the value of T in line 30, but by the execution time of the other BASIC statements in that part of the program.

There is yet another delay from the time the dog's tail is straightened out and then bent again. That is the cumulated delays between program line 135 and 115, a cycle that is made possible by the GOTO statement in line 150. It turns out that that delay interval is very much the same as the one between lines 115 and 135. Since both delays are longer than the eye-blinking delays, it figures that the dog's tail wags more slowly than the critters blink their eyes.

Where would you add more delays in order to slow down the tail wagging without affecting the duration of the eye blinks? How would you restructure the program so that the tail wagging could run faster without affecting the eye blinks?

## PROJECT 10–5

Reload Listing 10–3 from tape or disk, then add the program lines shown in Listing 10–5.

```
10 REM ** PROJECT 10-5
15 REM          DOG AND CAT -- SEQUENCES 1 AND 2
20 CLEAR 512:DEFSTR F,S
25 CLS:PRINT @ 410,"DOG AND CAT"
30 GOSUB 4000
100 REM ** CONTROL ROUTINE
105 D1=465:D2=421
110 CLS:GOSUB 1100:GOSUB 1200
115 FOR R1=0 TO RND(50)
120 GOSUB 1160
125 BD=RND(10):BC=RND(10)
130 IF BD<3 THEN GOSUB 1140
135 T=10:GOSUB 950:GOSUB 1130
140 GOSUB 1150
145 IF BC<3 THEN GOSUB 1240
150 T=10:GOSUB 950:GOSUB 1230
155 NEXT R1
160 FOR R2=0 TO RND(50)
165 MD=RND(10):BC=RND(10)
170 IF MD<3 THEN GOSUB 1120:GOSUB 1140
175 IF BC<3 THEN GOSUB 1240
180 T=10:GOSUB 950:GOSUB 1230
185 T=25:GOSUB 950:GOSUB 1110:GOSUB 1130
190 NEXT R2
195 GOTO 115
950 FOR TD=0 TO T:NEXT TD:RETURN
```

**LISTING 10-5** Initialization and control routine to be added to Listing 10-3 as described in Project 10-5

The sequence from the previous project is included in this listing, but now it runs only for a random number of cycles as determined by the statement in line 115. That first sequence now occupies lines 115 through 155. The new, second sequence is found between lines 160 and 195.

That second sequence causes the dog to bark at the cat at random intervals, closing its eye with every bark. The cat is nonplused, however. The cat still stands there, blinking its eyes at random intervals while the dog goes crazy. Here is a line-by-line analysis of the second animation sequence:

Line 165: Pick a pair of random numbers that will determine whether or not the dog will bark and the cat will blink its eyes during the current operating cycle. Variable MD applies to the dog's bark, and BC applies to the cat's blink.

Line 170: If the dog is supposed to bark (two chances out of ten), open its mouth and close its eye.

Line 175: If the cat is supposed to blink its eye, close the cat's eye.

Line 180: Do a short, fixed time delay, then open the cat's eye to end the blink cycle.

Line 185: Do a longer, fixed time delay, and then close the dog's mouth and open its eye to complete the barking cycle.

Line 190: Repeat the second segment.

The dog's barking and the cat's blinking are again synchronized through this routine, but as in the first case, the element of randomness eliminates the undesirable effect of "mechanical" behavior. Indeed, there seems to be no observable correspondence between the barking and blinking.

The timing of the barking sequence is quite different from the tail-wagging sequence in the first part of the program. When and if the dog's mouth is opened in line 170, there are two well-defined delays that always take place until the mouth is closed again. See those delays at the beginning of lines 180 and 185. The delay in line 180 is used directly to time the cat's eye-blinking operation, and the delay in line 185 adds more time for the dog's mouth to be open.

In this particular instance, tinkering with the time delay in line 185 can affect the barking effect without having the least effect on the cat's blinking. It is a more straightforward timing situation than the one required for the tail-wagging in the first sequence.

The synchronization of the events is masked by the random elements of the routine, but it is nevertheless an integral part of the scheme. Notice, for example, that the cat can blink its eyes only during the time the dog has an opportunity to open its mouth. The fact that the dog's mouth might or might not be open at the moment covers the synchronism of the matter.

The clever application of time delays, the arrangement of limited-segment framing and, above all, the use of random elements of behavior go a long way toward creating satisfying animations of two or more figures on the screen. But, alas, there are animation situations where covering up an underlying synchronism of the activity is very difficult or virtually impossible. Those situations call for doing away with the synchronized programming and running the two or more figures as entirely independent elements. That is asynchronous programming—the topic of the next section.

## ASYNCHRONOUS ANIMATION OF TWO OR MORE FIGURES

A computer can execute only one instruction at a time, so it is technically impossible to animate two or more figures simultaneously. A computer can run instructions quite quickly, however, so it is possible to create the illusion of animating figures simultaneously. In the previous section, animation control was switched back and forth between two different figures; a few simple steps were performed on one figure, then a few on the other. The programs were written so that the switching activity was synchronized, or bound into a tight sequential pattern. The fact that the figures were following a sequential, synchronous pattern was rather nicely covered by the use of some random selection of animation effects.

Not all multiple-figure animation sequences can be synchronized that way, though. There are situations where it is very difficult and, indeed, impossible to apply that technique effectively. A case in point is one where the animation sequence for one of the figures requires a relatively long time delay that must be executed while other figures are still performing. Generally speaking, the problem is one of controlling each figure independently. It is a matter of simulating the effect of running more than one animation program with an equal number of independent microprocessors. The technique is sometimes called *asynchronous multiplexing;* in the context of this book, we will call it *asynchronous animation*—totally independent animation of two or more figures.

Suppose you have two figures you want to control independently. Whatever one figure is doing at the moment must have absolutely no effect on the status of the other. Simple animation sequences for two such figures are outlined in Table 10–6. For the moment, regard them as wholly independent sets of programs.

The animation sequence for the first figure has four basic steps: draw a couple of segments, get a random value, draw the original segments again if X is equal to 1, or else draw two other segments and return to the start. A BASIC version of that sequence is shown with line number 100 through 120. It is a very simple control routine.

The second figure goes through a five-step control routine: draw a segment, get a random value for variable Y, go to Step 5 and draw a second segment if Y is equal to 1, do a fixed time delay if Y is not equal to 1, and then draw the second segment before looping back to the start of that

**TABLE 10-6**

TWO INDEPENDENT ANIMATION SEQUENCES; A VERBAL DESCRIPTION AND BASIC PROGRAMMING FOR IMPLEMENTING THE OPERATIONS

*FIGURE 1*

| Operation | | Basic Programming |
|---|---|---|
| Step 1 | Draw segments 1.1 and 1.2 | 100 GOSUB 1100:GOSUB 1200 |
| Step 2 | Get a random value for X | 105 X = RND(2) |
| Step 3 | If X is equal to 1, go back to Step 1 | 110 IF X = 1THEN 100 |
| Step 4 | Draw segments 1.3 and 1.4, and go back to Step 1 | 115 GOSUB 1300:GOSUB 1400<br>120 GOTO 100 |

*FIGURE 2*

| Operation | | Basic Programming |
|---|---|---|
| Step 1 | Draw segment 2.1 | 200 GOSUB 2100 |
| Step 2 | Get a random value for Y | 205 Y = RND(2) |
| Step 3 | If Y is equal to 1, go to Step 5 | 210 IF Y = 1 THEN 220 |
| Step 4 | Do a short, fixed time delay | 215 FOR T = 0 TO 50:NEXT T |
| Step 5 | Draw segment 2.2, and go back to Step 1 | 220 GOSUB 2200<br>225 GOTO 200 |

routine. The BASIC version uses program lines 200 through 225. That, too, is a simple control routine.

Both examples assume their respective drawing subroutines are in the system, even though they aren't shown here. Doing a RUN 100 will put figure 1 through its routine, and doing a RUN 200 will put the second figure through its paces. The animation situation, however, calls for running these two animation sequences simultaneously *and independently.* The routine for the first figure has to run without regard for the function of the programming for the second figure. At one moment, the computer can be running Step 1 for figure 1 while running Step 3 for figure 2. Some time later, the computer should be able to run Step 1 for figure 1 again, but while running Step 2 for figure 2. The two routines must not be synchronized in any way at all. The programming must be written in such a way that the two routines run asynchronously. Table 10–7 shows how such a control routine is developed.

The listing in Table 10–7A executes the series of operations for the first figure. The operation is divided into four distinct phases, and each phase is carried as a subroutine. In this particular case, variable P1 is the phase counter; it always carries the value of the phase that is to be executed. Line 100 shows P1 being initialized to 1. That means the sequence always starts with the operations for phase 1. According to the statement in line 105, having P1 equal to 1 sends control down to the subroutine at line 500. That subroutine draws two segments, sets P1 to 2, and then returns operation to line 110. Line 110 simply loops control back to line

**TABLE 10-7**

EVOLUTION OF SOME ASYNCHRONOUS PROGRAMMING FOR TWO INDEPENDENT FIGURES DESCRIBED IN TABLE 10-6: (A) FIRST FIGURE'S PROGRAMMING; (B) SECOND FIGURE'S PROGRAMMING; (C) THE FINISHED, COMPOSITE PROGRAM

```
100 P1=1
105 ON P1 GOSUB 500,505,510,515
110 GOTO 105
500 GOSUB 1100:GOSUB 1200:P1=2:RETURN
505 X=RND(2):P1=3:RETURN
510 IF X=1 THEN P1=1:RETURN
511 P1=4:RETURN
515 GOSUB 1300:GOSUB 1400:P1=1:RETURN
```

A

```
200 P2=1
205 ON P2 GOSUB 550,555,560,565,570
210 GOTO 205
550 GOSUB 2100:P2=2:RETURN
555 Y=RND(2):P2=3:RETURN
560 IF Y=1 THEN P2=5:RETURN
561 T2=0:P2=4:RETURN
565 T2=T2+1:IF T2=>50 THEN P2=5:RETURN
566 P2=4:RETURN
570 GOSUB 2200:P2=1:RETURN
```

B

```
100 P1=1:P2=1
105 ON P1 GOSUB 500,505,510,515
110 ON P2 GOSUB 550,555,560,565,570
115 GOTO 105
500 GOSUB 1100:GOSUB 1200:P1=2:RETURN
505 X=RND(2):P1=3:RETURN
510 IF X=1 THEN  P1=1:RETURN
511 P1=4:RETURN
515 GOSUB 1300:GOSUB 1400:P1=1:RETURN
550 GOSUB 2100:P2=2
555 Y=RND(2):P2=2:RETURN
560 IF Y=1 THEN P2=5:RETURN
561 T2=0:P2=4:RETURN
565 T2=T2+1:IF T2>=50 THEN P2=5:RETURN
566 P2=4:RETURN
570 GOSUB 2200:P2=1:RETURN
```

C

105, where, with P1 now equal to 2, control is sent to the subroutine at line 505.

Line 505 picks a random value for X, sets P1 equal to 3, and ultimately returns control to line 105 again. This time, P1 is equal to 3, so line 105 sends the system to the subroutine that begins at line 510.

Follow the programming in Table 10-7A all the way through, and you will see that it executes the same series of steps that are outlined for the first figure in Table 10-6. Every phase of the operation is carried by a subroutine that executes the steps in that particular operation and then sets the phase counter to the number representing the next operation to be performed. The ON . . . GOSUB line is home base for all the activity; that line, working in conjunction with the phase counter, points to the next series of steps to be performed.

Table 10-7B shows a similar sort of control routine for the second figure in Table 10-6. Run through the entire cycle, taking special note of how the time delay is executed—how variable T2 is allowed to increment until it is greater than or equal to 50.

Thus far in the analysis, the two routines run one at a time; doing a RUN 100 executes the series of operations for the first figure, and doing a RUN 200 runs the second figure.

The listing in Table 10-7C completes the task of creating a bit of asynchronous animation. There are no changes in the phase subroutines in lines 500 through 570. The steps the figures are to undergo are not changed. But look at lines 100 through 115.

Line 100 starts both figures with their respective phase-1 operations. Line 105 then causes figure 1 to execute its phase-1 operation; when that is done, line 110 causes figure 2 to execute its phase-1 operation. After that, there is no guarantee the two figures will ever be doing their phase-1 operations during the same multiplexing cycle again. They can run entirely independent of one another. That is the essence of asynchronous animation.

## PROJECT 10-6

Load Listing 10-3 into your system, then add the initialization and control routines as shown in Listing 10-6.

```
10 REM ** PROJECT 10-6
15 REM          DOG AND CAT -- SEQUENCES 1,2 AND 3
20 CLEAR 512:DEFSTR F,S
25 CLS:PRINT @ 410,"DOG AND CAT"
30 GOSUB 4000
100 REM ** CONTROL ROUTINE
105 D1=465:D2=421
110 CLS:GOSUB 1100:GOSUB 1200
```

(cont.)

```
115 FOR R1=0 TO RND(50)
120 GOSUB 1160
125 BD=RND(10):BC=RND(10)
130 IF BD<3 THEN GOSUB 1140
135 T=10:GOSUB 950:GOSUB 1130
140 GOSUB 1150
145 IF BC<3 THEN GOSUB 1240
150 T=10:GOSUB 950:GOSUB 1230
155 NEXT R1
160 FOR R2=0 TO RND(50)
165 MD=RND(10):BC=RND(10)
170 IF MD<3 THEN GOSUB 1120:GOSUB 1140
175 IF BC<3 THEN GOSUB 1240
180 T=10:GOSUB 950:GOSUB 1230
185 T=25:GOSUB 950:GOSUB 1110:GOSUB 1130
190 NEXT R2
195 GOSUB 1260
200 DP=1:CP=1
205 FOR R3=0 TO RND(50)
210 ON DP GOSUB 500,505,510,515,520
215 ON CP GOSUB 550,555,560,565,570
220 NEXT R3
225 GOSUB 1100:GOSUB 1200
230 GOTO 115
500 MD=RND(10):DP=2:RETURN
505 IF MD<3 THEN DP=3:RETURN
506 DT=0:DP=4:RETURN
510 GOSUB 1120:GOSUB 1140:DT=0:DP=4:RETURN
515 DT=DT+1
516 IF DT>1 THEN DP=5 ELSE DP=4
517 RETURN
520 GOSUB 1110:GOSUB 1130:DP=1:RETURN
550 PC=RND(10):CP=2:RETURN
555 IF PC<3 THEN CP=3:RETURN
556 CP=1:RETURN
560 FOR M=1 TO 4
561 ON M GOSUB 1220,1240,1280,1290
562 NEXT M
563 CT=0:CP=4:RETURN
565 CT=CT+1
566 IF CT>25 THEN CP=5 ELSE CP=4
567 RETURN
570 FOR M=1 TO 4
571 ON M GOSUB 1280,1270,1230,1210
572 NEXT M
573 CP=1:RETURN
950 FOR TD=0 TO T:NEXT TD:RETURN
```

**LISTING 10-6** Initialization and control routine to be used with Listing 10-3 as described in Project 10-6

The figures are the dog and cat that were featured in some earlier projects. The first two sequences, program lines 115–190, run exactly as before. A third animation sequence—an asynchronous one—is added at program lines 195 through 573.

Line 195 puffs up the cat's tail, and line 200 initializes the phase counters, DP and CP, for the dog and cat sequences, respectively. Line 205 sets up the sequence to run a random number of cycles.

The control lines for the asynchronous operations occupy program lines 210 and 215. Line 210 represents the five-phase operations for the dog, and line 215 is the five-phase sequence for the cat figure. Here is what those subroutines do:

Subroutine 500 (dog's phase 1): Pick a random value for variable MD; set up phase 2.

Subroutine 505 (dog's phase 2): If MD is less than 3, set up phase 3; otherwise, zero the dog's delay time (variable DT) and set up phase 4.

Subroutine 510 (dog's phase 3): Open the dog's mouth, close the dog's eye, zero the dog's delay time, and set up phase 4.

Subroutine 515 (dog's phase 4): Increment the delay time; if DT is greater than 1, then set up phase 5, otherwise set up phase 4 again.

Subroutine 520 (dog's phase 5): Close the dog's mouth, open its eye, set up phase 1 to begin the cycle from the start.

Subroutine 550 (cat's phase 1): Pick a random value for variable PC; set up phase 2.

Subroutine 555 (cat's phase 2): If PC is less than 3, set up phase 3; otherwise, zero the cat's delay time (variable CT) and set up phase 4.

Subroutine 560 (cat's phase 3): Open the cat's mouth, close its eye, and raise its paw; zero the time delay and set up phase 4.

Subroutine 565 (cat's phase 4): Increment the delay time; if CT is greater than 25, then set up phase 5; otherwise set for phase 4 again.

Subroutine 570 (cat's phase 5): Lower the cat's paw, open its eye, close its mouth, and set up to run the entire sequence again from phase 1.

While, indeed, the animation is rapidly switched back and forth between the dog and cat figures, there is no necessary synchronization of their activity through this sequence.

# 11 Moving Figures from Place to Place

Animating complex figures can be a meaningful and rewarding experience, but all of the animation sequences described thus far leave the animated figures in some fixed place on the screen. Animation effects can be greatly enhanced when figure animation is combined with some motion from place to place. Compare the COUNTRY GAL sequences in the previous chapter with the notion of having the figure of a man stroll across the screen. The COUNTRY GAL sequence was a rather complicated animation, but it was an in-place animation—the girl did her singing and dancing at one particular place on the screen. The STROLLING MAN sequence offered later in this chapter adds the dimension of place-to-place motion.

There are three categories of place-to-place figure animation. The simplest deals with single-space graphics; moving figures composed of a single graphic character. An example is moving a graphic–140 square around on the screen. The general procedure is to plot the graphic at some point on the screen, look to a tenative next position on the screen, and if the next position is a desirable one, erase the graphic from its old position and plot it in a new one.

The second type of place-to-place animation involves figures that are made up of two or more graphic symbols; usually there are two or more lines having two or more characters in each line. However, the figure does not change appearance as it moves. The figure of a rocket moving up the screen is an example. The programming must take into account the size and shape of the field that encloses the figure.

Finally, there are multiple-frame animations that cause the figure to change appearance as it moves around on the screen. The procedure is not as straightforward as one might expect; it isn't a simple matter of drawing the figure, setting up its next position on the screen, erasing the entire figure, and then redrawing it at that new place. Erasing the figure before redrawing a new frame at the next position occupies too much computer time, causing even moderately complex figures to flicker in an undesirable fashion. A more subtle erasing procedure is in order, and it is described later in this chapter.

## MOVING SINGLE-CHARACTER FIGURES

Fig. 11-1 is a flowchart for moving a single-character figure from place to place on the screen. The programming first establishes an initial position for the character. Immediately after that, the character is plotted onto the screen, and then the program looks to the next character position. If that next position doesn't carry the figure to some unwanted place on the screen, the program erases the figure from its old position and plots it in the new place. The program loops around and around, effectively moving the character from one place to the next, until the OK condition is no longer satisfied, that is, until the next step turns out to be one that would put the character at some undesirable point on the screen. Then the program comes to an end. That's a general view of the process.

There are a number of approaches to moving a single character, but this is the one used throughout this book. Note some of its features. First, the character is initialized as far as its position is concerned; then it is plotted on the screen. In other words, the character is set up and plotted before the moving routine begins. Once that is done, the graphic begins moving from a well-defined place.

The FIND NEXT POSITION operation is an important one in this scheme. The general idea is to look ahead at the character's next position on the screen before there is any thought of moving it to that point. Anticipating the next move in this fashion leads to smoother graphic control.

Perhaps one of the most important features of the scheme is that the

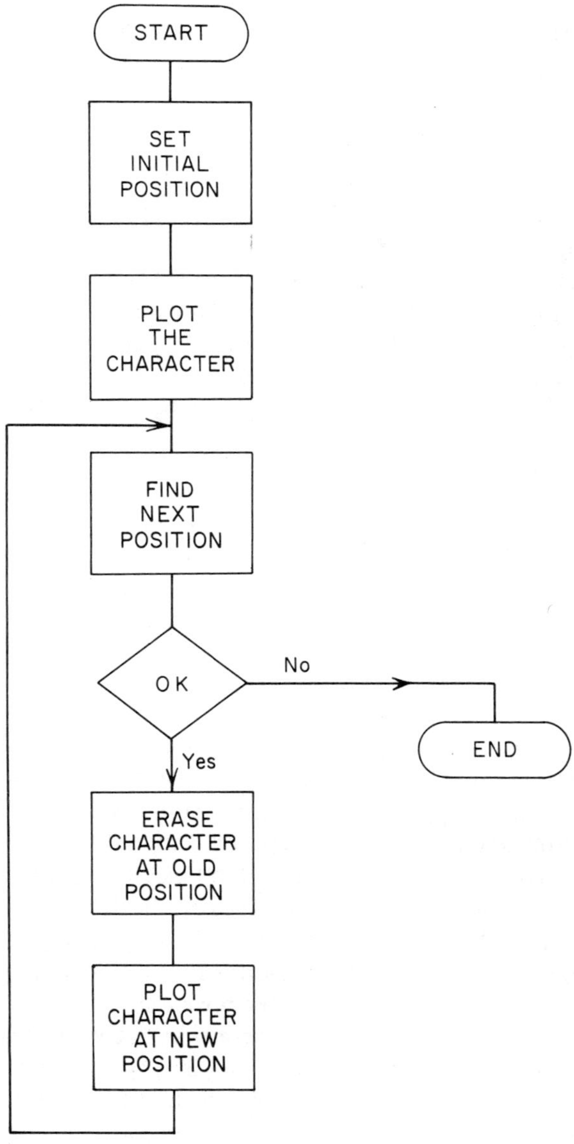


**FIGURE 11-1** Flowchart for moving single-character figures

character is erased from its old position immediately before it is drawn in its next position. It is possible to create the effect of place-to-place motion by having the operations separated by some other steps, but that method risks an impression of figure-flicker that is undesirable. Through all the moving-image projects, you will find the programming for drawing the figure separated from the erasing operation by one short and fast BASIC statement.

### vertical motion

Moving a character up and down on the screen is a matter of adding or subtracting 64 from its present screen position, since vertically adjacent positions on the screen are separated by 64 character spaces. To get a character to move up the screen, subtract 64 from the current screen position, and to get it to move downward, add 64 to the current position. Vertical motion takes place in increments of 64.

A general, up-moving sequence for a single character 191 might go like this:

```
100 CP=992
110 NP=CP-64
120 PRINT @ CP,CHR$(128);
130 CP=NP
140 PRINT @ CP,CHR$(191);
150 GOTO 110
```

Variable CP represents the character's current position on the screen, and variable NP stands for its next position. Line 100 thus sets the character position at 992; that's part of the initialization operation. Then, line 110 looks up one line, setting NP to that point. Line 120 erases the character from its old position—the current CP position—by plotting a space-graphic 128. Variable CP is then equated with NP in line 130, and the newly established CP value is used in line 140 for printing the graphic 191 in its new position. Line 150 simply loops operations back up to the point where the program establishes the next position, NP.

The program isn't complete in the context of the general flowchart in Fig. 11-1, but it does illustrate how subtracting a 64 from the current screen position can set the character up one line from its previous place.

Note how similar a down-moving sequence looks:

```
100 CP=32
110 NP=CP+64
120 PRINT @ CP,CHR$(128);
130 CP=NP
140 PRINT @ CP,CHR$(191);
150 GOTO 110
```

## PROJECT 11-1

Try Listing 11-1. It implements the features in Fig. 11-1 to make an arrow figure rise from the bottom of the screen and stop when it reaches the top.

```
10 REM ** PROJECT 11-1
15 REM          GO UP AND STOP
105 CLS
110 CP=992:BT=0
115 PRINT @ CP,CHR$(91);
120 NP=CP-64
125 IF NP<BT THEN END
130 PRINT @ CP,CHR$(128);
135 CP=NP
140 PRINT @ CP,CHR$(91);
145 GOTO 120
```

**LISTING 11-1** Programming for Project 11-1

Only lines 100 and 110 are different. Line 100 sets the initial screen position near the top of the screen, and line 110 sets up a downward motion by adding 64 to the current screen position.

Line 110 initializes the character position at 992, about halfway across the bottom line of the screen. Variable BT represents the upper boundary of the character's motion. With those two figures thus established, line 115 prints the character in its initial position.

Line 120 looks to the next position, one line higher on the screen from its present one. If that next position has a value that is less than BT—if the next position will carry the character higher on the screen than desired—the program comes to an end. Otherwise, line 130 erases the character from its current position, line 135 sets up the next position, and line 140 plots the character at that new position on the screen.

You can set the initial position of the character at just about any PRINT @ location. Try changing line 110 so that CP is set to 960; then run the program. Try some other initial values for CP: 156, 200, or 1022 for example. It isn't a good idea to try initializing the character from PRINT @ location 1023, the one at the very bottom, right-hand corner of the screen. PRINTing anything at location 1023 causes the display to scroll upward one line.

You can set the upper boundary of the motion by altering the value assigned to variable BT in line 110. Use any of the PRINT AT numbers along the left side of the TRS-80 video worksheet. In the listing, the upper boundary is set along the top line. Setting BT to 0 thus stops the motion anywhere along that line. Setting BT to 256, however, will stop the arrow figure at the fifth line from the top.

If you want to see continuous, vertical wraparound, change line 125 to look like this:

```
125 IF NP<BT THEN PRINT @ CP,CHR$(128);:GOTO 110
```

That modification causes the arrow figure to rise until it hits the specified upper-boundary line; then it is cleared from the screen and started again from its initial position.

The program is written so that the motion takes place at the highest possible speed. Slowing down the motion is a simple matter of inserting a time-delay routine just after the character is printed in its new position. For example:

```
142 FOR T=0 TO 10:NEXT T
```

The longer the counting range for variable T, the slower the character will rise up the screen.

Here is a short summary:

- Set the initial position for the upward-moving character by setting the initial value of CP at some valid PRINT @ location number.
- Set the upper-boundary line by specifying a value for variable BT that is found along the left side of the video worksheet, the PRINT @ values for the beginning of each line.
- Set the speed of motion by inserting a time-delay routine just after the character is printed in its new location.

Of course you ought to avoid a situation where the initial position number is smaller than the upper-boundary number. The character would never find the boundary in such a case, and the program would come to a halt with an FC error.

The program has the same general form as the previous one. In this case, however, the character is initialized near the top of the screen, and a lower boundary, variable BB, marks a line near the bottom of the screen. See program line 110.

Line 115 prints the character in its initial position, line 120 sets the new point downward one line from the current position, and line 125 checks to see whether or not the figure is at the lower boundary line. If the character is at the bottom line, the program goes into a loop at line 125 and latches up until you strike the BREAK key. Otherwise, the program moves the character by erasing it from its current position (line 130), setting the current position equal to the next position (line 135), and printing the character in that position (line 140).

## PROJECT 11-2

Try Listing 11-2. It uses the features of Fig. 11-1 to make an arrow figure drop from the top of the screen and stop when it reaches the bottom.

```
10 REM ** PROJECT 11-2
15 REM           GO DOWN AND STOP
105 CLS
110 CP=32:BB=1022
115 PRINT @ CP,CHR$(92);
120 NP=CP+64
125 IF NP>BB THEN GOTO 125
130 PRINT @ CP,CHR$(128);
135 CP=NP
140 PRINT @ CP,CHR$(92);
145 GOTO 120
```

**LISTING 11-2** Programming for Project 11-2

Experiment with the initial values in program line 110. In that line, CP represents the initial position of the character, and BB is the lower boundary number. Generally, you can specify a lower-boundary line by setting BB equal to one of the PRINT @ numbers along the right side of the video worksheet: 63, 127, 191, and so on. Notice that the lower boundary in Listing 11-2 is specified with a 1022 instead of the 1023 that appears at the end of that line on the video worksheet. This is a necessary exception to the rule for specifying lower-boundary lines because PRINTing anything in location 1023 causes the screen display to scroll upward one line.

Try changing program line 125 to read this way:

```
125 IF NP>BB THEN PRINT @ CP,CHR$(128);:GOTO 110
```

Now the arrow drops to the lower boundary, disappears, and then reappears at the initial position. It is an example of vertical motion wraparound in the downward direction.

Time delays can be inserted just after the character has been printed in its new position, between program lines 140 and 145. The idea, as with the upward-moving arrow project, is to lower the rate of motion.

In summary:

- Set the starting point of a downward-moving character by setting the initial value of CP at some valid PRINT @ location number.
- Set the lower-boundary line by specifying a value for BB that is found along the right side of the video worksheet, a PRINT @ location that marks the end of a line on the screen. *Exception:* Use 1022, instead of 1023, to indicate the bottom line as the lower-boundary line.

- Slow down the motion by inserting a time-delay routine just after printing the character in its new position.

The program cannot run properly if you set the character's initial position at a place that is lower than the lower-boundary line. In the initialization line, program line 110, CP must have a smaller value than BB does.

## PROJECT 11–3

Listing 11–3 causes a small square figure to bounce up and down on the screen. Try it for yourself.

```
10 REM ** PROJECT 11-3
15 REM          BOUNCE VERTICALLY
105 CLS
110 BT=192:BB=831
115 CP=223:J=1
120 PRINT @ CP,CHR$( 140 );
125 NP=CP+64*J
130 IF NP<BT OR NP>BB THEN J=J*-1:GOTO 125
135 PRINT @ CP,CHR$( 128 );
140 CP=NP
145 PRINT @ CP,CHR$( 140 );
150 GOTO 125
```

**LISTING 11–3** Programming for Project 11–3

This program combines the programming features for creating upward and downward motion. Notice how program line 110 establishes both upper and lower boundaries for the motion; those two values set the extreme limits of the character's motion.

Program line 115 sets up the character's initial position—along the upper boundary in this case.

Variable J determines the direction of vertical motion. As is shown by the next-position function in program line 125, the character moves downward whenever J is equal to 1, and upward whenever J is equal to −1. Line 115 thus sets up the character for an initial downward motion.

Line 130 is responsible for sensing when the character reaches one of the two boundary lines. Whenever that happens, the value of J is switched to its opposite sign; the direction of motion is changed.

Tinker with the initial values in program lines 110 and 115 to make sure you understand how the program works and how to modify it for your own purposes. As in the previous examples, slowing down the bouncing effect is a matter of inserting a time-delay routine after the character is printed in its next position, between program lines 145 and 150.

### horizontal motion

Moving a character one space to the right or left is a simple matter of adding or subtracting 1 from the current screen position. Incrementing the current position by one moves the character to the right, and decrementing the position by 1 moves it to the left. That is a simple idea, maybe even simpler than adding or subtracting multiples of 64 to create the effects of vertical motion.

What is a bit more difficult, however, is sensing the left and right boundaries during horizontal motion. The following projects show how to generate the effects of horizontal motion and sense the left and right boundaries.

## PROJECT 11-4

Try Listing 11-4. It sends a right-arrow figure from the left side of the screen to the right side. Once the arrow reaches that right boundary, it stops and the program comes to an end.

```
10 REM ** PROJECT 11-4
15 REM          RIGHT AND STOP
105 CLS
110 CP=128:BR=63
115 PRINT @ CP,CHR$(94);
120 NP=CP+1
125 IF NP>=BR+INT(NP/64)*64 THEN END
130 PRINT @ CP,CHR$(128);
135 CP=NP
140 PRINT @ CP,CHR$(94);
145 GOTO 120
```

**LISTING 11-4** Programming for Project 11-4

Program line 110 sets the initial CP value for the figure and establishes a right-side boundary value, BR. As in the case of the programs for vertical motion, program line 115 prints the character in its initial position. Line 120 then sets up the next screen position. The character is to be moving to the right in this project, so the next position is reckoned as one equal to the current position plus 1.

With the next position thus established, the function in line 125 determines whether or not the character has reached the right boundary line, an imaginary line running vertically along the right-hand edge of the screen. If the next-position value is greater than or equal to the right-boundary function value, the program comes to an end. Otherwise, the character is moved to its next position.

Setting the right-boundary value, variable BR in line 110, is a rather simple procedure. Since the right boundary is an imaginary vertical line, all you have to do is find the TAB number along the top of the video worksheet that marks the position of that line. In the sample listing, BR is set to 63, the rightmost TAB position on the screen. Try changing the value of BR to 31, and you will see the arrow stop moving about halfway across the screen.

To get a continuous left-to-right motion of the arrow character, change line 125 to show:

```
125 IF NP> =BR+INT(NP/64)*64 THEN PRINT @ CP,CHR$(128);:
GOTO 110
```

Now, when the character reaches the right boundary, it is cleared from the screen and started from its initial position once again.

The motion can be slowed by adding a time-delay routine after the character is printed in its new position, between program lines 140 and 145.

## PROJECT 11–5

Listing 11–5 moves the arrow character from an initial position near the right edge of the screen to a left boundary that is established near the left edge. Try it, comparing the results with previous projects.

```
10 REM ** PROJECT 11-5
15 REM          LEFT AND STOP
105 CLS
110 CP=319:BL=0
115 PRINT @ CP,CHR$(93);
120 NP=CP-1
125 IF NP<=BL+INT(NP/64)*64 THEN END
130 PRINT @ CP,CHR$(128);
135 CP=NP
140 PRINT @ CP,CHR$(93);
145 GOTO 120
```

**LISTING 11-5** Programming for Project 11-5

Line 110 sets the initial value for the character and establishes a left boundary, BL. In this particular example, the left boundary is along TAB position 0.

Line 120 is responsible for decrementing the current screen position, thus creating the effect of right-to-left motion. Line 125 senses contact with the left boundary by means of a function that is very similar to the one used in the previous project for sensing right boundary; the only difference is the use of a less-than expression and the BL variable.

See if you can modify line 125 to create a continuous character wraparound effect. Where would you insert a time-delay routine to slow the motion?

## PROJECT 11–6

Enter Listing 11–6. It combines the techniques for doing horizontal motion and sensing the left and right boundaries. In this case, the square of light oscillates back and forth between boundaries set at TAB positions 10 and 54.

```
10 REM ** PROJECT 11-6
15 REM          BOUNCE HORIZONTALLY
105 CLS
110 BL=10:BR=54
115 CP=523:I=1
120 PRINT @ CP,CHR$( 140 );
125 NP=CP+I
130 IF NP<=BL+INT( NP/64 )*64 OR NP>=BR+INT( NP/64 )*64 THEN I=I*-1:GOTO 125
135 PRINT @ CP,CHR$( 128 );
140 CP=NP
145 PRINT @ CP,CHR$( 140 );
150 GOTO 125
```

**LISTING 11-6** Programming for Project 11-6

In the light of previous discussions and projects in this chapter, you should have no difficulty understanding how and why this program works.

## PROJECT 11–7

Listing 11–7 runs a square of light around within a bordered area. The visual impression is that the light is bouncing off the segments of the border figure; the action reminds one of the popular Ping-Pong and Breakout electronic games. Try it.

```
10 REM ** PROJECT 11-7
15 REM          BOUNCING BALL
20 CLEAR 512
25 CLS
30 PRINT @ 0,STRING$( 64,176 );:PRINT @ 896,STRING$( 64,131 );
35 FOR N=0 TO 14:PRINT @ 64*N,CHR$( 191 );:NEXT N
40 FOR N=0 TO 14:PRINT @ 63+64*N,CHR$( 191 );:NEXT N
100 BT=64:BB=895:BL=0:BR=63
105 CP=542:I=1:J=1
110 PRINT @ CP,CHR$( 140 );
115 NP=CP+I+64*J
120 IF NP<BT OR NP>BB THEN J=J*-1:GOTO 115
125 IF NP<=BL+INT( NP/64 )*64 OR NP>=BR+INT( NP/64 )*64 THEN I=I*-1:GOTO 115
130 PRINT @ CP,CHR$( 128 );
135 CP=NP
140 PRINT @ CP,CHR$( 140 );
145 GOTO 115
```

**LISTING 11-7** Programming for Bouncing Ball, Project 11-7

Here is a section-by-section analysis of the program:

Lines 25–40: Clear the screen and draw the outside border figure.
Line 100: Set the four boundary values.
Line 105: Initialize the square's position and direction of motion.
Line 110: Print the square in its initial position.
Line 115: Figure the next screen position.
Line 120: If the square is at either the top or bottom boundary, switch the direction of vertical motion.
Line 125: If the square is at either the right or left boundary, switch the direction of horizontal motion.
Lines 130–140: Erase the character from its current position, set the next position, and redraw the character.
Line 145: Repeat the sequence indefinitely.

### summary of single-character motion

All single-character motion takes place by drawing the character, looking to the next position on the screen, and, if that position is a desirable one, erasing the character from its current position and drawing it in the new one. Horizontal motion occurs when the current position is incremented or decremented by 1; vertical motion takes place when the current position is increased or decreased by 64.

The next-position number is always used for determining whether or not the character has reached a designated top, bottom, left, or right boundary on the screen.

## MOVING MULTIPLE-CHARACTER FIGURES

The procedures for moving a multiple-character figure, a figure composed of two or more graphic characters, are practically identical to the single-character procedures just described. There is one additional feature, however, that must be taken into account: it is a rectangular field of characters, rather than a single character, that must be dealt with.

The variables for the figure's current position and next position are still applicable; those are variables CP and NP, respectively. In our present context, they apply to the first character in the first line of the multiple-character figure.

It is necessary to deal with a second critical place in the multiple-character figure: the last character in the last line of the figure. That place will be designated with variables CD and ND—current position of the diagonal point and next position of the diagonal point. That particular nomenclature reflects the fact that the last character in the last line in a rectangular field is situated diagonally from the first character in the first line. The only exception—a trivial one—is the case where the figure is composed of a single line of characters.

Figure 11-2 shows a rectangular field that just happens to measure 8 × 3; there are three lines having eight characters in each line. The objective is to move that field around on the screen, assuming of course that some meaningful, multiple-character figure is enclosed within it.

Motion variables CP and NP still apply, but they refer only to the first character in the first line of the field. The newly introduced variables play the same roles but refer only to the last character in the last line.

Vertical motion of the field is achieved by displacing the value of CP by 64. Assuming that the remaining characters in the field are keyed to the first one in the first line, adding 64 to the value of CP moves the entire field downward one line, and subtracting 64 from CP moves the entire field upward a line. Incrementing the value of CP by 1 moves the field to the right, and decrementing CP by 1 moves it to the left. Thus the procedure is identical to the one used for moving a single-character figure; the motion of a multiple-character figure is keyed to the motion of the character space located in the upper left-hand corner of the field. It is assumed that the remainder of the field is printed with reference to that one character position.

It is not enough, however, simply to draw the figure field as it moves from place to place. The field must be erased in some fashion prior to being redrawn in its next position. For the current series of projects, the field is erased by printing a field of the same dimensions that is filled with graphic 128s—blank spaces. Therefore if a PRINT @ CP,F(1) draws the figure field at position CP (upper left-hand corner of it), a PRINT @ CP,F(∅) can erase the figure from its current position. That supposes, of course, that string F(∅) is composed entirely of graphic 128s.

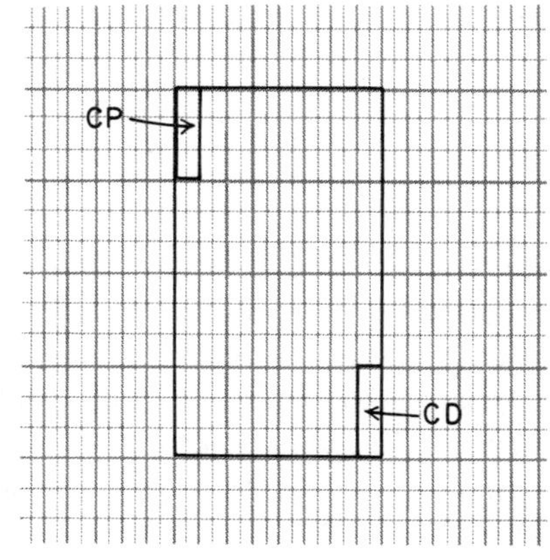


**FIGURE 11-2** An 8 × 3 image frame, showing the upper-left key point (CP) and the lower-right key point (CD)

Thus there are two strings for each field to be moved. One we will call F(1), the one that prints the multi-character figure, beginning from key position CP. The other field, called F(0), prints all spaces, also beginning from position CP.

A move one step to the right is thus accomplished by this sort of programming sequence:

```
PRINT @ CP,F(1);
NP=CP+1
PRINT @ CP,F(0);
CP=NP
PRINT @ CP,F(1);
```

The first statement prints the figure, the second establishes the next screen position, the third statement erases the figure from its current position, and the last two statements effectively draw the figure in its new position.

There is yet another special feature involved in moving multiple-character figures, and that is sensing the boundaries of motion. There is nothing different in this regard when you are working with the top and left boundaries of motion. The key character space, the one represented by values CP and NP, is located in the upper left-hand corner of the moving field; thus its next position is a reliable indicator of whether or not the figure is making contact with an upper or left boundary line. However, the rest of the character field is offset from that key character space in the upper left-hand corner; it is a fact that other parts of the field will make contact with bottom or right-side boundaries before the key character will.

With regard to Fig. 11–2, the purpose of the diagonal key point is to sense contact with a right or bottom boundary. The geometric relationship between the upper-left and lower-right keys in the field is a simple one. The position of the upper-left key is carried through the programming by variable CP, and the position of the diagonal, lower-right key is carried by variable CD. CD is mathematically related to CP in this way:

$$CD = CP + (s-1) + 64*(n-1)$$

Where *s* is the number of characters in each line of the field
*n* is the number of lines in the field.

As an example, the 8 × 3 character field in Fig. 11–2 might be situated on the screen where CP is equal to 500. That being the case, CD is located at PRINT @ location 635. When CP is incremented to position 501 (horizontal motion of the field), the current diagonal value, CD, increments to 636.

Also recall that the next-position variable, NP, plays a vital role in the technique for moving figures on the screen. Its diagonal counterpart, ND, is related to NP by:

ND = NP + (s–1) + 64*(n–1)

Again, *s* refers to the number of characters in each line of the field, and *n* represents the number of lines in the field.

The use of the following BASIC statements should thus make sense at this point:

NP = CP–1:ND = NP + 7 + 64*2
and
CP = NP:CD = ND

The first line is used for setting up the next position for the character field, a field that happens to be moving to the left and is made up of an 8 × 3 character configuration. That line establishes the next point for the upper-left key, NP, and the next point for the lower-right key, ND. Assuming the figure can move that one step to the left, it is cleared from the screen, and then the new positions for CP and CD are established by the second line in that example.

## PROJECT 11–8

Try in Listing 11–8 to draw a simple graphic that looks something like a white picture frame. It is enclosed in a 4 × 2 field, and it oscillates up and down on the screen.

```
10 REM ** PROJECT 11-8
15 REM      COMPLEX FIGURE -- VERTICAL
20 CLEAR 512:DEFSTR F
25 GOSUB 4000
100 REM ** CONTROL ROUTINE
105 CLS
110 CP=32:CD=CP+3+64
115 J=1
120 PRINT @ CP,F(1);
125 NP=CP+64*J:ND=NP+3+64
130 IF NP<0 OR ND>1022 THEN J=J*-1:GOTO 125
135 PRINT @ CP,F(0);
140 CP=NP:DP=ND
145 PRINT @ CP,F(1);
150 GOTO 125
4000 REM ** STRING-PACKING SUBROUTINE
4005 FOR N=0 TO 1
4010 GOSUB 4500:F(N)=F
4015 NEXT N:RETURN
4500 F=""
4505 READ A
4510 IF A=0 OR A=1 THEN RETURN
4515 IF A>1 THEN F=F+CHR$(A):GOTO 4505
4520 READ B:F=F+STRING$(ABS(A),B):GOTO 4505
5000 REM ** DATA LISTINGS
5010 DATA -4,128,26,-4,24,-4,128,1
5110 DATA 191,-2,131,191,26,-4,24,191,-2,176,191,1
```

**LISTING 11-8** Programming for Project 11-8

The program is formatted just like most of the string-packing routines described in earlier chapters. There is an initialization routine in lines 20 and 25, a control routine running from line 105 through 150, a string-packing subroutine that begins at line 4000, and a DATA listing that begins at line 5000.

The program packs two strings, F(Ø) and F(1). F(Ø) is the "erase" frame that fills two lines of four characters apiece; each character is a graphic-128 blank space. Note that it is packed as a single string variable; the control codes for dropping down a line and to the beginning of the next are included in that one string. String F(1) draws the picture-frame image.

The motion is generated by the control routine. It begins by setting the key point, CP, to 32—a spot at the top and near the middle of the screen. That same line also calculates the initial value for the diagonal key, CD. The frame is four characters wide and two lines long; thus CD is reckoned, by equations offered earlier, to be equal to CP plus 67.

Line 115 initializes the vertical motion in a downward direction, and line 120 simply prints the figure in its initial position. Notice that the printing operation refers to the upper-left key position; the figure is drawn in a left-to-right, top-to-bottom fashion, just as all the previous multiple-line drawings have been printed.

Line 125 sets up the next position for the figure, and line 130 tests the new positions to see whether or not the figure is making contact with the top or bottom boundary. And here is a vital point. The top boundary is fixed at zero in this example, and the figure must be at the top of the screen if NP is less than zero. Setting the top boundary is a matter of comparing the value of the NP figure with the top-boundary figure. The bottom boundary is set at 1022, but it is compared with the ND figure. You want the figure to stop moving upward when the top of the figure reaches the top boundary, but you want it to stop moving downward when the bottom of the figure reaches the bottom boundary. Thus, there is the need to compare upper key's next-point value with the upper-boundary value, and the lower key's next-point value with the bottom-boundary value. If the job is done any other way, the figure can slide off the top or bottom of the boundaries.

Line 135 uses the erase frame to clear the entire figure from its current position. Then line 140 adjusts the current key positions to their new positions, and line 145 completes the job by printing the figure in its new position.

Always use the upper-left key point for sensing top and left boundaries, and the lower-right key point for sensing bottom and right boundaries.

At this point you should be able to justify every function and statement in that control routine. See if you can figure out how to change the four boundary values.

## PROJECT 11–9

Enter and RUN Listing 11–9. It uses the same figure but moves it back and forth in a horizontal direction. Take special note of how the conditional statements in line 130 compare the upper-key position with the left-boundary value and the lower-key position with the right-boundary value.

```
10 REM ** PROJECT 11-9
15 REM      COMPLEX FIGURE -- HORIZONTAL
20 CLEAR 512:DEFSTR F
25 GOSUB 4000
100 REM ** CONTROL ROUTINE
105 CLS
110 CP=128:CD=CP+3+64
115 I=1
120 PRINT @ CP,F(1);
125 NP=CP+I:ND=NP+3+64
130 IF NP<=0+INT(NP/64)*64 OR ND>=63+INT(ND/64)*64 THEN I=I*-1:GOTO 125
135 PRINT @ CP,F(0);
140 CP=NP:DP=ND
145 PRINT @ CP,F(1);
150 GOTO 125
4000 REM ** STRING-PACKING SUBROUTINE
4005 FOR N=0 TO 1
4010 GOSUB 4500:F(N)=F
4015 NEXT N:RETURN
4500 F=""
4505 READ A
4510 IF A=0 OR A=1 THEN RETURN
4515 IF A>1 THEN F=F+CHR$(A):GOTO 4505
4520 READ B:F=F+STRING$(ABS(A),B):GOTO 4505
5000 REM ** DATA LISTINGS
5010 DATA -4,128,26,-4,24,-4,128,1
5110 DATA 191,-2,131,191,26,-4,24,191,-2,176,191,1
```

**LISTING 11-9** Programming for Project 11-9

## PROJECT 11–10

Listing 11–10 combines the horizontal and vertical motions from the two previous projects to create the visual impression of a bouncing picture frame. Enter and RUN it.

```
10 REM ** PROJECT 11-10
15 REM          BOUNCING COMPLEX FIGURE
20 CLEAR 512:DEFSTR F
25 GOSUB 4000
100 REM ** CONTROL ROUTINE
105 CLS
110 CP=128:CD=CP+3+64
115 I=1:J=1
120 PRINT @ CP,F(1);
125 NP=CP+I+64*J:ND=NP+3+64
130 IF NP<=0+INT(NP/64)*64 OR ND>=63+INT(ND/64)*64 THEN I=I*-1:GOTO 125
135 IF NP<0 OR ND>1022 THEN J=J*-1:GOTO 125
```

*(cont.)*

```
140 PRINT @ CP,F(0);
145 CP=NP:CD=ND
150 PRINT @ CP,F(1);
155 GOTO 125
4000 REM ** STRING-PACKING SUBROUTINE
4005 FOR N=0 TO 1
4010 GOSUB 4500:F(N)=F
4015 NEXT N:RETURN
4500 F=""
4505 READ A
4510 IF A=0 OR A=1 THEN RETURN
4515 IF A>1 THEN F=F+CHR$(A):GOTO 4505
4520 READ B:F=F+STRING$(ABS(A),B):GOTO 4505
5000 REM ** DATA LISTINGS
5010 DATA -4,128,26,-4,24,-4,128,1
5110 DATA 191,-2,131,191,26,-4,24,191,-2,176,191,1
```

**LISTING 11-10** Programming for Bouncing Complex Figure, Project 11-10

## MOVING ANIMATED FIGURES

For our purposes, a *moving animated figure* is one that changes appearance as it moves from place to place on the screen. Achieving this kind of high-level animation calls for combining the principles of successive framing described earlier in this book with the techniques for moving multiple-character figures.

In principle, it is a straightforward procedure. The task begins by defining the animation frames and packing those frames into string variables. Then you must create one or more erasing frames and pack them into some string variables, too. Finally, you write a control routine that coordinates the drawing of the frames with the principles of figure motion: draw one of the animation frames, set up the next position for the next animation frame, erase the first frame from its position, and draw the next frame in that next position on the screen. Indeed, the difficulty of the task is determined more by the complexity of the figure and its frames than by the animation and motion techniques.

In actual practice, however, there are some potential problems with image flickering. When you are animating figures that are to remain fixed in one place on the screen, you avoid image flickering by applying the technique of limited-segment animation, changing only small portions of the figure at any given moment. However, limited-segment animation is not appropriate when the figure has to move from place to place on the screen; moving just one segment of the figure at a time would distort the image in a wholly unsatisfactory way.

Thus, it would seem that the entire figure—the entire image frame—must be completely erased before the new frame can be drawn in its new position on the screen; and even frames of moderate size require an erasing time that produces an obvious flickering effect.

The way around the flickering difficulty in the case of moving figures is a technique called *trailing-edge* erasing. Instead of erasing an entire frame before drawing a new frame in the next position on the screen, you erase only the edge opposite the direction of the old frame. *The new frame is then drawn over the remaining elements of the old one.* The erasing operation is thus limited to a very few character spaces—those that do not contain any image information when the new frame is drawn.

The technique is perhaps better understood by being shown in a specific example.

## PROJECT 11–11

Use the three animation frames in Fig. 11–3 to create the impression of a man walking from left to right across the screen. Refer to the program in Listing 11–11.

```
10 REM ** PROJECT 11-11
15 REM          STROLLING MAN
20 CLEAR 512:DEFSTR F
25 CLS:PRINT @ 474,"STROLLING MAN"
30 GOSUB 4000
35 CLS
100 REM ** CONTROL ROUTINE
110 CLS
120 CP=512:CD=CP+64*5+9
125 GOSUB 1010
130 FOR S=1 TO 4
135 NP=CP+1:ND=NP+64*5+9
140 IF ND>=63+INT(ND/64)*64 THEN CLS:GOTO 120
145 GOSUB 1001
150 CP=NP:CD=ND
155 ON S GOSUB 1010,1020,1030,1020
160 NEXT S
170 GOTO 130
1000 REM ** DRAWING SUBROUTINES
1001 PRINT @ CP,F(0);:RETURN
1010 PRINT @ CP,F(1);:RETURN
1020 PRINT @ CP,F(2);:RETURN
1030 PRINT @ CP,F(3);:RETURN
4000 REM ** STRING-PACKING SUBROUTINE
4010 FOR N=0 TO 3
4015 F(N)=""
4020 GOSUB 4500
4030 F(N)=F(N)+F
4035 IF A=0 THEN F(N)=F(N)+CHR$(26)+STRING$(10,24):GOTO 4020
4040 NEXT N
4045 RETURN
4500 F=""
4505 READ A
4510 IF A=0 OR A=1 THEN RETURN
4515 IF A>1 THEN F=F+CHR$(A):GOTO 4505
4520 READ B:F=F+STRING$(ABS(A),B):GOTO 4505
4525 RETURN
5000 REM ** DATA LISTING
```

*(cont.)*

```
5001 DATA 128,26,24,128,26,24,128,26,24,128,26,24,128,26,24,128,1
5011 DATA 195,175,183,157,196,0
5012 DATA 195,184,191,148,196,0
5013 DATA 195,171,191,149,196,0
5014 DATA 195,175,191,149,196,0
5015 DATA 195,170,191,151,196,0
5016 DATA 195,-4,131,195,1
5021 DATA 195,175,183,157,196,0
5022 DATA 194,176,184,191,180,196,0
5023 DATA 193,190,151,171,191,151,173,144,194,0
5024 DATA 193,130,131,175,191,189,144,195,0
5025 DATA 195,170,191,159,189,-2,176,193,0
5026 DATA 195,-4,131,195,1
5031 DATA 195,175,183,157,196,0
5032 DATA 193,-2,176,184,191,148,196,0
5033 DATA 130,175,148,171,191,151,143,140,135,131,0
5034 DATA 195,175,191,189,176,195,0
5035 DATA 193,176,188,143,129,130,139,173,-2,176,0
5036 DATA 194,-2,131,129,197,1
```

**LISTING 11-11** Programming for Strolling Man, Project 11-11

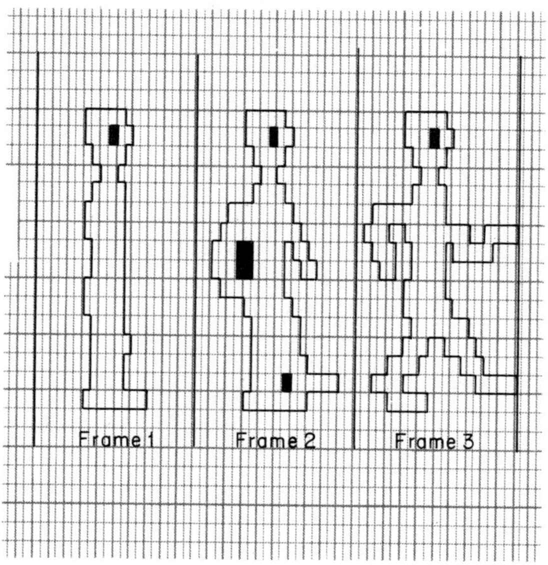


**FIGURE 11-3** Animation frames for Project 11-11

First load the program into your TRS-80 and give it a try so you can see it at work. Double-check the DATA listings, especially, if you have difficulty with the execution of this animation.

The basic walking sequence is generated by drawing of Frames 1, 2, 3, 2, 1 . . . . The motion of this animated figure is to be from left to right, so each frame is drawn after its upper-left key point, variable CP, has been incremented by 1. The overall sequence thus looks like this:

Draw Frame 1.
Increment CP.
Draw Frame 2.
Increment CP.
Draw Frame 3.
Increment CP.
Draw Frame 2.
Increment CP.
Draw Frame 1.
Increment CP.

That sequence is repeated until the figure reaches the right-hand side of the screen. In this particular program, the figure is then restarted from its initial position on the left side of the screen.

Obviously some sort of erasing has to take place before the incrementing and drawing of the next frame. Otherwise the figure would leave behind a trail of graphics that are situated in the first column of graphics on the left side of each frame. To get around that problem, the program uses a Frame 0. It is the trailing-edge erasing frame, and it is made up of six graphic 128s that are lined up vertically. Just prior to incrementing CP, Frame 0 is drawn at the current CP position, and that operation erases only the vertical line of graphics along the left-hand edge of the current frame, which in this case is the trailing edge. If the figure were moving to the left, the trailing edge would be along the right-hand edge of the figure field. If it were moving upward, the trailing edge would be along the bottom, and if the figure were moving downward, the trailing edge would be along the top of the frame.

This particular figure is built into a 10 × 6 field—six lines of ten characters each. Without the trailing-edge erasing technique, the program would have to clear 60 character locations before the next frame could be printed in its next position. Here, however, it is necessary to erase only six character locations, a 10:1 reduction in erasing speed. Thus there is virtually no flickering in the animation/motion sequence.

So this animation sequence actually calls for four frames: the three main drawing frames in Fig. 11–3 plus a trailing-edge erasing frame. If the figure had to move vertically as well, there would be a need for another erasing frame that would clear one line of ten characters at the top or bottom of the frame.

The trailing-edge frame is packed from the DATA in program line

5001. Notice that it is a single string composed of six graphic 128s that are positioned vertically by using the control sequence 26,24. The control 26 drops the cursor down a line, and the 24 backs it up one space. Thus drawing the string that is packed from DATA line 5001—doing a PRINT @ CP,F(0)—erases six successive, vertically arranged character spaces, beginning at screen position CP.

The Frame 1 string, F(1), is packed from DATA in lines 5011 through 5016. The entire field must be defined in each frame. Blank spaces must be represented by graphic codes that clear those spaces, and there can be no skip-over operations such as STRING$(10,25). The field does not have to be completely defined, and skip-over operations are often necessary when you are working with in-place animations and limited-segment animation. But here, every character space within the field must be defined in one way or another. Why? Because with the trailing-edge erasing technique a new figure is drawn over a significant portion of the old one, and leaving some of the character spaces undefined carries the risk of leaving behind some elements of the previous frame.

Using those same important guidelines, Frames 2 and 3 are packed into strings F(2) and F(3), using the DATA in lines 5021 through 5026, and lines 5031 through 5036.

Now notice that line 4035 in the string-packing subroutine is a bit more complicated than it has been in past programs. The idea is to save you the trouble of including a lot of 26, − 10,24 sequences in each DATA line that must be ended with control codes to point to the beginning of the next line in the field. Every time the string-packing subroutine READs a zero, it inserts the control codes for resuming the drawing at the beginning of the next line in the frame or field.

The drawing subroutines in program lines 1000 through 1030 are quite simple. They simply draw their respective string-packed frames and return to the control routine. Actually, there is nothing in the drawing subroutines, string-packing subroutine, and DATA listings that tell one that the figure will be moving from place to place on the screen. That is all handled by the control routine in lines 100 through 170.

Looking over the control routine, you should see that it closely resembles a routine for moving a multiple-character figure from left to right across the screen. Line 110 clears the screen, line 120 sets the initial positions for the upper-left and lower-right key points in the frame, and line 125 draws Frame 1 in that position.

The FOR . . . NEXT statement surrounds the operations in lines 135 through 155. Those operations represent the four phases of the walking cycle. Notice, for example, the ON . . . GOSUB statement in line 155. As S is incremented from 1 through 4, line 155 causes the program to draw Frames 1, 2, 3, and 2 in that sequence.

Line 135 sets the next position for the frame, line 140 tests the position of the lower-right diagonal to see whether or not the figure has reached the right boundary limit of the motion, line 145 does the trailing-edge erasing operation, line 150 equates the current frame position with the tested next-position figures, and line 155 draws the appropriate frame in that new position. Line 160 simply causes the entire framing cycle to start over from Frame 1.

# 12 Keyboard Control and Contact Sensing

After you have mastered the techniques for drawing, animating, and moving figures on the screen, it is perhaps inevitable that you begin thinking about arcade-type games—games that are programmed so that a player can interact with the ongoing animations in some meaningful fashion. Virtually all of the previous discussions have dealt with procedures for setting up prescribed sequences of animation effects, but setting up some games calls for introducing control mechanisms that have not yet been described in much detail.

Any interactive game requires some manual control on the part of the players. The only manual control mechanism available on the standard TRS–80 system is its keyboard, so it should come as no surprise that keyboard control is a vital part of the programming for arcade-type games.

A second kind of control for animated games is contact sensing. Program routines must be able to sense a contact between two different figures, and that contact must eventually lead to an appropriate response.

This chapter deals with the programming for keyboard controls and sensing contact between two figures. It concludes with a simple missile-shooting game that demonstrates some of the control mechanisms.

## KEYBOARD CONTROL

There are three different ways to work with the TRS–80 keyboard from BASIC programs. The two most common ones, those using INPUT and INKEY$ statements, can be used quite effectively under many circumstances. The third technique, directly addressing the keyboard, can be used in any situation requiring a keyboard input; the technique is equally effective through BASIC and machine language programming.

The first project shows how to use the INKEY$ function to initiate some animated activity.

### PROJECT 12–1

Listing 12–1 is a short key-controlled program that "launches" a graphic 191 whenever the RETURN key is depressed. Enter and RUN it.

```
10 REM ** PROJECT 12-1
15 REM          KEY-INITIATED MOTION
20 DEFSTR F
25 F0=CHR$(128):F1=CHR$(191)
100 REM ** CONTROL ROUTINE
105 CLS
110 CP=927:J=0
115 PRINT @ CP,F1
120 IF INKEY$<>CHR$(13) THEN 120 ELSE J=-1
125 NP=CP+64*J
130 IF NP<=0 THEN PRINT @ CP,F0:GOTO 110
135 PRINT @ CP,F0
140 CP=NP
145 PRINT @ CP,F1
150 GOTO 125
```

**LISTING 12-1** Programming for Project 12-1

Upon running this program, you will see a graphic 191 rectangle situated near the bottom middle of the screen. It remains there until you strike the ENTER key. At that moment the "missile" rises toward the top of the screen. Once it reaches the top, it is automatically returned to its initial position, and launching it again is a matter of releasing and striking the ENTER key once again.

Notice in program line 110 that the motion of the figure, variable J, is set to 0. That holds it fixed on the screen until the program reaches line 120.

The ASCII control code for the ENTER key is 13, so as long as the

ENTER key is not depressed, the INKEY$ statement in line 120 continually loops to itself. However, once you strike the ENTER key, motion variable J is set to −1, and the program begins executing from line 125. That portion of the program moves the figure upward until line 130 senses contact with the top of the screen. At that moment, the figure is cleared and control loops back to program line 110, where the whole routine is initialized once again.

Other keys could be used for initiating the activity in this demonstration. Using CHR$(70) in place of CHR$(13) in line 120 would launch the figure when you strike the *F* key. The idea is to use an ASCII code number for the key that is to initiate the action.

In that particular program, program activity is essentially halted at line 120 until the ENTER key is depressed. Halting the entire program until a key depression occurs is not always desirable; it is often necessary to continue some sort of screen activity, then alter the nature of that activity when the key is depressed. That can be accomplished by jumping to some portion of the program other than the line that carries the INKEY$ statement.

A good many experienced TRS-80 programmers believe that the INKEY$ function is usually more troublesome than helpful, however. Also, for in-line game-playing purposes, the INPUT function is unquestionably more troublesome than it's worth. (The INPUT function definitely stops all ongoing activity.) The alternative is to address the keyboard directly.

Table 12-1 shows the decimal addresses and read-only data from the TRS-80's keyboard. Only the lower-case characters are represented here, but that is usually a more-than-adequate listing.

Suppose you want to know whether or not the ENTER key is depressed. According to the table, PEEKing into address location 14440 will turn up a data value of 1 if, indeed, that key (and only that one) is depressed. That feature can be used in the previous program listing by replacing line 120 with this one:

```
120 IF PEEK(14440)<>1 THEN 120 ELSE J=-1
```

Suppose you want to take some action that is determined by the left- and right-arrow keys. If the right-arrow key is depressed, PEEK (14440) will yield a value of 64. If the left-arrow key is depressed, PEEK (14440) will be equal to 32. If both the right- and left-arrow keys are depressed at the same time, PEEK (14440) will turn up a value of 96—the sum of their individual values.

Enter the program and play with it for a while. See if you can work out an INKEY$-type procedure for doing the same thing. It isn't easy.

The direction of motion of the graphic is determined by program lines 120 and 125. Line 120 is satisfied if the left-arrow key is depressed, if

**TABLE 12-1**

KEYBOARD CODES FOR THE LOWER-CASE KEYS

| *Key* | *Peek Addr.* | *Data* |
|---|---|---|
| @ | 14337 | 1 |
| A | 14337 | 2 |
| B | 14337 | 4 |
| C | 14337 | 8 |
| D | 14337 | 16 |
| E | 14337 | 32 |
| F | 14337 | 64 |
| G | 14337 | 128 |
| H | 14338 | 1 |
| I | 14338 | 2 |
| J | 14338 | 4 |
| K | 14338 | 8 |
| L | 14338 | 16 |
| M | 14338 | 32 |
| N | 14338 | 64 |
| O | 14338 | 128 |
| P | 14340 | 1 |
| Q | 14340 | 2 |
| R | 14340 | 4 |
| S | 14340 | 8 |
| T | 14340 | 16 |
| U | 14340 | 32 |
| V | 14340 | 64 |
| W | 14340 | 128 |
| X | 14344 | 1 |
| Y | 14344 | 2 |
| Z | 14344 | 4 |
| 0 | 14352 | 1 |
| 1 | 14352 | 2 |
| 2 | 14352 | 4 |
| 3 | 14352 | 8 |
| 4 | 14352 | 16 |
| 5 | 14352 | 32 |
| 6 | 14352 | 64 |
| 7 | 14352 | 128 |
| 8 | 14368 | 1 |
| 9 | 14368 | 2 |
| : | 14368 | 4 |
| ; | 14368 | 8 |
| , | 14368 | 16 |
| - | 14368 | 32 |
| . | 14368 | 64 |
| / | 14368 | 128 |
| ENTER | 14440 | 1 |
| CLEAR | 14440 | 2 |
| BREAK | 14440 | 4 |
| ↑ | 14440 | 8 |
| ↓ | 14440 | 16 |
| ← | 14440 | 32 |
| → | 14440 | 64 |
| (SPACE) | 14440 | 128 |

## PROJECT 12-2

Try Listing 12-2. It lets you set the horizontal position of a graphic 191, using the left- and right-arrow keys as control keys. Depressing the left-arrow key moves the graphic to the left; it moves at a constant speed as long as that key is depressed and the figure has not reached the extreme left side of the screen. Releasing the key stops the motion. The figure is moved to the right when the right-arrow key is depressed. The motion also stops whenever both keys are depressed at the same time.

```
10 REM ** PROJECT 12-2
15 REM          KEY-CONTROLLED MOTION
20 DEFSTR F
25 F0=CHR$(128):F1=CHR$(191)
100 REM ** CONTROL ROUTINE
105 CLS
110 CP=927:I=0
115 PRINT @ CP,F1;
120 IF PEEK(14440)=32 THEN I=-1:GOTO 135
125 IF PEEK(14440)=64 THEN I=1:GOTO 135
130 GOTO 120
135 NP=CP+I
140 IF NP<=INT(NP/64)*64 OR NP>=63+INT(NP/64)*664 THEN 120
145 PRINT @ CP,F0;
150 CP=NP
155 PRINT @ CP,F1;
160 GOTO 120
```

**LISTING 12-2** Programming for Project 12-2

PEEK (14440) equals 32. That being the case, the horizontal motion vector, I, is set to −1, line 125 sets the next position, line 140 checks for the edges of the screen, and lines 145 through 155 move the figure to its next position if the edge of the screen is not immediately at hand.

The PEEK statement in line 125 is satisfied if the right-arrow key is depressed. Then the horizontal motion vector is set to 1, resulting in motion to the right.

If both keys happen to be depressed at the same time, the PEEK statement will turn up a data value of 96, and neither line 120 nor 125 will be satisfied. In that case, the program defaults to line 130, which loops the program back up to line 120.

Incidentally, if no key is depressed, the PEEKs in lines 120 and 125 will turn up data values of 0, and that satisfies neither of the figure-moving conditions.

Check your understanding of the technique by devising a similar program that uses the up- and down-arrow keys to position the graphic in the vertical direction.

Aside from combining a couple of different keyboard control techniques, the program also shows how two different graphics can be moved

## PROJECT 12-3

Listing 12-3 combines the INKEY$ and keyboard PEEK techniques. Upon running the program, you will see a graphic 191 rectangle with an up-arrow figure perched on top of it. Working the right- and left-arrow keys, you can position those graphics anywhere along the bottom of the screen. Striking the ENTER key "fires" the arrow from its current launch position. The arrow rises until it reaches the top of the screen. After that, the arrow is returned to the launch position, and the assembly can be moved back and forth until the arrow is launched again.

```
10 REM ** PROJECT 12-3
15 REM          ROCKET LAUNCHER
20 DEFSTR F
25 F0=CHR$(128):F1=CHR$(191):F2=CHR$(91)
100 REM ** CONTROL ROUTINE
105 CLS
110 CP(1)=927:CP(2)=CP(1)-64:I=0:J=0
115 PRINT @ CP(1),F1;:PRINT @ CP(2),F2;
120 IF PEEK(14440)=32 THEN I=-1:GOTO 140
125 IF PEEK(14440)=64 THEN I=1:GOTO 140
130 IF INKEY$=CHR$(13) THEN J=-1:GOTO 170
135 GOTO 120
140 NP(1)=CP(1)+I
145 IF NP(1)<=INT(NP(1)/64)*64 OR NP(1)>=63+INT(NP(1)/64)*64 THEN 12
150 PRINT @ CP(1),F0;:PRINT @ CP(2),F0;
155 CP(1)=NP(1):CP(2)=CP(1)-64
160 PRINT @ CP(1),F1;:PRINT @ CP(2),F2;
165 GOTO 120
170 NP(2)=CP(2)+64*J
175 IF NP(2)<=0 THEN PRINT @ CP(2),F0;:CP(2)=CP(1)-64:GOTO 115
180 PRINT @ CP(2),F0;
185 CP(2)=NP(2)
190 PRINT @ CP(2),F2;
195 GOTO 170
```

**LISTING 12-3** Programming for Project 12-3

together under one set of circumstances, then moved independently under another set of circumstances.

The key controls appear in program lines 120, 125, and 130. The PEEK statement in line 120 is sensitive to a depression of the left-arrow key; when it is satisfied, the figures move to the left. Line 125 looks for a depression of the right-arrow key, moving the figures to the right. Line 130 is sensitive to striking the ENTER key, the action that launches the arrow figure.

The figures are defined in line 25. F0 is the clearing figure, F1 represents the graphic 191 "arrow launcher," and F2 is defined as the arrow figure itself. Line 110 initializes the program, using CP(1) as the current position of the launcher and CP(2) as the current position of the arrow. Note that CP(2) is equal to CP(1)−64; that fixes the arrow on the character space directly above the launcher.

Whenever the figures are to be moved to the left or right, lines 120 and 125 send program control down to line 140. At that point, the program sets up the next position for the launcher figure; if it isn't an off-screen position, both figures are erased from their current positions (line 150 in the program), the current values are adjusted to the next-position values (program line 155), and both figures are printed in their new positions (program line 160). Wherever the launcher goes, so goes the arrow.

When the RETURN key is depressed, line 130 is satisfied and the vertical motion vector, J, is set to −1. The program then runs the routine that begins at line 170. That line sets the next position of the arrow figure one line higher on the screen; if the figure has not already reached the top of the screen, it is first erased (program line 180) and then drawn in its new position (program line 190). In this case, control returns to the keyboard-checking lines only after the figure reaches the top of the screen. Once the arrow is launched, there is no stopping it—and no moving the launcher.

## PROJECT 12–4

The program in Listing 12–4 lets you move the graphic horizontally, vertically, and in directions that combine horizontal and vertical motion. The key controls in lines 120 through 127 are the central features of this particular demonstration. Try it for yourself.

```
10 REM ** PROJECT 12-4
15 REM          2-DIMENSIONAL KEY CONTROL DOMO
20 DEFSTR F
25 F0=CHR$(128):F1=CHR$(191)
100 REM ** CONTROL ROUTINE
105 CLS
110 CP=927:I=0:J=0
115 PRINT @ CP,F1;
120 IF PEEK(14440)=8 THEN I=0:J=-1:GOTO 130
121 IF PEEK(14440)=16 THEN I=0:J=1:GOTO 130
122 IF PEEK(14440)=32 THEN I=-1:J=0:GOTO 130
123 IF PEEK(14440)=40 THEN I=-1:J=-1:GOTO 130
124 IF PEEK(14440)=48 THEN I=-1:J=1:GOTO 130
125 IF PEEK(14440)=64 THEN I=1:J=0:GOTO 130
126 IF PEEK(14440)=72 THEN I=1:J=-1:GOTO 130
127 IF PEEK(14440)=80 THEN I=1:J=1:GOTO 130
128 I=0:J=0:GOTO 120
130 NP=CP+I+64*J
135 IF NP<=INT(NP/64)*64 OR NP>=63+INT(NP/64)*64 THEN 120
140 IF NP<=0 OR NP>=1022 THEN 120
145 PRINT @ CP,F0;
150 CP=NP
155 PRINT @ CP,F1;
160 GOTO 120
```

**LISTING 12–4** Programming for Project 12–4

It is possible to modify the program so that the launcher can be moved while the arrow figure is rising, but that would call for some multiplexing routines that would obscure the main points of this demonstration.

Enter this program and give it a try. You should be able to situate the graphic anywhere on the screen you choose. If you save the program on tape or disk, you will save time when working with several other programs suggested in this chapter.

The key-control routines in lines 120 through 127 are responsible for setting the horizontal and vertical motion vectors to values that reflect the directions of the four arrow keys. If, for instance, you depress only the up-arrow key, you want the graphic to move straight upward, but if you depress the down-arrow key, the graphic should move downward. See those two controls in program lines 120 and 121. The left- and right-arrow keys are checked individually in lines 122 and 125.

We want to move the figure diagonally as well, and that means checking for depressions of one of the horizontal and one of the vertical keys. Line 123, for example, looks for data value 40—the sum of 8 and 32—up-arrow and left-arrow keys depressed simultaneously. If that condition is satisfied, the motion vectors are both set to negative values, causing the figure to move upward and toward the left.

Any PEEK(14440) value other than those listed in program lines 120 through 127 are considered invalid—holding down the left- and right-arrow keys at the same time, for instance. Such invalid key conditions allow the program to execute line 128, and that line stops the motion, keeping it stopped until a valid key combination occurs.

After saving this program on tape or disk, see if you can alter it so that the figure moves according to depressions of the *U, D, L* and *R* keys: up, down, left, and right.

## SENSING CONTACT BETWEEN FIGURES

While manual key controls can be used for altering the sequence of events in a program, there should also be some automatic means for doing the same thing. Contact sensing is the automatic counterpart of manual key control.

Actually, most of the programs in the previous chapter and all of them presented so far in this one use a very common kind of contact sensing: sensing contact with the top, bottom, left, or right edges of the screen. The techniques for sensing contact between two different figures use a similar kind of thinking, but implementing the thinking is often much more difficult.

There are two general philosophies regarding contact sensing. The one used most often through this book is really a form of position sensing. Sensing contact with the edges of the screen is a fine example of position sensing: the contact is sensed by comparing of the next-position value of the moving figure with some equations that represent the edges of the screen. Constant comparison of the positions of two or more moving figures can also result in sense contact between any of them—contact occurs whenever any two figures have some position elements in common. The figures need not be drawn in this case; sensing contact by comparing of screen positions works equally well with drawn and "invisible" figures.

True figure contact sensing is not position-dependent. Before a figure is moved to a new position on the screen, a short programming routine searches the path immediately ahead of the figure. If that search-ahead routine sees a clear path, the figure is allowed to move, but if the routine does a PEEK-type operation and finds some relevant graphic in the path ahead, it knows that a figure contact is about to occur. Unfortunately, the search-ahead mechanism runs too slowly in BASIC to be of much use under most circumstances.

### single-point contact

The simplest kind of position-dependent contact-sensing situation is one that calls for sensing contact between two single-graphic figures. If the next-position value for one of the figures is exactly equal to the current-position value for a second figure, contact has surely taken place.

## PROJECT 12–5

Listing 12–5 demonstrates single-point contact between two one-character figures. The "target" figure in this case is an asterisk located near the middle of the screen. You can move a graphic 191 figure through two dimensions as described in an earlier project. Whenever contact occurs, the target figure blinks on and off for a moment; then you are free to move the rectangle around and make contact from a different position.

```
10 REM ** PROJECT 12-5
15 REM          SINGLE-POINT CONTACT
20 DEFSTR F
25 F0=CHR$(128):F1=CHR$(191):F2=CHR$(42)
100 REM ** CONTROL ROUTINE
105 CLS
110 CP=927:I=0:J=0:OP=479
115 PRINT @ CP,F1;:PRINT @ OP,F2
120 IF PEEK(14440)=8 THEN I=0:J=-1:GOTO 130
121 IF PEEK(14440)=16 THEN I=0:J=1:GOTO 130
122 IF PEEK(14440)=32 THEN I=-1:J=0:GOTO 130
```

(cont.)

```
123 IF PEEK(14440)=40 THEN I=-1:J=-1:GOTO 130
124 IF PEEK(14440)=48 THEN I=-1:J=1:GOTO 130
125 IF PEEK(14440)=64 THEN I=1:J=0:GOTO 130
126 IF PEEK(14440)=72 THEN I=1:J=-1:GOTO 130
127 IF PEEK(14440)=80 THEN I=1:J=1:GOTO 130
128 I=0:J=0:GOTO 120
130 NP=CP+I+64*J
135 IF NP<=INT(NP/64)*64 OR NP>=63+INT(NP/64)*64 THEN 120
140 IF NP<=0 OR NP>=1022 THEN 120
145 IF NP=OP THEN I=0:J=0:GOSUB 200:GOTO  120
150 PRINT @ CP,F0;
155 CP=NP
160 PRINT @ CP,F1;
165 GOTO 120
200 FOR N=1 TO 10
205 PRINT @ OP,F0;
210 FOR T=0 TO 10:NEXT T
215 PRINT @ OP,F2;
220 FOR T=0 TO 10:NEXT T
225 NEXT N
230 RETURN
```

**LISTING 12-5** Programming for Project 12-5

The key-control routines, program lines 120 through 128, can be preloaded from cassette or disk if you have saved them as suggested in Project 12-4. Of course, you will have to modify parts of that listing in order to make it match Listing 12-5.

The contact-sensing routines are located in program lines 135 through 145. Line 135 looks for contact at the extreme vertical edges of the screen, and line 140 senses contact with the horizontal edges. Both are intended to keep the graphic 191 figure from running off the screen. There is nothing new in those two lines.

Program line 145 represents the real objective of the project. That line compares the next-position value of the moving figure, NP, with the screen position of the stationary object, OP. Whenever those two figures are equal, the moving figure has indeed made contact with the stationary one. As a result, both motion vectors are set to zero in order to stop the motion of the moving figure, the program goes to a subroutine that begins at line 200 (to flash the stationary figure), then it returns the system to line 120 to do the key-control routine again.

When both figures are represented by single characters, sensing contact is a simple matter of comparing the next position of the moving figure with the current position of the other. When they are equal, contact has occurred. The idea works equally well when both figures are moving: just compare the next-position value of one figure with the current-position value of the other.

What if there are more than two figures, and the reaction of the program depends on which two come into contact with one another? Suppose you are trying to "shoot down" two different graphics—say, an asterisk and a graphic 149. Let's say the scoring for the asterisk has to be different from that of hitting the graphic 149. It's no real problem as long as the program is keeping track of the position values for all three characters—the missile and the two targets. Assuming the targets themselves are separated, contact with either of them is sensed when the next-position value of the moving missile is equal to the current-position value of one of the targets, and the current-position value of the target that is hit is a reliable indication of which target it is.

See if you can add a graphic 149 target to Listing 12–5. Work things out so that contact with the asterisk makes the asterisk blink and contact with the graphic 149 makes that blink.

### horizontal-line contact

Sensing contact between a single graphic and a horizontal line of two or more graphics is only a bit more complicated. It is a matter of comparing the next-position value of the moving character with the current position of the left- and right-hand ends of the horizontal graphic. If the next-position value is greater than or equal to the position of the left end *AND* less than or equal to the position of the right end, contact has taken place.

## PROJECT 12–6

Modify the previous listing to look like the one shown in Listing 12–6. Upon running the program, you will see a horizontal line of 16 graphic-191s running across the middle of the screen. You will be able to move a single 191 graphic around on the screen. Whenever it makes contact with the long target, anywhere along its length, the target figure will blink off and on for a moment. That blinking signals that the program has indeed sensed a contact.

```
10 REM ** PROJECT 12-6
15 REM      HORIZONTAL-LINE CONTACT
20 DEFSTR F
25 F0=CHR$(128):F1=CHR$(191)
26 F2=STRING$(16,191):F3=STRING$(16,128)
100 REM ** CONTROL ROUTINE
105 CLS
110 CP=927:I=0:J=0:OP=479
115 PRINT @ CP,F1;:PRINT @ OP,F2
120 IF PEEK(14440)=8 THEN I=0:J=-1:GOTO 130
121 IF PEEK(14440)=16 THEN I=0:J=1:GOTO 130
122 IF PEEK(14440)=32 THEN I=-1:J=0:GOTO 130
123 IF PEEK(14440)=40 THEN I=-1:J=-1:GOTO 130
124 IF PEEK(14440)=48 THEN I=-1:J=1:GOTO 130
125 IF PEEK(14440)=64 THEN I=1:J=0:GOTO 130
126 IF PEEK(14440)=72 THEN I=1:J=-1:GOTO 130
```

(cont.)

```
127 IF PEEK(14440)=80 THEN I=1:J=1:GOTO 130
128 I=0:J=0:GOTO 120
130 NP=CP+I+64*J
135 IF NP<=INT(NP/64)*64 OR NP>=63+INT(NP/64)*64 THEN 120
140 IF NP<=0 OR NP>=1022 THEN 120
145 IF NP>=OP AND NP<=OP+15 THEN I=0:J=0:GOSUB 200:GOTO 120
150 PRINT @ CP,F0;
155 CP=NP
160 PRINT @ CP,F1;
165 GOTO 120
200 FOR N=1 TO 10
205 PRINT @ OP,F3;
210 FOR T=0 TO 10:NEXT T
215 PRINT @ OP,F2;
220 FOR T=0 TO 10:NEXT T
225 NEXT N
230 RETURN
```

**LISTING 12-6** Programming for Project 12-6

Program line 145 represents the contact-sensing routine. The ends of the string-packed, horizontal target are located at screen positions OP and OP+15. Contact has taken place whenever the NP value of the moving character falls within that range of screen positions.

It is possible to rewrite the program so that the horizontal target figure moves, too. Line 145 need not be changed at all; all that has to be done is to write a simple motion routine for string F2, then work out a multiplexing scheme that would let the two figures move simultaneously and independently.

### vertical-line contact

Sensing contact between a vertical line of characters and a single moving character is more complicated. It is easy to reckon a contact at the extreme ends of the line, but sensing contact with the segments between the two ends is a different situation.

A process of elimination is the most efficient way to approach the problem. If the next-position value of the missile is less than the current-position of the top of the target, contact is *not* being made. If the next-position value of the missile is greater than the current-position value of the bottom of the vertical target, contact is *not* being made. However, not all of the screen-position numbers between those extremes are part of the target figure. If the next-position value of the missile is greater than or equal to the position of the top of the line, and it is less than or equal to the bottom of the target line, that simply means the two figures are sharing the same line—the same vertical region of the screen. Whether or not they are actually in contact also depends on their horizontal positions. If both the vertical and horizontal elements are the same, contact is being made. Otherwise it is not.

## PROJECT 12–7

Listing 12–7 draws a vertical target near the middle of the screen. Load the program and run it. You will notice that the target blinks on and off whenever you touch it with the key-controlled "missile."

```
10 REM ** PROJECT 12-7
15 REM       VERTICAL-LINE CONTACT
20 DEFSTR F
25 F0=CHR$(128):F1=CHR$(191)
26 GOSUB 4000
100 REM ** CONTROL ROUTINE
105 CLS
110 CP=927:I=0:J=0:OP=479
115 PRINT @ CP,F1;:PRINT @ OP,F2
120 IF PEEK(14440)=8 THEN I=0:J=-1:GOTO 130
121 IF PEEK(14440)=16 THEN I=0:J=1:GOTO 130
122 IF PEEK(14440)=32 THEN I=-1:J=0:GOTO 130
123 IF PEEK(14440)=40 THEN I=-1:J=-1:GOTO 130
124 IF PEEK(14440)=48 THEN I=-1:J=1:GOTO 130
125 IF PEEK(14440)=64 THEN I=1:J=0:GOTO 130
126 IF PEEK(14440)=72 THEN I=1:J=-1:GOTO 130
127 IF PEEK(14440)=80 THEN I=1:J=1:GOTO 130
128 I=0:J=0:GOTO 120
130 NP=CP+I+64*J
135 IF NP<=INT(NP/64)*64 OR NP>=63+INT(NP/64)*64 THEN 120
140 IF NP<=0 OR NP>=1022 THEN 120
145 IF NP-INT(NP/64)*64<>OP-INT(OP/64)*64 THEN 150
146 IF NP<OP OR NP>OP+64*3 THEN 150
147 I=0:J=0:GOSUB 200:GOTO 120
150 PRINT @ CP,F0;
155 CP=NP
160 PRINT @ CP,F1;
165 GOTO 120
200 FOR N=1 TO 10
205 PRINT @ OP,F3;
210 FOR T=0 TO 10:NEXT T
215 PRINT @ OP,F2;
220 FOR T=0 TO 10:NEXT T
225 NEXT N
230 RETURN
4000 REM ** STRING-PACKING SUBROUTINE
4005 F2="":F3=""
4010 FOR N=1 TO 4
4015 F2=F2+CHR$(191)+CHR$(26)+CHR$(24)
4020 F3=F3+CHR$(128)+CHR$(26)+CHR$(24)
4025 NEXT N
4030 RETURN
```

**LISTING 12-7** Programming for Project 12–7

The contact-sensing operations take place in program lines 145, 146, and 147. Line 145 compares the horizontal positions of the two figures. If they are not the same, they cannot be in contact with one another, and normal motion of the missile is called at line 150. However, if the horizontal positions are identical, then it is time to check their vertical positions in program line 146. If they do not share the same lines of screen positions, the missile is allowed to move. Whenever the program reaches line 147, the process of elimination is complete, and by default the figures must be in contact with one another. That line stops the motion of the moving figure and causes the target to flash on and off for a moment.

### rectangular-field contact

Figures to be used as targets are often made up of a rectangular field of characters rather than just a single point or a straight line of them. Sensing contact with a figure that is built within a rectangular field is a matter of combining the techniques for sensing contacts with horizontal and vertical lines of characters.

## PROJECT 12–8

Try Listing 12–8 to draw a 16 × 4 rectangle near the middle of the screen. That is the stationary target. The moving missile is controlled from the keyboard, as in the three previous projects. Contact with any part of the target (or, to be more exact, any segment of the outside edge) causes the target to flash on and off several times.

```
10 REM ** PROJECT 12-8
15 REM    RECTANGULAR-FIELD CONTACT
20 CLEAR 512:DEFSTR F
25 F0=CHR$(128):F1=CHR$(191)
26 GOSUB 4000
100 REM ** CONTROL ROUTINE
105 CLS
110 CP=927:I=0:J=0:OP=479
115 PRINT @ CP,F1;:PRINT @ OP,F2
120 IF PEEK(14440)=8 THEN I=0:J=-1:GOTO 130
121 IF PEEK(14440)=16 THEN I=0:J=1:GOTO 130
122 IF PEEK(14440)=32 THEN I=-1:J=0:GOTO 130
123 IF PEEK(14440)=40 THEN I=-1:J=-1:GOTO 130
124 IF PEEK(14440)=48 THEN I=-1:J=1:GOTO 130
125 IF PEEK(14440)=64 THEN I=1:J=0:GOTO 130
126 IF PEEK(14440)=72 THEN I=1:J=-1:GOTO 130
127 IF PEEK(14440)=80 THEN I=1:J=1:GOTO 130
128 I=0:J=0:GOTO 120
130 NP=CP+I+64*J
135 IF NP<=INT(NP/64)*64 OR NP>=63+INT(NP/64)*64 THEN 120
140 IF NP<=0 OR NP>=1022 THEN 120
145 IF INT(NP/64)<INT(OP/64) THEN 150
146 IF INT(NP/64)>INT((OP+64*3)/64) THEN 150
147 IF NP-INT(NP/64)*64<OP-INT(OP/64)*64 THEN 150
148 IF NP-INT(NP/64)*64>OP+15-INT((OP+15)/64)*64 THEN 150
149 I=0:J=0:GOSUB 200:GOTO 120
150 PRINT @ CP,F0;
155 CP=NP
160 PRINT @ CP,F1;
165 GOTO 120
```

```
200 FOR N=1 TO 10
205 PRINT @ OP,F3;
210 FOR T=0 TO 10:NEXT T
215 PRINT @ OP,F2;
220 FOR T=0 TO 10:NEXT T
225 NEXT N
230 RETURN
4000 REM ** STRING-PACKING SUBROUTINE
4005 F2="":F3=""
4010 FOR N=1 TO 4
4015 F2=F2+STRING$(16,191)+CHR$(26)+STRING$(16,24)
4020 F3=F3+STRING$(16,128)+CHR$(26)+STRING$(16,24)
4025 NEXT N
4030 RETURN
```

**LISTING 12-8** Programming for Project 12-8

The target sensing is carried out by program lines 145 through 149. The scheme uses a process of elimination; as long as the conditions in lines 145 through 148 are met, the missile cannot be in contact with the target figure. Only when all four of those conditions fail is the contact made. As a result, the reaction in program line 149 occurs: the missile is stopped, the target is flashed, and control is returned to program line 120.

If line 145 is true, the missile is above the target figure, or at least to the left of its upper-left corner. If line 146 is true, the missile is below or to the right of the lower-right corner of the target figure. If lines 145 and 146 *both* fail, the missile is on the same screen lines as the target.

If line 147 is true, the missile is to the left of the target, and if line 148 is true, the missile is to the right. Those two conditions must fail before line 149, the contact-response line, is executed.

## contacts between multiple-character figures

The discussion thus far has dealt only with a single-character missile making contact with a single- or multiple-character target. There are many situations where the contacts to be sensed are between two or more multiple-character figures. In such cases, general equations for sensing contacts are too complex and slow in execution to be of any practical use. Instead, such situations have to be handled on a case-by-case basis.

Matters are much simpler, for example, if two multiple-character fields contact one another from the same direction at all times. That being the case, there is no need to cover all possible contact situations, but just those that are allowed to occur in the context of the animation sequence at hand. The principles follow those just described for contacts between single-character and multiple-character figures; it is a matter of making a wise selection regarding which characters in the two fields will be sensitive to one another.

### summary of contact-sensing expressions

The following summary of logical expressions assume that one figure is moving and the other is stationary. Variable NP(1) is the next-position value of some critical character in the moving figure, and variable CP(2) is the current-position value of the upper-left key character in the stationary figure. Variables *n* and *s* represent the number of lines and number of spaces per line in the stationary figure field.

Contact is being made if *all four* of the following conditions are met:

```
IF INT(NP(1)/64<INT(CP(2)/64)
IF INT(NP(1)/64)>INT((CP(2) 64*(n-1)/64)
IF NP(1)-INT(NP(1)/64)*64<CP(2)-INT(CP(2)/64)*64
IF NP(1)-INT(NP(1)/64)*64>CP(2)+(s-1)-INT((CP(2)+(s-1))/64)*64
```

The condition that one figure is moving and that the other is stationary is not as restrictive as it might sound at first. The overall effect could be that both are moving, but as explained in an earlier chapter, a single microprocessor cannot move more than one figure at a time. Getting the effect of two or more moving figures calls for some multiplexing techniques, by which one figure can be moving while the other must be stationary.

## AN EXAMPLE: A MISSILE SHOOT GAME

It's game-playing time, time to put together the ideas about keyboard controls and contact sensing and combine them with some multiplexed, moving-figure animation. It all adds up to a one-player arcade game of the shoot-down variety.

## PROJECT 12–9

Listing 12–9 is a simple MISSILE SHOOT game. Load it into your system, double-check the listing, and run it.

```
10 REM **  PROJECT 12-9
15 REM          MISSILE SHOOT
20 DEFSTR F
25 GOSUB 4000
100 REM ** CONTROL ROUTINE
110 CLS
115 CP(1)=927:CP(2)=CP(1)-64:I=0
120 PRINT @ CP(1),F1;:PRINT @ CP(2),F2;
125 P1=1:P2=1
130 ON P1 GOSUB 500,575
135 IF HF=1 THEN P2=3
```

```
140 ON P2 GOSUB 605,625,650
145 GOTO 130
500 REM          LAUNCHER AND MISSILE ROUTINES
505 I=0
510 IF PEEK(14440)=1 THEN P1=2:RETURN
515 IF PEEK(14440)=32 THEN I=-1:GOTO 525
520 IF PEEK(14440)=64 THEN I=1 ELSE P1=1:RETURN
525 NP(1)=CP(1)+I
530 IF NP(1)<=INT(NP(1)/64)*64 THEN 555
535 IF NP(1)>=63+INT(NP(1)/64)*64 THEN 555
540 PRINT @ CP(1),F0;:PRINT @ CP(2),F0;
545 CP(1)=NP(1):CP(2)=CP(1)-64
550 PRINT @ CP(1),F1;:PRINT @ CP(2),F2;
555 P1=1:RETURN
575 NP(2)=CP(2)-64
580 IF NP(2)>=CP(3) AND NP(2)<=CP(3)+4 THEN HF=1:GOTO 590
585 IF NP(2)>=0 THEN 595
590 PRINT @ CP(2),F0;:CP(2)=CP(1)-64:PRINT @ CP(2),F2;:P1=1:RETURN
595 PRINT @ CP(2),F0;:CP(2)=NP(2):PRINT @ CP(2),F2;:P1=2:RETURN
600 REM           FLYING SAUCER ROUTINES
605 I(3)=RND(3)-2:IF I(3)=0 THEN 605
610 CP(3)=(RND(7)-1)*64
615 IF I(3)<0 THEN CP(3)=CP(3)+59
620 P2=2:RETURN
625 NP(3)=CP(3)+I(3)
630 IF NP(3)<=INT(NP(3)/64)*64 THEN PRINT @ CP(3),F4;:P2=1:RETURN
635 IF NP(3)+4>=63+INT((NP(3)+4)/64)*64 THEN PRINT @ CP(3),F4;:
    P2=1:RETURN
640 PRINT @ CP(3),F4;:CP(3)=NP(3):PRINT @ CP(3),F3;
645 P2=2:RETURN
650 FOR N=1 TO 5
655 PRINT @ CP(3),F3;
660 FOR T=0 TO 5:NEXT T
665 PRINT @ CP(3),F4;
670 FOR T=0 TO 10:NEXT T
675 NEXT N
680 HF=0:P2=1:RETURN
4000 REM ** STRING-PACKING SUBROUTINE
4005 F0=CHR$(128)
4010 F1=CHR$(191)
4015 F2=CHR$(91)
4020 F3=CHR$(160)+CHR$(184)+CHR$(174)+CHR$(172)+CHR$(176)
4025 F4=STRING$(5,128)
4030 RETURN
```

**LISTING 12-9** Missile Shoot game, Project 12-9

The two figures located near the bottom of the screen, an up-arrow perched on top of a graphic 191, represent your missile and its launcher. The figure moving to the left or right at a place higher on the screen is your target—a little flying saucer invader.

You fire the missile, presumably at the flying saucer, by striking the ENTER key. You can adjust the horizontal position of the launcher by working the left- and right-arrow keys. That launch adjustment is possible only when the missile is still perched on top of it.

When the missile is launched, it rises toward the top of the screen. One of two events can take place after that. Either the missile strikes the target, or it misses the target and rises all the way to the top of the screen. In either case, the missile returns to the launcher. However, if it strikes the target, the target figure blinks on and off to indicate a score.

The key control feature of the game is demonstrated by the ability to adjust the horizontal position of the launcher and fire the missile. Contact sensing is demonstrated in several ways: limiting the horizontal motion of the launcher and flying saucer to the edges of the screen, limiting the rise of the missile to the top of the screen, and detecting a hit between the missile and flying saucer figures.

Since more than one figure can appear to be moving at the same time, the routines must be multiplexed.

### the string-packed figures

The launcher and missile are both single-character figures. If you note the statements in the string-packing subroutine (program lines 4000–4030), you will see that the launcher is carried as string variable F1, and the missile is represented by variable F2. They are both movable objects, so there is a one-character "erase" variable, F0.

The flying saucer figure fits into a 1 × 5 frame; it is made up of one line having five characters in it. Its string is packed as variable F3, and its "erase" string is a string of five successive 128s, F4.

The one-character launcher or missile is thus moved by printing F0 in the current position and then printing an F1 or F2 in the next position. The flying saucer is moved by printing an F4 in the current position, followed by printing an F3 in the next position.

### the program variables

The most important variables in the program are defined this way:

F0: Printable string that erases the launcher and missile figures
F1: Printable string for the launcher figure
F2: Printable string for the missile figure
F3: Printable string for the flying saucer figure
F4: Printable string that erases the flying saucer figure
CP(1): Current-position value for the launcher
NP(1): Next-position value for the launcher
CP(2): Current-position value for the missile
NP(2): Next-position value for the missile
CP(3): Current-position value for the left key character in the flying saucer figure

NP(3): Next-position value for the left key character in the flying saucer figure

NP(3)+4: Next-position value for the right key character in the flying saucer figure

I: Horizontal motion vector for the launcher (−1 to move left and 1 to move right)

I(3): Horizontal motion vector for the flying saucer (−1 to move left and 1 to move right)

HF: Hit flag (0 if target has not been hit, 1 if target has been hit)

P1: Multiplexing phase for the launcher and missile (1 or 2)

P2: Multiplexing phase for the flying saucer (1, 2, or 3)

N,T: Variables for timing the blinking effect that occurs whenever the missile strikes the flying saucer

### initializing the play

After the strings are defined and packed by lines 20 and 25, the game is initialized in program lines 110 through 125. Line 110 clears the screen, and line 115 sets the initial positions of the launcher and missile figures. Note that the missile, variable CP(2), is set directly above the launcher figure. That particular program line concludes by setting the launcher's motion vector, I, to zero—no motion.

Line 120 simply prints the launcher and missile figures in their initial positions, and line 125 sets both operating phases of the multiplexing to phase 1.

### multiplexing phases for the launcher and missile

Line 130 implies that there are just two multiplexing phases for the launcher and missile. Phase 1 begins at program line 500, and phase 2 begins at line 575.

Phase 1 occupies lines 505 through 555, and the analysis of events goes something like this:

Line 505: Set the motion vector to zero.

Line 510: If the ENTER key is depressed, initiate the missile-launch phase, phase 2, and return.

Line 515: If the left-arrow key is depressed, set the launcher's motion vector to −1 and jump down to the launcher/missile motion routine at line 525.

Line 520: If the right-arrow key is depressed, set the launcher's motion vector to 1; otherwise, set up to repeat phase 1 and return.

Line 525: Set up the next-position value for the launcher figure.

Line 530: If the launcher is against the left edge of the screen, jump to line 555—don't move.

Line 535: If the launcher is against the right edge of the screen, jump to line 555—don't move.

Line 540: By default, the launcher/missile assembly must be free to move. Erase both figures from their current positions.

Line 545: Set the new positions, keeping the missile located directly over the launcher.

Line 550: Print the launcher and missile figures in their new position.

Line 555: Set up to repeat phase 1 and return.

Phase 1 operations thus deal solely with the procedures for moving the launcher/missile figures to the left or right on the screen. If the motion is to take place, it covers just one space each time the phase is executed.

Phase 2 operations for the missile/launcher system is concerned with moving the missile figure upward on the screen. That phase occupies program lines 575 through 595, and they do these jobs:

Line 575: Set next upward position for the missile.

Line 580: If the missile is making contact with any portion of the flying saucer figure, set the HF variable to 1, and jump down to line 590.

Line 585: If the missile figure has *not* reached the top of the screen, jump down to line 595 to move it.

Line 590: This line is executed if the missile strikes the flying saucer figure or reaches the top of the screen. The statements clear the missile figure from its current position, situates and redraws it atop the launcher figure, and sets up the multiplexing for returning to phase 1 operations.

Line 595: This line is executed if the missile is rising freely. It is a basic character-move operation that concludes by setting up a repeat of these phase-2 operations.

The launcher and missile figures are really independent figures, but they are multiplexed as though they are a single figure.

## multiplexing phases for the FLYING SAUCER

Line 140 in the program points to one of three possible multiplexing phases for the flying saucer figure. Those phases begin at program lines 605, 625, and 650.

The phase 1 operations are responsible for setting a random altitude and direction of motion for the saucer.

Line 605: Pick a random motion vector; −1 or 1.

Line 610: Pick a random line number; 0, 64, 128, 192, 256, 320, or 384.

Line 615: If the motion is to the left, move the initial position 59 spaces to the right—to the right side of the screen. (If the motion is to the right, the initial position is now equal to the value picked in line 610, a place at the left-hand side of the screen.)

Line 620: Set up phase 2 operations and return.

Phase 2 operations move the flying saucer figure across the screen:

Line 625: Set the next position for the flying saucer.

Line 630: If it has reached the left side of the screen, erase the figure, set up phase 1 operations, and return.

Line 635: If the flying saucer has reached the right side of the screen, erase the figure, set up phase 1 operations, and return.

Line 640: When the program reaches this line, the figure must be free to move on the screen, so the instructions execute the move to the next position.

Line 645: Set up to repeat phase 2, and return.

The phase 3 operations occupy program lines 650 through 680. They simply cause the flying saucer figure to blink on and off at its current position on the screen. When that blinking cycle is done, the last line clears the hit-flag variable, HF, to zero, then sets up phase 1 operations.

Phase 3 of the flying saucer routines is run only when line 135 is satisfied—when the missile has made contact with the flying saucer figure.

# 13 Perspective Animation

One of the common-sense notions of visual perception is that things appear to grow smaller and less distinct as they move into the distance, but larger and more distinct as they move into the foreground. One can take advantage of that notion to create the illusion of depth on the CRT, making use of a technique commonly known as *perspective drawing*. What's more, the technique of perspective drawing can be extended to include animated figures that appear to move away from or toward the foreground plane of the CRT screen. That is the subject of this chapter.

Perspective animation can add a great deal of meaning and visual interest to an animation sequence that otherwise appears primitive and flat. Being able to zoom figures in and out of an imaginary point in the distance—the *vanishing point*—literally adds a new dimension to animation sequences.

A perspective animation sequence is a special sort of animation sequence that is implemented by plotting a carefully designed sequence of image frames on the screen. The design of those frames, and the planning of their placement, sets perspective animation apart from the other animation sequences.

Here are a few special principles that must be borne in mind while you are planning a perspective animation sequence:

1. Objects appear to grow smaller as they move from the foreground toward the vanishing point, but larger as they move from the vanishing point toward the foreground.
2. Objects seem to grow less distinct in appearance as they move toward the vanishing point, but more distinct as they move toward the foreground.
3. Objects appear to shrink at a slower rate as they move toward the vanishing point, but grow at a faster rate as they approach the foreground.
4. The larger the number of frames incorporated in the sequence, the smoother the animation appears.
5. The faster the animation frames are sequenced, the faster the figure appears to move toward or from the vanishing point.

Those seem to be simple, common-sense principles. But their practical implementation calls for a lot of work and, quite often, some rather distasteful compromises.

It isn't difficult to plan the image frames in order to make the object appear to grow smaller or larger as it zooms toward or away from the vanishing point. The frames are simply designed so that the figure appears successively smaller or larger.

The matter of making the figure in successive frames appear less distinct as it approaches the vanishing point is automatically handled by the inherent nature of the TRS-80 graphics system. The fixed size of the graphics elements on the screen actually makes it impossible to put a lot of detail into small figures. Large figures, on the other hand, cover a broader area of the screen and can take advantage of the larger number of graphic elements available. Actually, you will probably find that there aren't enough graphic elements available for the medium-distance animation frames; there will be more than the desired amount of spatial distortion. That's one of those compromises we must learn to live with or find some clever way to overcome.

Making figures seem to shrink more slowly as they recede toward the vanishing point is an effect that beginners sometimes overlook. Setting up a perspective animation sequence that shows the figure shrinking the same amount in each frame actually creates the illusion that it moves faster as it goes into the distance. Creating the appearance of constant-speed motion calls for adjusting the size of the figure at different rates.

Generally, therefore, there will be more animation frames devoted to the figure when it is away from the foreground.

Certainly any animation sequence appears smoother as the number of frames devoted to it increases. However, there is a practical limit to the number of frames we all choose to draw, encode, and write into the computer program. It is thus necessary to trade off a smooth animation effect against the amount of time and work we care to put into the sequence. We are going to take a very practical approach to the situation: try a few frames, and if the animation appears too jerky, add a few more.

The rate at which the frames are sequenced can be traded off against the number of frames in the perspective animation. In any case, the apparent rate of motion to or from the vanishing point is dictated by the frequency of plotting—and that brings up the problem of computer drawing speed. The faster the frames can be plotted, the faster the figure can appear to move (and the smoother the animation will be). To this particular end, every animation frame will be designed so that it fits into a single string variable; furthermore, the frames will be planned so that they plot the new figure and erase elements of the previous figure at the same time.

All of these ideas can be incorporated in a special procedure for developing perspective animation sequences.

Here are the steps in that procedure:

1. Make a preliminary perspective drawing of the sequence on a video worksheet, showing simple rectangles where the figures are to be plotted.
2. Separate the rectangles into individual frames (on a different video worksheet), showing the area to be plotted and the areas to be erased.
3. Use the drawings of individual frames to determine the graphics codes, and use the preliminary perspective drawing to determine the screen position for each frame.
4. Write the frames into a BASIC program and run the program to check the accuracy of the work and the smoothness of the animation.
5. Make any necessary adjustments in the work thus far, then draw the desired figure into the rectangles, the area originally plotted as image planes.
6. Adjust the graphics-code listing to accommodate the figure.

This is a six-step procedure that can get a bit tedious at times, but if it is followed conscientiously, it promises a working perspective animation sequence. A haphazard approach guarantees confusion, frustration, and wasted work. Do it "by the numbers," and things will work out a lot better in the long run.

## NEAR-CENTER PERSPECTIVE ANIMATION

The procedure for generating a satisfactory perspective animation sequence is illustrated here with one of the simplest kinds of sequences: making an object appear to zoom straight in or out of the screen.

Fig. 13-1 represents the preliminary perspective drawing for this sequence. There are six image planes labeled P1 through P6. P1 represents the frontmost drawing plane, P2 represents the same plane as it is moved back a bit toward the vanishing point, P3 represents the next one back, and so on. Plane P6 marks the vanishing point of the sequence. If these planes are drawn in rapid sequence, beginning with P1, the viewer will get the impression of a square figure moving back into the distance. If the planes are sequenced in the reverse order, P6 to P1, the visual impression is that of a square moving from the vanishing point toward the foreground.

Notice that there is an attempt to make the sizes of the image planes decrease at a slower rate as they approach the vanishing point. Plane P2, for instance, is two character spaces smaller all around than plane P1 is, whereas plane P3 is just one "square" smaller than P2. Ideally, plane P4 would be ½ "square" smaller than P3, but that cannot be done with this graphics system. This is another one of those compromises we have to tolerate in order to achieve anything at all.

Along that same line of thinking, notice that the plane at the vanishing point, plane P6, is not centered within the other squares. That's another one of the compromises: it simply cannot be done within the format imposed by the TRS-80 graphics system. So that small plane has to be situated a bit off center.

In this particular case, the number of planes that can be used is dictated by the size of the largest one. It would be difficult to use more image planes and yet have each one a bit smaller than the preceding one.

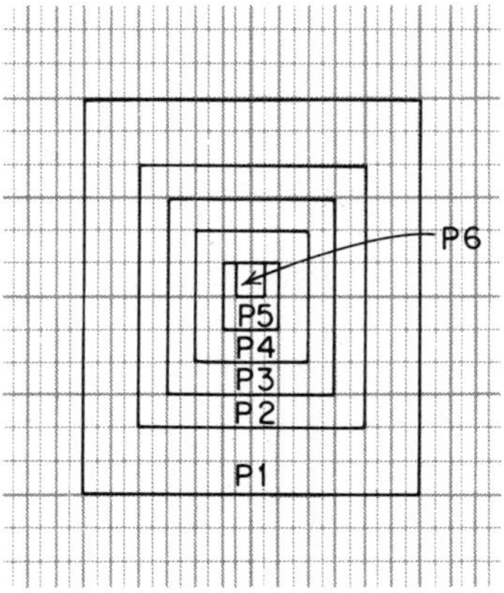


**FIGURE 13-1** Preliminary perspective drawing of six image planes for an on-center perspective animation

That is the preliminary perspective drawing. The image planes could have a rectangular shape; the relative dimensions of the planes are determined by the nature of the figure that will eventually be drawn on them. In this case, the figure will have a rather squarish shape.

The second step in the procedure is to develop a frame for each image plane, designing them so that they both plot the image plane as white and erase any vestiges of a previously drawn plane. That is done for you in Fig. 13-2.

Those frames show the drawing planes individually, along with the surrounding areas that have to be erased. Plane P1, for instance, is shown as Frame F(1). Here there is no need to erase portions of a larger, preceding frame because there is none preceding it.

Frame F(2) draws plane P2, but also has an erasing border that deletes segments of Frame F(1). Likewise, Frame F(3) draws image plane

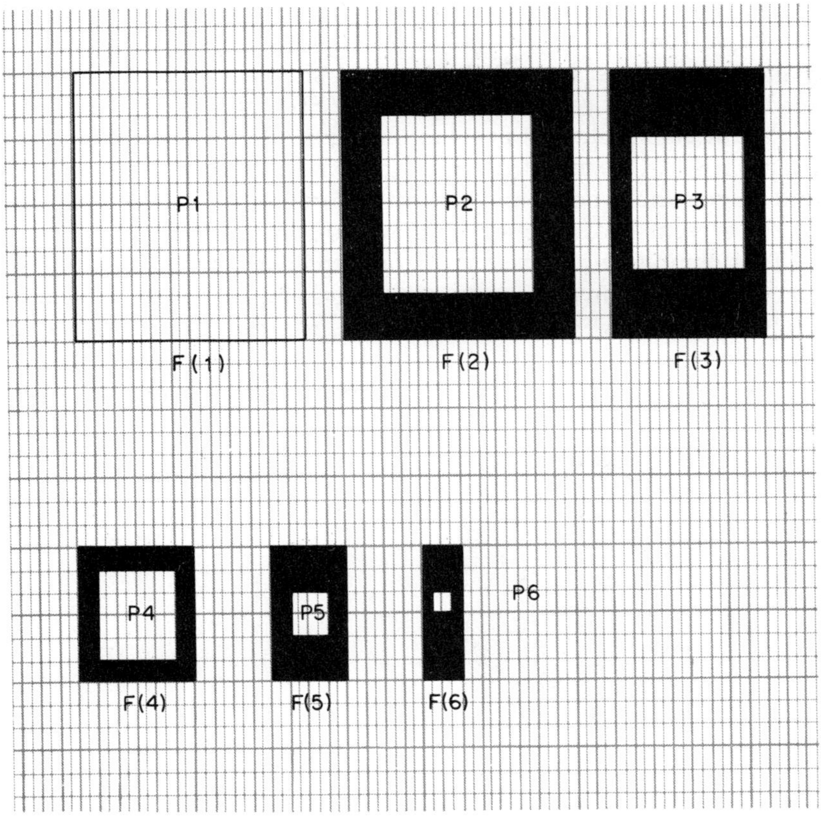


**FIGURE 13-2** The six frames required for plotting the image planes and erasing segments of larger ones

F3 and erases unwanted segments of Frame F(2). The same idea follows all the way down to Frame F(6).

Also notice that the frames are planned such that it makes no difference whether the planes are sequenced from P1 down to P6 or from P6 up to P1. Consider Frame F(3), for example. If the perspective animation calls for moving the frames into the distance, Frame F(2) will precede F(3); and F(2) has the drawing and erasing elements necessary for wiping out any part of F(2) that might otherwise remain on the screen. If the sequence calls for making the planes appear to be moving outward from the vanishing point, Frame F(4) will precede F(3). Still, the plotting and erasing areas of F(3) are adequate for clearing away any part of Frame F(4).

In short, every frame in a perspective animation sequence ought to be designed in such a way that it can clear out portions of a frame that precedes it from either direction.

Figure 13–3 shows two additional frames, F(0) and F(7). The purpose of these frames is to erase the first and last drawing planes in the sequence. Whenever the planes are to be moved toward the vanishing point, for example, one should get the visual impression that the figure finally vanishes into the distance. Doing that is a simple matter of erasing plane P6 at the end of the sequence, and Frame F(7) fulfills that requirement.

By the same token, it is sometimes desirable to erase plane P1 as it appears in F(1). One might do that when the planes are being moved out from the vanishing point and reach the foreground before disappearing from the screen. The erase-only frame, F(0), does that job.

That completes the second major step in the procedure for developing a perspective animation sequence. Bear in mind that some meaningful graphic figures will eventually be drawn into the plotting areas of the frames. For now, we are just setting things up.

The next step is one of the simpler ones: coming up with the

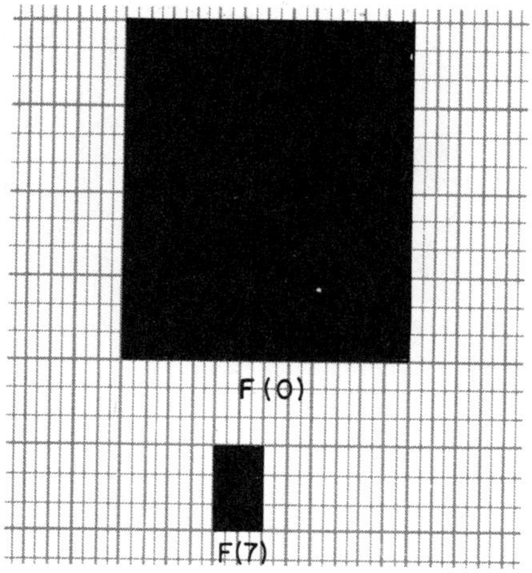


**FIGURE 13–3** Two additional "erase-only" frames required for the on-center perspective animation sequences

character codes for each of the frames. With the frame drawings used as guides, a line-by-line listing of the drawing codes look like those in Table 13–1.

Some of the codes, you will notice, are underlined. Those represent plotting areas for the image planes; they are the places where we will eventually substitute graphics codes for drawing a particular image. The codes that are *not* underlined must never be changed; they represent the erasing areas and control codes for packing the entire frame into a single, fast-printing string variable.

The scheme isn't ready for running on the computer yet. It is first necessary to determine the screen position for the upper-left key point in each frame, and that's a task that calls for some clear-headed thinking.

Suppose you want to key Frame F(1) to screen position 0. That will plot it so that its upper-left key point is in the upper left-hand corner of the

**TABLE 13-1**

CHARACTER AND CONTROL DATA FOR THE PERSPECTIVE ANIMATION FRAMES IN FIG. 13–2

```
-- FRAME 0 --
204,26,-12,24
204,26,-12,24
204,26,-12,24
204,1
      -- FRAME 1 --
-12,191,26,-12,24
-12,191,26,-12,24
-12,191,26,-12,24
-12,191,1
      -- FRAME 2 --
194,-8,176,194,26,-12,24
194,-8,191,194,26,-12,24
194,-8,191,194,26,-12,24
194,-8,131,194,1
      -- FRAME 3 --
200,26,-8,24
193,-6,191,193,26,-8,24
193,-6,191,193,26,-8,24
200,1
      -- FRAME 4 --
193,-4,188,193,26,-6,24
193,-4,143,193,1
      -- FRAME 5 --
193,-2,176,193,26,-4,24
193,-2,131,193,1
      -- FRAME 6 --
160,144,26,-2,24
194,1
      -- FRAME 7 --
194,1
```

screen. That's easy. Where should you set the key point for Frame F(2)? To answer that question, you must compare the perspective drawing in Fig. 13-1 with the frame drawings in Fig. 13-2. Doing that, you will see that the upper-left key point for F(2) is identical in position to that of F(1).

That wasn't too bad. What about Frame F(3)? That's a different story. Frame F(3) has the same height as the previous two frames, but it's narrower. It begins at a printing location that is two spaces to the right of F(2). Thus the printing position of Frame F(3) is 2.

Frame F(4) is both narrower and shorter than F(3). Relative to F(3), Frame F(4) begins one space to the right and one line lower. That means the printing position for F(4) is equal to that of F(3) plus 1 plus 64. Putting the information all together, that means Frame F(4) is plotted at position 67.

Applying the same line of thinking a couple of more times, it turns out that F(5) should be printed at position 68, and F(6) should be at position 69. Using the same ideas for the erase-only frames, F(0) is at zero, and F(7) is at position 69.

It is not a difficult idea, but it is one that demands your full concentration. One little miscalculation anywhere along the way can mess up the placement of all the remaining frames.

At this point, you are ready to type the information into the computer and give it a try.

## PROJECT 13-1

Use the frames just developed to show a sequence of square image planes zooming into the vanishing point. See the suggested program in Listing 13-1.

```
10 REM ** PROJECT 13-1
15 REM          PERSPECTIVE ANIMATION DEMO #1
20 CLEAR 1024:DEFSTR F,P
30 GOSUB 4000
100 REM ** CONTROL ROUTINE
105 CLS
110 FOR N=1 TO 7
115 M=3*N+1:D=VAL(MID$(P,M,3))
120 PRINT @ D+0,F(N);
125 FOR T=0 TO 50:NEXT T
130 NEXT N
135 GOTO 110
4000 REM ** STRING-PACKING SUBROUTINE
4005 FOR N=0 TO 7
4010 GOSUB 4500
4015 F(N)=F
4020 NEXT N
4025 P=""
4030 FOR N=1 TO 8:READ F:P=P+F:NEXT N
4495 RETURN
4500 F=""
```

```
4505 READ A
4510 IF A=0 OR A=1 THEN RETURN
4515 IF A>1 THEN F=F+CHR$(A):GOTO 4505
4520 READ B:F=F+STRING$(ABS(A),B):GOTO 4505
5000 REM ** CHARACTER LISTINGS
5001 DATA 204,26,-12,24
5002 DATA 204,26,-12,24
5003 DATA 204,26,-12,24
5004 DATA 204,1
5010 REM         -- FRAME 1 --
5011 DATA -12,191,26,-12,24
5012 DATA -12,191,26,-12,24
5013 DATA -12,191,26,-12,24
5014 DATA -12,191,1
5020 REM         -- FRAME 2 --
5021 DATA 194,-8,176,194,26,-12,24
5022 DATA 194,-8,191,194,26,-12,24
5023 DATA 194,-8,191,194,26,-12,24
5024 DATA 194,-8,131,194,1
5030 REM         -- FRAME 3 --
5031 DATA 200,26,-8,24
5032 DATA 193,-6,191,193,26,-8,24
5033 DATA 193,-6,191,193,26,-8,24
5034 DATA 200,1
5040 REM         -- FRAME 4 --
5041 DATA 193,-4,188,193,26,-6,24
5042 DATA 193,-4,143,193,1
5050 REM         -- FRAME 5 --
5051 DATA 193,-2,176,193,26,-4,24
5052 DATA 193,-2,131,193,1
5060 REM         -- FRAME 6 --
5061 DATA 160,144,26,-2,24
5062 DATA 194,1
5070 REM         -- FRAME 7 --
5071 DATA 194,1
6000 REM ** DISPLACEMENT DATA **
6001 DATA 000,000,000,002,067,068,069,069
```

**LISTING 13-1** Program for demonstrating the perspective animation sequence developed from Figs. 13-1 and 13-2; see Project 13-1

The program listing appears much like any other kind of animation program. The seven different frames are packed into strings F(0) through F(7), following the nomenclature already established during the preliminary work. The displacement data—the PRINT @ values for each frame—are offered here in a different form, however. Notice in program line 6001 how the eight different PRINT @ values are designated in sequence, using three-digit numerals. Recall that the frames are to be printed at 0,0,0,2,67,68,69, and 69 respectively. Those displacement values are entered at program line 6001 as three-digit figures and packed into a single string, P, at program line 4030. The displacement values are then pulled out of that string by line 115 in the control routine. It is the nature of that program line that makes it necessary to specify the displacement values in line 6001 as three-digit numerals.

The control routine is quite simple. The FOR . . . NEXT loop between lines 110 and 130 cycle through the frames one at a time, beginning with frame F(1) and ending with frame F(7). That creates the impression of the square zooming into the distance. Line 135 merely makes the entire zoom begin all over again.

During that seven-frame sequence, program line 115 fetches the designated key point for the current frame and line 120 prints it on the screen.

Do you want to change the speed of motion? Alter the value of the timing constant in program line 125.

Do you want to change the screen position of the animation? Substitute some other PRINT @ value for the zero in program line 120.

Do you want to make the square zoom out from the vanishing point? Change program line 110 to read:

```
110 FOR N=6 TO 0 STEP -1
```

Indeed, there is a great deal of flexibility built into this animation scheme.

The purpose of entering and running the program at this point is merely to test the configuration of the frames and their respective displacement values. If there are any errors in the design thus far, they generally show up as bits and pieces of the image planes being scattered or left on the screen when and where they should not be. Whenever that happens, it is time to take a calm, careful look at the data generated thus far.

Assuming the program runs as you expect it should, the next step is to draw the desired figure into the available image planes.

Fig. 13-4 shows the frames with a house figure drawn into them. Frame F(6) isn't shown here because it is too small to have any significant part of the house figure drawn into it; it will be left unchanged from the earlier programming.

This is perhaps the most creative part of the job. The earlier work is highly technical; this demands an artist's eye if you hope to carry out the animation successfully. The main problem is to draw the figure into the smaller framing areas in such a way that it resembles the larger versions.

Work out the graphics codes for your final figures, then insert them into the program where the white squares were originally defined; insert them where the underlined characters appear in Table 13-1.

Getting that figure data into the program's DATA listing is the final step. Run the program to check the overall visual impression, and make any necessary changes. At this point in the procedure, the only changes should concern the appearance of the figure. Don't tamper with the framing sizes or displacement values now; things might get so far out of hand that it would be better to start all over from the beginning.

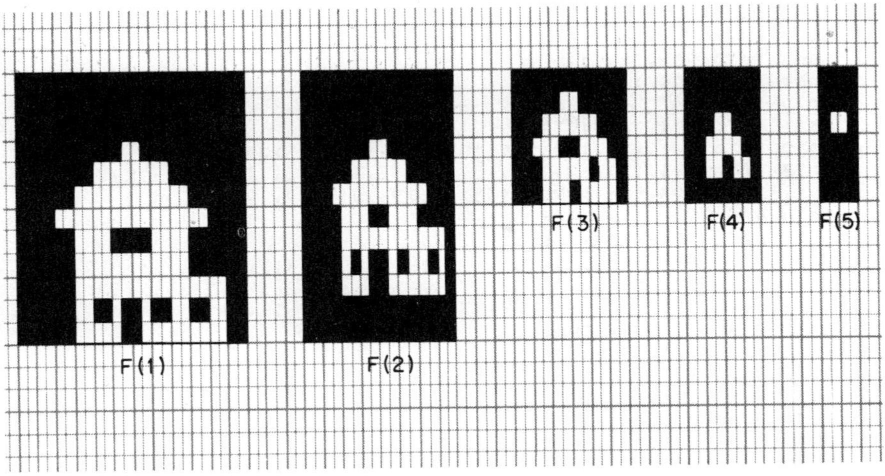


**FIGURE 13-4** A house figure fit into the image planes and frames for the on-center perspective animation

## PROJECT 13–2

Modify the program in Listing 13–1 to show the house figure receding into the distance. See Listing 13–2.

```
10 REM ** PROJECT 13-2
15 REM          PERSPECTIVE ANIMATION HOUSE
20 CLEAR 1024:DEFSTR F,P
30 GOSUB 4000
100 REM ** CONTROL ROUTINE
105 CLS
110 FOR N=1 TO 7
115 M=3*N+1:D=VAL(MID$(P,M,3))
120 PRINT @ D+0,F(N);
125 FOR T=0 TO 25:NEXT T
130 NEXT N
135 GOTO 110
4000 REM ** STRING-PACKING SUBROUTINE
4005 FOR N=0 TO 7
4010 GOSUB 4500
4015 F(N)=F
4020 NEXT N
4025 P=""
4030 FOR N=1 TO 8:READ F:P=P+F:NEXT N
4495 RETURN
4500 F=""
4505 READ A
4510 IF A=0 OR A=1 THEN RETURN
4515 IF A>1 THEN F=F+CHR$(A):GOTO 4505
4520 READ B:F=F+STRING$(ABS(A),B):GOTO 4505
5000 REM ** CHARACTER LISTINGS
```

(cont.)

```
5001 DATA 204,26,-12,24
5002 DATA 204,26,-12,24
5003 DATA 204,26,-12,24
5004 DATA 204,1
5010 REM        -- FRAME 1 --
5011 DATA 204,26,-12,24
5012 DATA 195,176,188,190,189,188,176,195,26,-12,24
5013 DATA 194,131,-2,191,-2,179,-2,191,131,194,26,-12,24
5014 DATA 195,191,179,151,171,179,191,179,191,193,1
5020 REM        -- FRAME 2 --
5021 DATA 194,200,194,26,-12,24
5022 DATA 194,193,160,184,190,189,180,144,193,194,26,-12,24
5023 DATA 194,194,159,157,174,175,156,148,194,26,-12,24
5024 DATA 194,194,131,129,130,-2,131,129,194,1
5030 REM        -- FRAME 3 --
5031 DATA 200,26,-8,24
5032 DATA 193,193,160,184,180,144,193,193,26,-8,24
5033 DATA 193,193,171,189,174,187,148,193,26,-8,24
5034 DATA 200,1
5040 REM        -- FRAME 4 --
5041 DATA 193,193,160,144,193,193,26,-6,24
5042 DATA 193,193,143,139,132,193,1
5050 REM        -- FRAME 5 --
5051 DATA 193,-2,176,193,26,-4,24
5052 DATA 193,-2,131,193,1
5060 REM        -- FRAME 6 --
5061 DATA 160,144,26,-2,24
5062 DATA 194,1
5070 REM        -- FRAME 7 --
5071 DATA 194,1
6000 REM ** DISPLACEMENT DATA **
6001 DATA 000,000,000,002,067,068,069,069
```

**LISTING 13-2** Programming for the perspective-animated house figure suggested in Project 13-2

The next series of comments concern the same general project, but offsetting the perspective slightly. See the preliminary perspective drawing in Fig. 13-5 and the corresponding image-plane frames in Fig. 13-6.

Up to this point we have gone through the first major phase of the

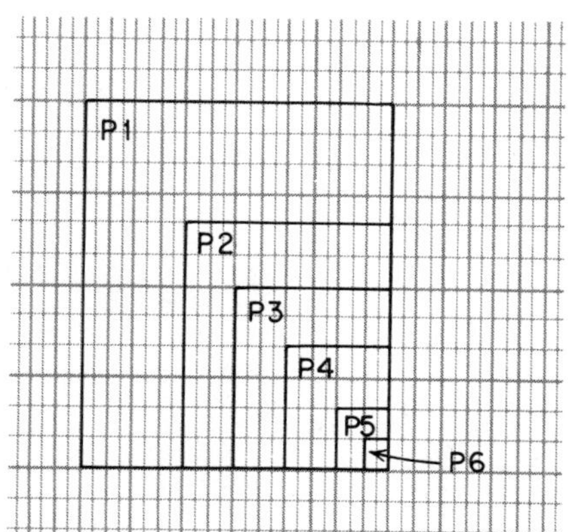


**FIGURE 13-5** Preliminary perspective drawing for a near-center perspective animation sequence

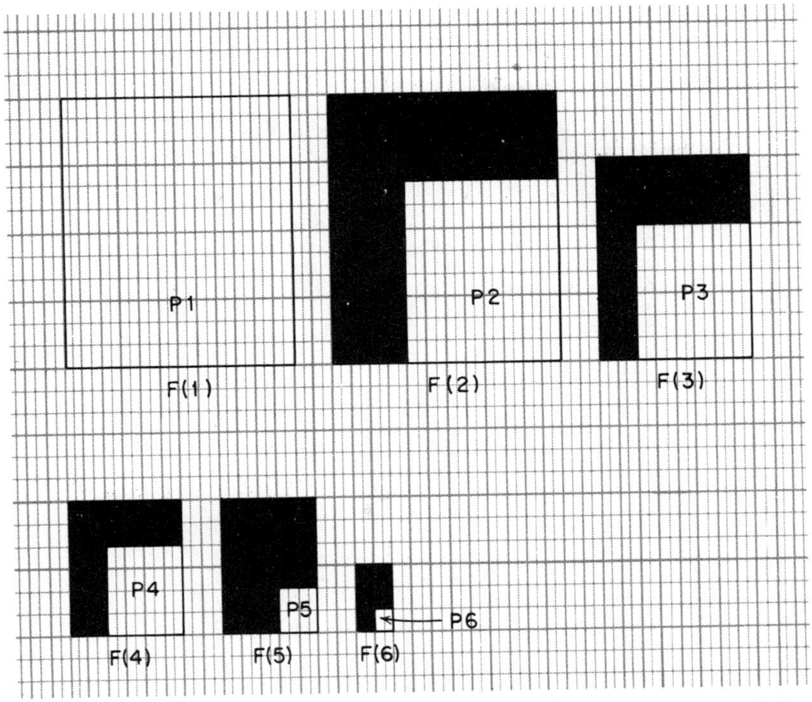


**FIGURE 13-6** Animation frames for the perspective planes in Fig. 13–5; the erase-only frames for erasing planes P1 and P6 are not shown, but they are included in the programming for the sequence

## PROJECT 13–3

Use the frame data and displacement information available from Figs. 13–5 and 13–6 to write a BASIC program that shows the offset perspective planes zooming out from the vanishing point. See Table 13–2 and Listing 13–3.

```
10 REM ** PROJECT 13-3
15 REM      PERSPECTIVE ANIMATION DEMO #2
20 CLEAR 1024:DEFSTR F,P
30 GOSUB 4000
100 REM ** CONTROL ROUTINE
105 CLS
110 FOR N=1 TO 7
115 M=3*N+1:D=VAL(MID$(P,M,3))
120 PRINT @ D+0,F(N);
125 FOR T=0 TO 25:NEXT T
130 NEXT N
135 GOTO 110
4000 REM ** STRING-PACKING SUBROUTINE
```

(cont.)

```
4005 FOR N=0 TO 7
4010 GOSUB 4500
4015 F(N)=F
4020 NEXT N
4025 P=""
4030 FOR N=1 TO 8:READ F:P=P+F:NEXT N
4495 RETURN
4500 F=""
4505 READ A
4510 IF A=0 OR A=1 THEN RETURN
4515 IF A>1 THEN F=F+CHR$(A):GOTO 4505
4520 READ B:F=F+STRING$(ABS(A),B):GOTO 4505
5000 REM ** CHARACTER LISTINGS
5001 DATA 204,26,-12,24
5002 DATA 204,26,-12,24
5003 DATA 204,26,-12,24
5004 DATA 204,1
5010 REM          -- FRAME 1 --
5011 DATA -12,191,26,-12,24
5012 DATA -12,191,26,-12,24
5013 DATA -12,191,26,-12,24
5014 DATA -12,191,1
5020 REM          -- FRAME 2 --
5021 DATA 204,26,-12,24
5022 DATA 196,-8,191,26,-12,24
5023 DATA 196,-8,191,26,-12,24
5024 DATA 196,-8,191,1
5030 REM          -- FRAME 3 --
5031 DATA 200,26,-8,24
5032 DATA 194,-6,191,26,-8,24
5033 DATA 194,-6,191,1
5040 REM          -- FRAME 4 --
5041 DATA 194,-4,176,26,-6,24
5042 DATA 194,-4,191,1
5050 REM          -- FRAME 5 --
5051 DATA 197,26,-5,24
5052 DATA 195,-2,188,1
5060 REM          -- FRAME 6 --
5061 DATA 193,176,1
5070 REM          -- FRAME 7 --
5071 DATA 193,1
6000 REM ** DISPLACEMENT DATA **
6001 DATA 000,000,000,068,134,135,202,203
```

**LISTING 13-3** Program for demonstrating the perspective animation sequence developed from Figs. 13-5 and 13-6; see Project 13-3

perspective animation development procedure a second time. Once the program in Listing 13-3 is run and debugged, the house images can be fit into the frames and the corresponding data worked into the program.

## OFF-CENTER PERSPECTIVE ANIMATION

Fig. 13-7 shows a full-screen perspective drawing of six image planes. The first, the foreground plane, is drawn near the lower left-hand corner of the screen; when the planes are plotted in numerical sequence, they create

**TABLE 13-2**

CHARACTER AND CONTROL DATA FOR THE PERSPECTIVE ANIMATION FRAMES IN FIG. 13-6

```
        -- FRAME 0 --
204,26,-12,24
204,26,-12,24
204,26,-12,24
204,1
      -- FRAME 1 --
-12,191,26,-12,24
-12,191,26,-12,24
-12,191,26,-12,24
-12,191,1
      -- FRAME 2 --
204,26,-12,24
196,-8,191,26,-12,24
196,-8,191,26,-12,24
196,-8,191,1
      -- FRAME 3 --
200,26,-8,24
194,-6,191,26,-8,24
194,-6,191,1
      -- FRAME 4 --
194,-4,176,26,-6,24
194,-4,191,1
      -- FRAME 5 --
197,26,-5,24
195,-2,188,1
      -- FRAME 6 --
193,176,1
      -- FRAME 7 --
193,1
```

## PROJECT 13-4

Complete this revised near-center zooming animation by fitting the house images into the previous program. See Listing 13-4.

```
10 REM ** PROJECT 13-4
15 REM        PERSPECTIVE HOUSE #2
20 CLEAR 1024:DEFSTR F,P
30 GOSUB 4000
100 REM ** CONTROL ROUTINE
105 CLS
110 FOR N=6 TO 0 STEP -1
115 M=3*N+1:D=VAL(MID$(P,M,3))
120 PRINT @ D+0,F(N);
125 FOR T=0 TO 25:NEXT T
130 NEXT N
135 GOTO 110
4000 REM ** STRING-PACKING SUBROUTINE
4005 FOR N=0 TO 7
```

*(cont.)*

```
4010 GOSUB 4500
4015 F(N)=F
4020 NEXT N
4025 P=""
4030 FOR N=1 TO 8:READ F:P=P+F:NEXT N
4495 RETURN
4500 F=""
4505 READ A
4510 IF A=0 OR A=1 THEN RETURN
4515 IF A>1 THEN F=F+CHR$(A):GOTO 4505
4520 READ B:F=F+STRING$(ABS(A),B):GOTO 4505
5000 REM ** CHARACTER LISTINGS
5001 DATA 204,26,-12,24
5002 DATA 204,26,-12,24
5003 DATA 204,26,-12,24
5004 DATA 204,1
5010 REM        -- FRAME 1 --
5011 DATA 204,26,-12,24
5012 DATA 195,176,188,190,189,188,176,195,26,-12,24
5013 DATA 194,131,-2,191,-2,179,-2,191,131,194,26,-12,24
5014 DATA 195,191,179,151,171,179,191,179,191,193,1
5020 REM        -- FRAME 2 --
5021 DATA 204,26,-12,24
5022 DATA 196,193,160,184,190,189,180,144,193,26,-12,24
5023 DATA 196,194,159,157,174,175,156,148,26,-12,24
5024 DATA 196,194,131,129,130,-2,131,129,1
5030 REM        -- FRAME 3 --
5031 DATA 200,26,-8,24
5032 DATA 194,193,160,184,180,144,193,26,-8,24
5033 DATA 194,193,171,189,174,187,148,1
5040 REM        -- FRAME 4 --
5041 DATA 194,193,160,144,193,26,-6,24
5042 DATA 194,193,143,139,132,1
5050 REM        -- FRAME 5 --
5051 DATA 197,26,-5,24
5052 DATA 195,-2,188,1
5060 REM        -- FRAME 6 --
5061 DATA 193,176,1
5070 REM        -- FRAME 7 --
5071 DATA 193,1
6000 REM ** DISPLACEMENT DATA **
6001 DATA 000,000,000,068,134,135,202,203
```

**LISTING 13-4** Programming for the animated-house sequence suggested in Project 13-4

the impression of zooming toward a vanishing point situated a bit above the center of the screen. This is an example of an off-center perspective animation sequence.

The six major plotting frames for this sort of perspective animation are somewhat more difficult to design than they are for on- or near-center perspectives, especially when they have to be designed so that the motion can be run in either direction. Fig. 13–8 shows those main plotting frames. Indeed, they have some unusual, or irregular, shapes, but using those strange shapes for the plotting and erasing effects allows somewhat shorter drawing times than using full rectangles would.

Notice how each frame is planned so that it plots its image plane and

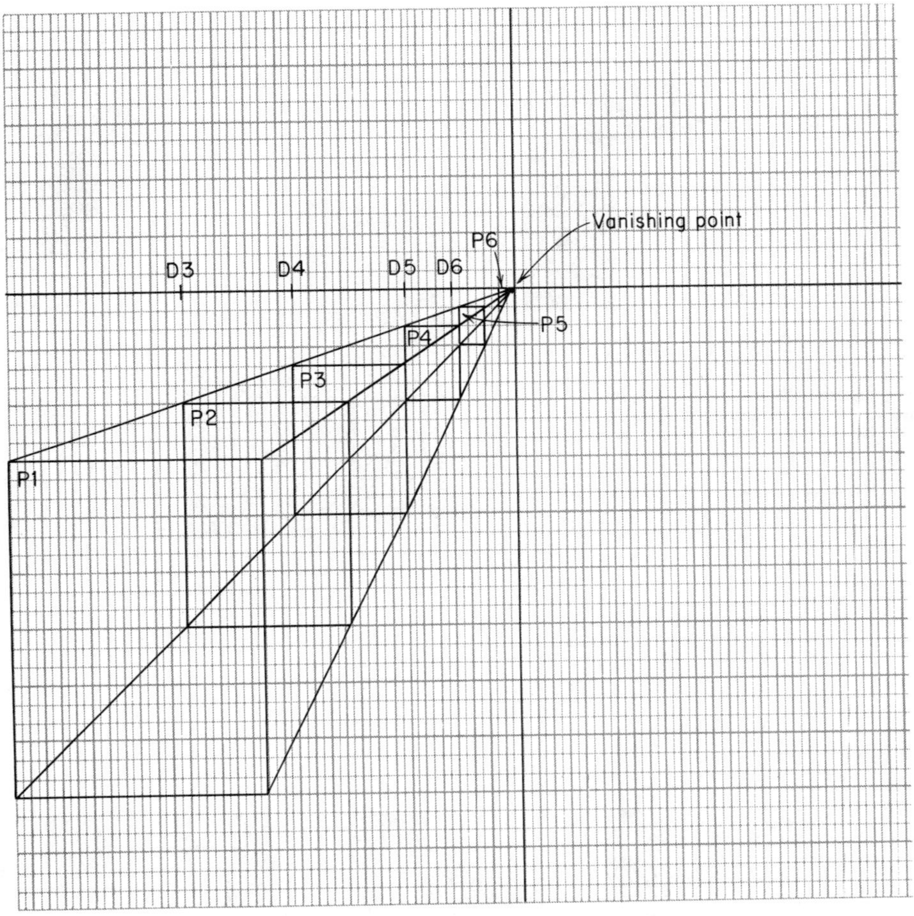


**FIGURE 13-7** Preliminary perspective drawing of six planes for an off-center perspective animation sequence; points D0 through D6 are screen locations for frames that are developed in the next step of the procedure

erases vestiges of the plane that might be plotted ahead or behind it in the animation sequence. Frame F(2), for instance, plots the image plane for P2 and erases segments of planes P1 and P3.

Of course the framing sequence should also include a frame F(0) for erasing P1 and a frame F(7) for erasing P6. Those two erase-only frames are not shown here, but they will be included in the DATA listings.

The displacement values—the key plotting points for each frame—are shown on both figures.

Table 13-3 shows the character data and control codes for generating the eight frames in this perspective animation sequence. The

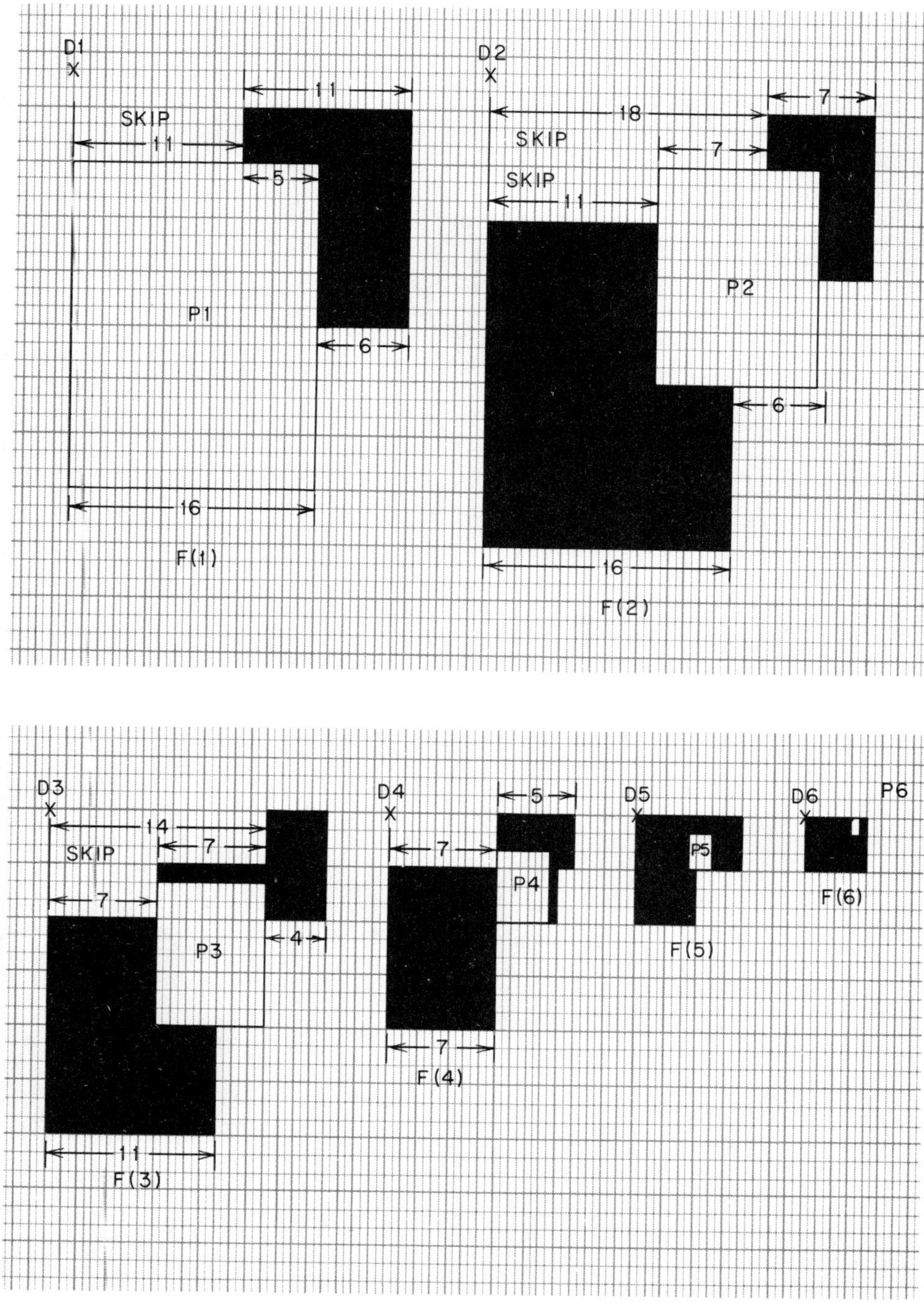


**FIGURE 13-8** Image frames for the off-center animation sequence specified in Fig. 13-7; The points D1 through D6 indicate the upper-left key points for drawing the frames on the CRT

**TABLE 13-3**

CHARACTER AND CONTROL DATA FOR THE PERSPECTIVE ANIMATION FRAMES IN FIG. 13-8

```
-- FRAME 0 --
208,26,-16,24
208,26,-16,24
208,26,-16,24
208,26,-16,24
208,26,-16,24
208,1
     -- FRAME 1 --
-11,25,203,26,-22,24
-16,191,198,26,-22,24
-16,191,198,26,-22,24
-16,191,198,26,-22,24
-16,191,26,-16,24
-16,191,26,-16,24
-16,191,1
     -- FRAME 2 --
-18,25,199,26,-14,24
-10,191,149,195,26,-25,24
203,-10,191,149,195,26,-25,24
203,-10,191,149,26,-22,24
203,-10,191,149,26,-22,24
208,26,-16,24
208,26,-16,24
208,1
     -- FRAME 3 --
-14,25,196,26,-11,24
-7,188,196,26,-18,24
199,-7,191,26,-14,24
199,-7,191,26,-14,24
203,26,-11,24
203,1
     -- FRAME 4 --
-7,25,-3,176,144,193,26,-12,24
199,-3,191,149,26,-11,24
199,26,-7,24
199,1
     -- FRAME 5 --
195,168,188,194,26,-7,24
196,1
     -- FRAME 6 --
195,129,1
     -- FRAME 7 --
193,1
```

underlined data indicate those places that can carry more meaningful figure data when it is time to fit a figure into the planes.

## PROJECT 13–5

Write a BASIC program that implements the perspective animation just described. Show the image planes zooming out from the vanishing point. See the suggested programming in Listing 13–5.

```
10 REM ** PROJECT 13-5
15 REM       PERSPECTIVE ANIMATION DEMO #3
20 CLEAR 1024:DEFSTR F,P
30 GOSUB 4000
100 REM ** CONTROL ROUTINE
105 CLS
110 FOR N=6 TO 0 STEP -1
115 M=3*N+1:D=VAL(MID$(P,M,3))
120 PRINT @ D+0,F(N);
125 FOR T=0 TO 5:NEXT T
130 NEXT N
135 GOTO 110
4000 REM ** STRING-PACKING SUBROUTINE
4005 FOR N=0 TO 7
4010 GOSUB 4500
4015 F(N)=F
4020 NEXT N
4025 P=""
4030 FOR N=1 TO 8:READ F:P=P+F:NEXT N
4495 RETURN
4500 F=""
4505 READ A
4510 IF A=0 OR A=1 THEN RETURN
4515 IF A>1 THEN F=F+CHR$(A):GOTO 4505
4520 READ B:F=F+STRING$(ABS(A),B):GOTO 4505
5000 REM ** CHARACTER LISTINGS
5001 DATA 208,26,-16,24
5002 DATA 208,26,-16,24
5003 DATA 208,26,-16,24
5004 DATA 208,26,-16,24
5005 DATA 208,26,-16,24
5006 DATA 208,1
5010 REM          -- FRAME 1 --
5011 DATA -11,25,203,26,-22,24
5012 DATA -16,191,198,26,-22,24
5013 DATA -16,191,198,26,-22,24
5014 DATA -16,191,198,26,-22,24
5015 DATA -16,191,26,-16,24
5016 DATA -16,191,26,-16,24
5017 DATA -16,191,1
5020 REM          -- FRAME 2 --
5021 DATA -18,25,199,26,-14,24
5022 DATA -10,191,149,195,26,-25,24
5023 DATA 203,-10,191,149,195,26,-25,24
5024 DATA 203,-10,191,149,26,-22,24
5025 DATA 203,-10,191,149,26,-22,24
5026 DATA 208,26,-16,24
5027 DATA 208,26,-16,24
```

```
5028 DATA 208,1
5030 REM        -- FRAME 3 --
5031 DATA -14,25,196,26,-11,24
5032 DATA -7,188,196,26,-18,24
5033 DATA 199,-7,191,26,-14,24
5034 DATA 199,-7,191,26,-14,24
5035 DATA 203,26,-11,24
5036 DATA 203,1
5040 REM        -- FRAME 4 --
5041 DATA -7,25,-3,176,144,193,26,-12,24
5042 DATA 199,-3,191,149,26,-11,24
5043 DATA 199,26,-7,24
5044 DATA 199,1
5050 REM        -- FRAME 5 --
5051 DATA 195,168,188,194,26,-7,24
5052 DATA 196,1
5060 REM        -- FRAME 6 --
5061 DATA 195,129,1
5070 REM        -- FRAME 7 --
5071 DATA 193,1
6000 REM ** DISPLACEMENT DATA **
6001 DATA 512,448,384,331,338,345,348,351
```

**LISTING 13-5** Program listing for demonstrating the off-center perspective animation developed from Figs. 13-7 and 13-8; see Project 13-5

Run the program to make sure the planes zoom out of the vanishing point in a clear and regular fashion. Any errors in the programming will generally show up as irregular rectangles that blink or remain fixed on the screen.

Reverse the direction of the zooming effect by altering line 110 to read:

```
110 FOR N - 1 TO 7
```

Change the position of the vanishing point by replacing the zero in program line 120 with a positive or negative number, a number representing the character-space displacement from the original vanishing point.

Alter the zoom rate by changing the range of values counted in the time delay loop in program line 125.

Fig. 13-9 shows the image of a hitchhiker drawn into the available frames.

## PROJECT 13-6

Fit the character data from Fig. 13-9 into the frame data in Listing 13-5. When the program is run, you should get the impression that you are driving along a road passing some hitchhikers at regular intervals. See my version in Listing 13-6.

```
10 REM ** PROJECT 13-6
15 REM          HITCHIKER
20 CLEAR 1024:DEFSTR F,P
30 GOSUB 4000
100 REM ** CONTROL ROUTINE
105 CLS
110 FOR N=6 TO 0 STEP -1
115 M=3*N+1:D=VAL(MID$(P,M,3))
120 PRINT @ D+0,F(N);
125 FOR T=0 TO 5:NEXT T
130 NEXT N
135 GOTO 110
4000 REM ** STRING-PACKING SUBROUTINE
4005 FOR N=0 TO 7
4010 GOSUB 4500
4015 F(N)=F
4020 NEXT N
4025 P=""
4030 FOR N=1 TO 8:READ F:P=P+F:NEXT N
4495 RETURN
4500 F=""
4505 READ A
4510 IF A=0 OR A=1 THEN RETURN
4515 IF A>1 THEN F=F+CHR$(A):GOTO 4505
4520 READ B:F=F+STRING$(ABS(A),B):GOTO 4505
5000 REM ** CHARACTER LISTINGS
5001 DATA 208,26,-16,24
5002 DATA 208,26,-16,24
5003 DATA 208,26,-16,24
5004 DATA 208,26,-16,24
5005 DATA 208,26,-16,24
5006 DATA 208,1
5010 REM         -- FRAME 1 --
5011 DATA -11,25,203,26,-22,24
5012 DATA 194,168,-2,188,144,202,198,26,-22,24
5013 DATA 193,176,178,187,183,177,144,194,168,176,197,198,26,-22,24
5014 DATA 190,177,176,-3,191,-5,131,197,198,26,-22,24
5015 DATA 194,130,-3,191,202,26,-16,24
5016 DATA 195,-3,191,196,184,140,180,195,26,-16,24
5017 DATA 194,136,143,135,143,140,132,193,-5,143,194,1
5020 REM         -- FRAME 2 --
5021 DATA -18,25,199,26,-14,24
5022 DATA 193,138,175,157,199,195,26,-25,24
5023 DATA 203,190,179,-2,191,173,176,180,196,195,26,-25,24
5024 DATA 203,193,130,-2,191,199,26,-22,24
5025 DATA 203,193,160,159,191,144,168,190,191,189,148,193,26,-22,24
5026 DATA 208,26,-16,24
5027 DATA 208,26,-16,24
5028 DATA 208,1
5030 REM         -- FRAME 3 --
5031 DATA -14,25,196,26,-11,24
5032 DATA 193,172,148,196,196,26,-18,24
5033 DATA 199,142,191,159,141,142,194,26,-14,24
5034 DATA 199,160,191,181,193,184,180,193,26,-14,24
5035 DATA 203,26,-11,24
5036 DATA 203,1
5040 REM         -- FRAME 4 --
5041 DATA -7,25,160,144,194,193,26,-12,24
5042 DATA 199,171,151,176,193,26,-11,24
5043 DATA 199,26,-7,24
```

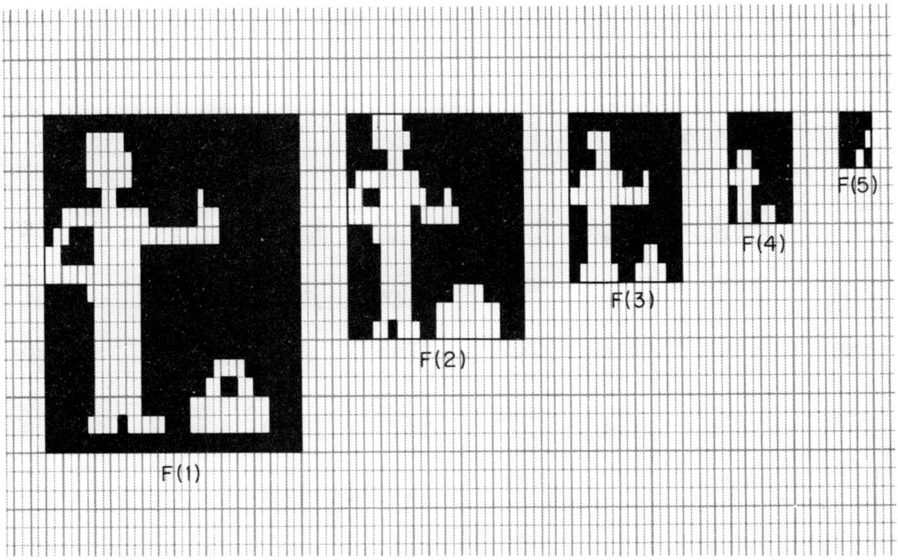


**FIGURE 13-9** Images of a hitchhiker as they fit into the image planes for the off-center perspective animation sequence

```
5044 DATA 199,1
5050 REM         -- FRAME 5 --
5051 DATA 195,193,152,194,26,-7,24
5052 DATA 196,1
5060 REM         -- FRAME 6 --
5061 DATA 195,129,1
5070 REM         -- FRAME 7 --
5071 DATA 193,1
6000 REM ** DISPLACEMENT DATA **
6001 DATA 512,448,384,331,338,345,348,351
```

**LISTING 13-6** Programming for the hitchhiker sequence suggested in Project 13-6

See if you can modify the hitchhiker program to include some interesting background detail, a roadway, and some random delays between appearances of the figure.

# APPENDIX A -- TRS-80 GRAPHICS SET

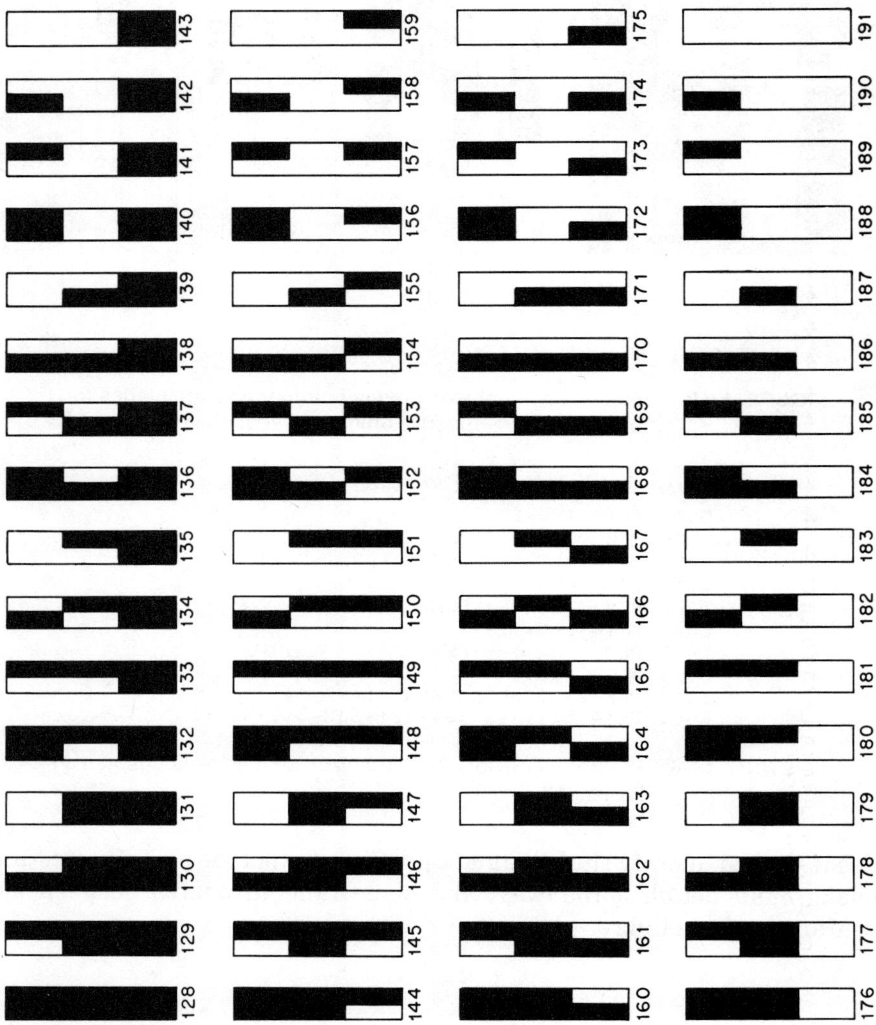

# APPENDIX B -- TRS-80 ALPHANUMERIC CHARACTER SET

| ASCII CODE | CHARACTER | ASCII CODE | CHARACTER |
|---|---|---|---|
| 32 | (space) | 64 | @ |
| 33 | ! | 65 | A |
| 34 | " | 66 | B |
| 35 | # | 67 | C |
| 36 | $ | 68 | D |
| 37 | % | 69 | E |
| 38 | & | 70 | F |
| 39 | ' | 71 | G |
| 40 | ( | 72 | H |
| 41 | ) | 73 | I |
| 42 | * | 74 | J |
| 43 | + | 75 | K |
| 44 | , | 76 | L |
| 45 | - | 77 | M |
| 46 | . | 78 | N |
| 47 | / | 79 | O |
| 48 | 0 | 80 | P |
| 49 | 1 | 81 | Q |
| 50 | 2 | 82 | R |
| 51 | 3 | 83 | S |
| 52 | 4 | 84 | T |
| 53 | 5 | 85 | U |
| 54 | 6 | 86 | V |
| 55 | 7 | 87 | W |
| 56 | 8 | 88 | X |
| 57 | 9 | 89 | Y |
| 58 | : | 90 | Z |
| 59 | ; | 91 | [ |
| 60 | < | 92 | \ |
| 61 | = | 93 | ] |
| 62 | > | 94 | ↑ |
| 63 | ? | 95 | ← |

# APPENDIX C -- TRS-80 CURSOR CONTROL CODES

| | |
|---|---|
| 8 | BACKSPACE AND ERASE CURRENT CHARACTER |
| 13 | LINEFEED/CARRIAGE RETURN |
| 14 | TURN ON CURSOR |
| 15 | TURN OFF CURSOR |
| 24 | BACKSPACE CURSOR |
| 25 | ADVANCE CURSOR |
| 26 | DOWNWARD LINEFEED CURSOR |
| 27 | UPWARD LINEFEED CURSOR |
| 28 | CLEAR THE SCREEN AND HOME THE CURSOR |
| 29 | CURSOR TO BEGINNING OF CURRENT LINE |
| 30 | ERASE TO END OF CURRENT LINE |
| 31 | CLEAR TO END OF FRAME |

# Index